❀ The Bells in Their Silence

THE BELLS IN THEIR SILENCE

Travels through Germany

MICHAEL GORRA

PRINCETON UNIVERSITY PRESS

PRINCETON AND OXFORD

Library of Congress Cataloging-in-Publication Data

Gorra, Michael Edward.
    The bells in their silence : travels through Germany / Michael Gorra.
       p.   cm.
    Includes bibliographical references and index.
    ISBN 0-691-11765-9 (alk. paper)
    1. Germany—Description and travel.   2. Travel writing—History.
    3. Germany—In literature.   I. Title.

  DD21.5.G67   2004
  914.304′882—dc22   2003056474

British Library Cataloging-in-Publication Data is available

This book has been composed in Sabon

Printed on acid-free paper. ∞

www.pupress.princeton.edu

Printed in the United States of America

10   9   8   7   6   5   4   3   2   1

For B. B.

We ramble about in open country so as to learn how to ramble about in the singularly dusty world of books.
—Wilhelm Heinrich Riehl,
The Natural History of the German People

✸ Contents

The Wanderer Above the Sea of Fog

Rain again, and wind, the kind of wind that drives the water sideways and makes an umbrella seem useless even when it doesn't turn the thing inside out. I had known it would rain when I went out for a late-afternoon walk — the skies had already looked theatrical and the forecast had put the odds at fifty-fifty. Here in Hamburg that doesn't mean it might stay dry, but rather that it will pour one minute out of two. Yet while there's nothing unexpected about it, I'd still rather wait out the storm inside, and so I splash another hundred yards along and into the city's Kunsthalle. Shake myself dry, check my coat. And then I climb the stairs to wander through a dozen rooms of old masters, looking at winter scenes by Ruisdael and van Goyen, a Claesz still life, and a Cranach triple-portrait in which you can see the brutish familial resemblance in a clutch of Saxon dukes, all bullet eyes and pinched noses. It's not my first visit and I stop only at the pictures I already know I like, while trying simultaneously to delay arriving at my favorites for as long as I can. But it's too much, and in the end I find myself skipping past whole rooms, hurried along by my desire for one painting in particular.

In the foreground, a solitary figure stands on a promontory, looking out over a fog that seems to foam like the ocean itself.

He's got a walking stick in one hand, though it's too thin to have helped him much in reaching this wild lookout, and his clothes, too, have an elegance at odds with the place: a bottle-green velvet suit that makes me imagine he's got a coach waiting somewhere just outside the frame. There he stands, as if alone, Caspar David Friedrich's 1817 "Wanderer Above the Sea of Fog." His sandy hair tosses in the wind and he keeps his back turned to us, so that we don't look at him so much as at what he himself sees; as always with Friedrich, who seems never to have painted a full clear view of the human face. Nor does the scene that opens at the wanderer's feet show any trace of human habitation. In the middle distance, a ridge breaks through the mist, a mouth of broken teeth against which the fog seems to smash itself; far away behind looms something indistinct, a shape like the Sphinx or a butte from Monument Valley; and then, beyond, the shrouded mountains rise. It is the most iconic German painting since Dürer, a picture that seems to encapsulate the whole of European Romanticism; an image of the Kantian sublime, as if in gazing out at this white and formless haze the wanderer were peering into the murky deep of his own mind. Looking at it, I think of Wordsworth on Snowdon, at the end of *The Prelude*, his vision of "a silent sea of hoary mist/ . . . [of] solid vapours stretched,/ In Headlands, tongues, and promontory shapes." And I think too of Goethe, who was himself suspicious of Friedrich's appeal: the poet as one who has surmounted the storm and the stress of his own emotion and can now serenely gaze upon them from above.

I had the painting to myself for a few minutes that afternoon, enabling me to look at what even the best reproductions don't show, such as the tufts of moss at the wanderer's feet or the layered wash of color that shimmers through the the high glaze of its surface, tinging the fog with blue and green and gray. But no matter how long I stood there — and no matter how often — the picture still held its secrets tight. Is the sky misting or clearing, the fog coming or going? And what, after all, does it hide? Lakes, villages, sheep, an approaching hiker, an impassable crevasse? What about that wanderer: what does he look like, and what's he doing on this vertiginous height? Any chance he'll jump? Friedrich's work speaks always of the longing for something just beyond our understanding, glimpsed but not grasped, the face that never quite turns toward us, the road that disappears in the forest. And this particular painting, with its depiction of a man contemplating a mystery, has always seemed to me an emblem of the idea of travel itself. We stand above the fog of a foreign place, wondering what — if anything — lies hidden there, trying to figure out the shape of that peak or this valley. If only we could stand there long enough! Then the clouds would break, and everything would become quite clear. Or would it?

That mist hangs with a special weight over Friedrich's own country. Indeed the news magazine *Der Spiegel* once put Friedrich's wanderer on its cover, poised on "the precipice of the German horror," as the art historian Werner Hofmann calls it, with a half-seen collage of twentieth-century nightmares replacing the mountains of the painting itself. The Nazis spoke of masking their actions in *Nacht und Nebel*, night and fog. They did not succeed, and yet the fog endures. Germany is a land about which we all have questions but where answers remain elusive. Indeed those clouds hang so heavily still as to produce this curious fact: nobody in the Anglo-American world writes travel books about contemporary Germany. There are works of reportage, like Jane Kramer's *The Politics of Memory*, dozens of them: books in which the writer takes the temperature of The German Problem as it exists today. And there are hundreds more about the way in which the Germans themselves have tried to come to terms with their past. But not travel books, not if one means the kind of impressionistic work of literary nonfiction that Robert Byron made from his Iranian experiences in *The Road to Oxiana* or that Eleanor Clark produced in *Rome and a Villa*. So in writing this book I have had to ask why, and whatever answers I've come up with have as much to do with the generic limits of the travel narrative itself as they do with the peculiarities of German history. Doing that has made this a work of criticism as well as a description of place: a traveller's tale that also offers an account of the rather ramshackle genre to which it belongs.

Colin Thubron has defined the travel book as the work of an amateur in an age of professionalization. The form belongs to the unspecialist, someone who "reaches his destination wide-eyed," both acknowledging his own subjectivity and allowing for the accidents of the road. Certainly there was something accidental about my own first encounter with Germany itself. I was a student of nineteenth- and twentieth-century fiction, a teacher who described his field as stretching from Jane Austen to last week—but in English, and only in English. Germany wasn't something I had ever thought I would have to grapple with—and then I found myself living there. I first went to the country in 1993 on what was frankly an academic junket, part of a faculty exchange with the University of Hamburg: give a lecture, stay a month. My sense of its history had been shaped by Hollywood, and I didn't know more of the language than would help me order a sausage. As the days went by, however, I was startled to find I was enjoying myself, startled because once you get past the idea of Oktoberfest, the words "enjoy" and "Germany" don't, for an American, seem to belong together. Or they hadn't, except that now I was in love with the sober elegance of Hamburg's streets and the nervy edge of its nightlife. So I began to wonder about what it meant to have fun in a place where so much wrong had happened, a place, moreover, that I was perfectly free to avoid.

Or was I? I don't mean that question in any kind of large historical sense. No, I simply mean that you don't really choose the objects of your own fascination, and almost everything in Germany intrigued me. There were small things, such as the way every corner optician's shop seemed to turn itself into a museum: a single pair of eyeglasses on display in an austere vitrine, half jewelry and half industrial design, or a cascade of frames wired together into a piece of statuary. But there were big things, too, like the careful maintenance of war-time ruins in the heart of the city in a way that made them seem a source of civic pride. In the end, that first visit proved a kind of scouting expedition, and I went back to Hamburg during the academic year 1997–98. Only this time I wasn't alone. I had gotten married in the meantime and was now a drone on sabbatical following in the trail of my wife Brigitte, who was directing a study-abroad program for the New England college where we both teach. So I cooked and ran errands, poured drinks, and tried not to talk to our students in English. For I had learned some German by then, enough at least to buy groceries, to make reservations, and to chat with the patient and well-disposed. After a few weeks, I could no longer distinguish the white noise of a German café from the white noise of English; still, my language never became easy and it never stopped seeming strange. I kept hearing superlatives — *kürzesten, gesündesten* — as though they were the names of Central Asian republics, and I couldn't accept the idea that imperatives required an exclamation mark: *"Der Nächste!"* when you reach the head of the post-office line. Impossible, with that punctuation, to imagine it as spoken softly, and even a request like "Pass the butter!" seems made peremptory by its very grammar.

The German language never wore itself into smooth familiarity — and that may have been a good thing. I might otherwise have made myself too comfortable. I had my routines, I read and wrote, we saw friends and went out to restaurants and concerts, and it sometimes took the absence of my own language to remind me that I wasn't entirely at home. In our apartment's basement storage locker I found a bicycle, and for the only time in my adult life began to ride regularly, at first to make the shopping easier, then for exercise, and at last for exploration, heading off without a map and seeing where the streets would take me. And from those streets I would set off on more ambitious journeys as well.

This book offers a partial account of those explorations, and its form requires a touch of explanation. Most travel books employ a linear narrative that is mimetic of the journey itself. One's itinerary provides a structural spine, and no matter how much one may from moment to moment digress, the book never strays far from an already determined sucession of one place after another; Paul Theroux's *Great Railway Bazaar* provides a good example, with one train leading seamlessly on to the next in a linear unfolding of time and space. But our stay in Germany had no itinerary as such. We were not so much travellers as residents and spent most of our time in Hamburg itself, walking the same streets, visiting and revisiting the same places.

In consequence, these pages neither move smoothly through the year nor attempt to cover the country as a whole. Instead, each chapter takes an aspect of our stay in Germany — a cluster of anecdotes, a visit to some historically important place — and bounces it off a wall of other texts. My third chapter, for example, uses Italo Calvino's *Invisible Cities* as a way to approach both the old Holy Roman Empire *and* the role of figurative language in travel writing; while the fifth starts in a Hamburg bookstore and ends by enlisting Walter Benjamin in a reading of the city's shopping arcades. Each of them enacts a dialogue between my hours in a library and the ones I passed on the ground itself, and I've skipped over those travels that didn't push me toward some sustained textual encounter. The Harz is here, but not the broad highway of the Rhine or the marzipan pilgrimage churches of the Catholic south; indeed Germany's south hardly figures here at all, except for purposes of comparison. Sometimes I rely on a novel, using Theodor Fontane's tales of nineteenth-century Berlin as a way to understand the boomtown of the 1990s. But most of the texts I look at are explicitly concerned with travel itself, though not always in Germany; I have in particular drawn on the rich tradition of Italian journeys as a way to establish a generic norm.

Travel books are about process — the process of movement and of understanding, too. They tell the tale of the journey toward knowledge and play up the delights of discovery, and the voyage matters more than any one destination. In this, they have long anticipated the attempts of some postmodern forms of scholarship to foreground the search for understanding, to shift our attention to the quest for knowledge and away from its final fruits. In my own case, that search is a double one: an attempt both to pierce the wanderer's fog and to understand the nature of the genre to which this book belongs. Most travel narratives do not, admittedly, need that self-reflexive awareness of their own operations; but then most travel books are not about Germany. In *The Texture of Memory*, James Young identifies a tradition of what he calls "countermonuments" in the German remembrance of the Holocaust—"brazen, painfully self-conscious memorial spaces conceived to challenge the very premises of their being," monuments that seem certain only of their own inadequacy. This book is an essay in that spirit.

✺ The Bells in Their Silence

✸ ONE

Cultural Capital

Hamburg, Hannover, Göttingen, and Kassel. There were other trains: the tracks to the dull marshy west toward Bremen and Osnabrück (change for Amsterdam), or the maddeningly slow and infrequent service to Berlin, whose cars were always crowded with students. There was the boat-train north to Denmark and the local to Lübeck. But this was the one we took most often from our temporary home, the white and bullet-nosed InterCity Express that dropped south at a speed America could only dream of—Hamburg to Frankfurt in three hours and a half, Munich in just over six. Though today I wasn't going quite so far. "*Grüssen Sie Thüringen von mir,*" the happy pink-faced conductor had said when he punched my ticket. Say hello to Thuringia for me. He was young and plump, with a ginger mustache; I had trouble with his accent and wondered when he'd left.

In the café car, I spread the *Herald-Tribune* under coffee and rolls and looked up from "Doonesbury" as, south of Hannover, the north German lowlands began to ripple into hills. I finished my breakfast and the ripples turned into folds, the hills began to offer something like a prospect. A landscape has to be uneven before you can see it—the bands of fields and forests, the villages settled in valleys, confined and bordered, framed, and yet because of that open and legible, in a way that the flat countryside around Hamburg almost never is. Then the train was at Göttingen, the university town of the Brothers Grimm, unvisited. And then Kassel, where six months before Brigitte had led me around the Documenta, building after building of oddly undemanding contemporary art. Kassel: change for Weimar. It was a slow train now, along rivers and through tight-packed hills, a postcard landscape with every town tucked neatly in a bend of the stream, unbombed and old-fashioned and no longer quite so gray as they would have been when this was still the East.

And then Weimar. I wheeled my bag downhill from the station, past the set of brooding administrative buildings that the Nazis had built, along the tree-lined Schillerstrasse, through the crowded Marktplatz with its vendors of fruit and *Fleisch* and blue Bohemian pottery, and into the lobby of the Hotel Elephant. And so began my jog around this small and architecturally modest city that has nevertheless figured on the traveller's shopping list for two centuries and more. Every reader of German literature knows the story: how the Dowager Duchess Anna Amalia of Saxe-Weimar-Eisenach, widowed young and ambitious in a way that her son's small realm couldn't satisfy, started inviting poets and thinkers to make their home in his capital. Wieland came, to serve as tutor to Anna Amalia's son Karl August, and Herder took over the city's largest church. The most important invitation, however, was that extended by the young duke himself, who in 1775 picked out the day's hottest talent and asked him to visit, a writer who though only in his twenties was already a bestseller, a notorious maker of taste and of fashion. Goethe came, he saw, he stayed. He picked up a title, supervised Weimar's finances, established the theater, chaired the War Commission, oversaw the duchy's mines, and always, always kept his pen moving. Schiller joined him 1787, and long after Goethe's death the place remained attractive enough to become Liszt's base of operations.

Now you can buy their faces on plates and mugs, and in Goethe's case on much more besides. He has, for example, given his name to a popular mark of brandy, whose labels carry a detail from the portrait that his friend Tischbein did in Rome: the poet in a wide-brimmed gray hat that turns him into something like a German *gaucho*. In fact Tischbein's Goethe is as much an icon in Germany as Gilbert Stuart's Washington is in America. I've seen it on the sign of an Italian restaurant in Berlin and on a mirror advertising a brand of beer, while Andy Warhol once modeled a poster on it, whose hot pink and yellow make the poet look as though he were his own acid trip. It is in truth a very bad picture — not in the handling of the face, where Tischbein has perfectly caught Goethe's long straight typically Teutonic nose, but in the body, whose legs are comically out of proportion. Much better is the simpler portrait that Angelica Kauffman did on that same Italian journey, in which Goethe looks both less grand and more interesting, full-faced and with his brown hair pulled back, hatless and dark-eyed and shrewdly sensual.

The Weimar of today isn't the city in which Goethe lived, but it *is* an elaboration of it, a town decked out with memorials to the one he lived in. I've never been in a place so small that had so many statues and monuments. Goethe and Schiller, standing in bronze together in front of the theater; Karl August on horseback, done up as though he were Marcus Aurelius; the plaque put up for Bach, who spent almost a decade here: all these one understands. Yet Shakespeare? Did he visit too? Indeed the whole atmosphere reminds me of Stratford — no, that's unfair. Stratford can offer nothing beyond the bare fact of Shakespeare's birth and death. He lived and worked elsewhere, and not much is known about any of it; so the city, having only what Henry James called "The Birthplace," in all its odd mingling of presence and absence, has rushed to fill the vacuum with that peculiar English genius for the tacky souvenir. Weimar has almost nothing tacky about it, there's hardly even any kitsch beyond those plates and something called a "Goethe barometer." Nor has the town's poet given his name to an undistinguished bit of chocolate-covered marzipan, as Mozart has in Salzburg. There are souvenirs aplenty — but they sit next to full racks of books, and it's the latter that seem to have the quickest turnover. For there is no vacuum here. Imagine a Shakespeare about whom *everything* was known: his letters to his parents and his notes to Jonson or Donne, his wife's relations with some third person, a secretary's record of what he thought about Marlowe and said to the Queen, or even what he ate on Thursdays.

Imagine that and you will have the six thousand pages of Robert Steiger's *Goethe's Life from Day to Day*, a documentary record, in eight volumes, of the letters Goethe wrote and received, the hours of statecraft, the conversations with Eckermann and others, the poems he worked on and the guests he saw. Goethe was from a very early age a tourist attraction in his own right: everybody who came to Weimar wanted to meet him, and everybody wrote about it, as though he were the Colosseum or Niagara Falls. Of all the reminiscences, the one I like most is that of Thackeray, who arrived in Weimar in 1830, two years before the poet's death. The *Engländer* was just nineteen; he had left Cambridge without a degree and was busy squandering his fortune. Drifting through Europe he found that he liked the statelet's relaxed approach to morality and stayed for six months; it later became the "Pumpernickel" of *Vanity Fair.* He thought the court's sense of protocol absurd, but for any visiting Englishman who seemed (still) to have money, it was nevertheless "most pleasant and homely," and so he worked away at flirting in German and bought a sword alleged to have been Schiller's. Eventually, with what he called a "perturbation of spirit," he found himself presented to the genius of the place. He must have been one of the last Englishmen to have seen the poet plain and wrote that he could imagine "nothing more serene, majestic, and *healthy* looking than the grand old Goethe," noting in particular the "awful splendour" of his eyes. But he added, in a letter to his mother, that the German, though "a noble poet . . . is little better than an old rogue" and was both astonished and "somewhat relieved" to find that he "spoke French with not a good accent."

Twenty years later, another English writer who wasn't yet famous came to Weimar. Marian Evans had just run away with G. H. Lewes; it was 1854 and it would be a few years yet before she turned herself into George Eliot. They spent three months in the town, while Lewes worked on his still-readable biography of Goethe, three months in a place that, though there were as yet few statues up, was already busy turning itself into a memorial. They met Clara Schumann, whose husband had just been shut away, and Liszt, whose playing made her feel that "for the first time in my life I beheld real inspiration." But for Evans — Eliot — Weimar had "a charm independent" of the great names associated with it. Even allowing for the fact that she was on her honeymoon, I'm inclined to agree and to locate that charm precisely where she did: in the park that lies along the Ilm, Weimar's little stream, and which ran from the Duke's *Schloss* in town to the rococo hilltop villa called the Belvedere a few miles to the south. It's laid out on an English model, and its planning seems reflected in the discussion of landscape architecture in *Elective Affinities,* where Goethe writes that one should try to "take advantage of and enhance every existing good feature . . . of the landscape in its original natural condition." In Eliot's mind that illusion of artlessness had met with complete success, producing a park "which would be remarkably beautiful even among English parks . . . the walks are so ingeniously arranged, and the trees so luxuriant and various, that it takes weeks to learn the turnings and windings by heart." It remains a pretty piece of landscape still, dotted with small buildings, each of them with a folklore of its own, like the Roman temple built for Karl August, or the garden house in which Goethe spent his first Weimar years.

As for Goethe himself, Eliot's account of Weimar makes her sound surprised by reports that he was rather fond of sausage; it didn't fit her conception of what such a man might eat. (In fact the local *Thüringer Bratwurst* are among Germany's best, fat and juicily seasoned, much choicer than a grape for bursting against a palate, however fine. I ate one for lunch on the market square within a few minutes of my arrival, holding it in my fingers and dunking the bitten end in a pool of sharp mustard.) She visited Goethe's large house in town and found herself sharply critical of his heirs, who hoped to turn the place into cash and had curtailed the tourist's access. And like all visitors who write, she was profoundly moved by Goethe's study and library, "with its common deal shelves, and books containing his own paper marks," shelves that now indeed sag under the weight of those books; a library designed for use, not show, marked not by fine bindings but by cramped corners and bookcases squeezed in at odd angles to save space. They made her pensive, these rooms, reminding her "that the being who has bequeathed to us immortal thoughts . . . had to endure the daily struggle . . . [and] sordid cares of this working-day world." And so she looked "through the mist of rising tears at the dull study with its two small windows," this woman still inclined to hero-worship, who could not yet know that out of her own workroom in Regent's Park would come the greatest of all English novels.

It seems I have always known the "Erlkönig" in Walter Scott's translation, but like most readers of English I have otherwise come to Goethe late and only in part. *Elective Affinities*, yes, and the "Novelle" and even the "Conversations of German Refugees," but I haven't sorrowed with young Werther and remain innocent of *Faust*. The Goethe I know best is instead the man who — traveling alone and under an assumed name — jumped into a mail coach in 1786 on the first leg of the sabbatical from power that would become his *Italian Journey*. "I slipped out of Carlsbad at three in the morning," he writes, "otherwise I would not have been allowed to leave"; and if he exaggerates the danger of his friends detaining him, he nevertheless did have to write Karl August to ask for his belated permission to go. Goethe's sense of escape seems real, and it grows with each mile he moves south. The degrees of latitude tick by, and his mood improves long before he reaches the Alps: "I am writing this on the forty-ninth parallel . . . a glorious day . . . the air is extraordinarily mild." In Munich he eats his first figs, and once over the Brenner Pass is thrilled by "the first hillside vineyards . . . [and] a woman selling pears and peaches"; later there will be the richly-laden olive. "How happy I am," he cries, "that, from now on, a language I have always loved will be the living common speech." He hopes for a kind of inner renovation, asking himself if "the grooves of old mental habits [can] be effaced," wondering whether he will indeed begin to "look at things with clear, fresh eyes."

It's an oddly reassuring book, one that gives a kind of license to enthusiasm; if even Goethe can admit to being "overwhelmed . . . swept off my feet," by the grandeur that was Rome, then how can anyone play it cool? A month before visiting Weimar, I'd joined a long line at Hamburg's Fuhlsbüttel airport, waiting on a cold March morning to check my bag for a flight to Milan. It was a Friday and there were, it's true, a few gray suits around me, carrying their briefcases and not much else, setting out for a day's work building Europe. I myself was moving on to Venice for a conference. But most of the people around me looked headed for a pleasure unmitigated by even the illusion of work, and they wore an air of relaxed expectation. It was a line of loose suede jackets and open collars, of sunglasses and fine silk scarves, and nearly everybody in it had already put in a few hours at the tanning salon. Two couples traveling together and laughing; whole families with the parents in jeans. Nobody looked worried, fathers seemed patient with their teenaged children, and I remembered Dr. Johnson's claim that "the noblest prospect which a Scotchman ever sees, is the high road that takes him to England." So perhaps, I thought, the happiest moment in any German's life today is that in which the Alitalia ticket counter comes into view. Goethe himself had wanted a break from Germany, though he was hardly the first: the medieval emperors, those Ottos and Heinrichs and Friedrichs, had all preferred sunning themselves on the Adriatic to shivering on the Rhine.

Nor was Goethe the last—even leaving Alitalia aside. Twenty years after the poet's exhilarating trip, a young Frenchman who would eventually call himself Stendhal dreamt of Italy while working as a civil servant in Braunschweig, a lesser position than Goethe's, but in the service of a greater master. And when after that master's fall, the now-unemployed Henri Beyle decided to write up the time he'd spent in the land where the lemon trees bloom, he took for his name that of a Saxon town and depicted himself as a cavalry officer setting out from Berlin: "I open the letter which grants me four months leave—I am transported with joy, my heart beats faster!" Yet if their elation at the moment of departure seems similar, Goethe and Stendhal are in almost nothing else alike, and in comparing them it's possible to locate a set of contrasting desires and beliefs that even now determines the range of the traveler's responses—and not only about Italy. To Stendhal the peninsula is above all the site for "pure pleasure." In Milan, La Scala puts him in a "feverish daze" of delight, though he also claims that "there is no pleasanter occupation . . . than walking aimlessly about." Consistency is for Stendhal no virtue, it plays one's momentary perceptions false, and Italy is for him "in truth merely an occasion for sensations." Above all, for the sensation of beauty—or rather, that of happiness. For in one of his most famous aphorisms, the two seem to merge, making "beauty . . . nothing more than the promise of happiness," and, of course, the beauty that most attracts him is that of Milan's woman, beauty so overwhelming that it "obliges one to turn one's eyes away," as if he could hardly bear such joy. Still, the pursuit of the one is that of the other as well, and if we catch the euphemism that makes "happiness" a synonym for sexual fulfillment, we may also hear an echo of Jefferson in this admirer of written constitutions and "bicameral government."

One could hardly imagine a greater contrast to Goethe, whose attitude toward pleasure and indeed toward Italy itself seems considerably more ambivalent if not necessarily more complex. In Rome, Stendhal tastes the delight of "wandering almost at random . . . without thinking about [his] duty to see." Goethe will have none of that, and reminds himself that "I am not here simply to have a good time, but to devote myself to the noble objects about me, to educate myself . . ." For "like true Germans, we cannot refrain from making plans to work," and Italy isn't a place for pleasure so much as it is for *Bildung*—though that education can itself produce a "joyous composure" and the "presence of such noble objects makes me feel very happy." Nor can those objects, those buildings and statues and paintings, ever lose for him "their freshness . . . for I did not grow up with them." Goethe's visual sense awakens, and he feels "the moral effect of having lived in a larger world," one that has changed him "to the very marrow of [his] bones."

Stendhal travels, as Dennis Porter writes, "to be ravished by the spectacle of beauty"; Goethe to locate himself in relation to the past. "My purpose in making this wonderful journey," the latter writes, "is not to delude myself but to discover myself in the objects I see." It would be easy to read that sentence uncharitably, to hear in it the traveler from the north projecting himself onto the warm landscape of the south and finding in it some analogue for his inner life. That is what Graham Greene did in his *Journey Without Maps*, turning West Africa — "the past from which one has emerged . . . [the] true primitive source" — into an emblem for all the fears of his own early childhood. But I don't want to see Goethe's statement as such an act of appropriation, even though he quite consciously presents himself as an awestruck inheritor of Rome's never-vanished glory. He doesn't impose himself on Italy so much as he hopes that Italy will impose itself on him. He wants to be flooded by it and to use his experience of the place as a way to test himself. Just as he finds it "impossible to understand the present without knowing the past," so he hopes to discover his own soul through the contemplation of the great city around him. St. Peter's makes him "realize that Art, like Nature, can abolish all standards of measurement," and it is precisely through such struggles to apprehend a world outside his own experience that the poet comes to know himself.

The French writer doesn't test himself in that way. He does, admittedly, test himself as a lover, seeing how well (not well) he can manage what he already knows how to do, but he doesn't have Goethe's sense of discovery. Not at any rate about the self. In making other kinds of discoveries, however, the advantage is all Stendhal's. Goethe writes that "What I want to see is the Everlasting Rome, not the Rome which is replaced by another every decade," and that sense of the everlasting does indeed dominate the *Italian Journey*. He describes the Carnival and offers a memorable account of Neapolitan street life, but his primary interest lies in monuments, not manners. Stendhal's concerns are very different. Most tourists, he argues, content themselves with giving a reliable description of works of art, but he is bored by such counting of columns and wants instead to capture "the inner, secret life of Italy." Some of those secrets are, of course, political ones. His *Rome, Naples, and Florence in 1817* is marked by republican longings in a time of reaction, and Stendhal himself was expelled from Italy in 1821 because of his involvement with the *Carbonari*. He doesn't want an everlasting Italy, he wants a new one, and the very specificity of his title suggests the possibility that the country may soon be different. But in the meantime, and in the absence of political change, he is content to limn the moment — fascinated by the everyday life that Goethe eschews, noting down the details of this year's clothes, music, manners, love affairs.

Pleasure, learning, monuments, mores — it's perhaps a sign of the complex and richly varied role Italy plays in the European imagination that both their approaches should seem equally plausible and equally valid. Nevertheless these very different writers do have one crucial thing in common. To each of them, Italy provides the opportunity for both an expansion and a record of the self. Travel writing may take many forms. It can describe a journey of adventure or discovery, of exploration and endurance, the kind of trip that involves physical risk, whether those risks are the product of nature or of politics. At one extreme, as Porter writes, it may tend toward an act of political witness, and at another toward the fieldwork of ethnography. Taken together, however, the Italian journeys of Goethe and Stendhal do provide a norm for a particular kind of traveler's tale, for the account of a journey made in safety if not always in comfort, the tale that neither bears witness nor depends on reliable reporting so much as it provides an idiosyncratic record of one's own individual experience. Yet what about the land from which Goethe in fact and Stendhal in fiction had set out? What possibilities, and what problems, does Germany hold for the traveler, and the travel writer?

I made the stations of the tour: stopped in the church where Herder preached and saw the Cranachs in the museum that now fills Weimar's large shambling *Schloss*. I waited in line, the only American, with a busload of elderly Germans, to admire the Borromini-like curves of the bookcases and stairs in the ducal library. I saw the building where the Bauhaus had gotten its start and found to my surprise how little Weimar had to do with Weimar — that is, with the Weimar Republic, whose 1919 declaration here owed less to cultural history than to the city's relative isolation and calm. I hiked to the Belvedere — not worth it — and saw Goethe's house with its pretty back garden and wide handsome staircase, and the library in which Eliot had found herself so moved. But she was less impressed with the rest of the place, finding that Goethe's "collection of casts, pictures, cameos, etc. . . . is utterly insignificant except as having belonged to him." And perhaps that judgment can stand for one of Weimar itself. It's charming enough — indeed more than that as one walks through the park — but it's interesting because of what happened here and not because of any physical remains. Eliot herself wrote that it "does *not* shine in its buildings!" Which makes it rather curious. The town lives on its past, and yet that past left its principal relics not in the form of things you must go there to see but rather in that of words, which you can read anywhere. Do we actually need to visit a writer's haunts and houses, do they ever really tell us anything that the work itself cannot? Weimar doesn't have much to say about what gave Goethe his range and his strength, though perhaps — perhaps — the Frankfurt of his childhood could, the free city that fostered what Thomas Mann called his "middle-class love of order . . . a carefulness and caution."

And yet the one piece of architecture that quickened into life for me did seem to have some explanatory power. When she passed control of Weimar to her son, Anna Amalia moved out of the ducal *Schloss* and into the *Wittumspalais* — the dower house — in the city center. It was just a few minutes walk, but several centuries away in the ease and informality of its rooms. The Rococo was beginning to lighten into the spare clean lines that would be called Biedermeier, and there, in rooms furnished with comfortable tables and chairs, where the walls were painted a delicate lime-sherbet green, on floors of simple polished boards, beneath ceilings of a moderate height — in rooms that would have suited a German Jane Austen, were such a thing conceivable — the Dowager Duchess served coffee to her friends. They are rooms in which you want to stay and talk; and many people did. I looked hard at the portraits of Anna Amalia that hung in the *Wittumspalais*. She was still in her teens when her husband died, a young woman and pretty, and though Weimar's manners were lax enough, one still wonders what her life would have been like. Was it all invitations to poets and supervising her son's education, or did she have the chance for affairs that weren't of state? Standing before her picture, and thinking of this city that she more than anyone else had made, I found myself hoping that she had had a good time.

I don't know what kind of good times my hotel might have been able to produce, though it did offer some curious cable channels, but I didn't at all enjoy staying there. The Elephant sits on a corner of Weimar's main square, holding down a spot where you can imagine there's been an inn for as long as there's been a city. Certainly it was already old in Goethe's time. Its corridors provide the setting for a part of Mann's *Lotte in Weimar*, his 1939 novel about the writer whom he saw always as both his model and his competition; while Thackeray borrowed its name for Becky Sharp's disreputable Pumpernickel lodging, where she lives happily in a society of students and tumblers. Such raffish ease is now long past, though the hotel's long hallway was indeed full of theatrical memorabilia, souvenirs of the guests who had come to play at Weimar's state theater. And I appreciated the fact that the hotel put its history on display, that it sought to cultivate a sense of its own past. Or a part of it anyway, for the Elephant has another and much more oppressive history, not the stuff in the display cases but the one that seemed to shout from every detail of its construction.

Because the Nazi leadership, all the way up to Hitler himself, liked the Elephant so much that they remade it in their own image, gutting the old building and replacing it with one of a severely rationalized modernity. Even my locally published guidebook admits that "the relation of the hotel . . . to the plain block architecture of those years cannot be denied." I had already had a taste of that architecture, walking in from the train station past what was called the Gauforum, the headquarters for the Nazis' regional administration, and which still today houses local government offices. Long lines of low and absolutely regular archways, balconies that could double as reviewing stands, a plinth that must once have supported a swastika, and all of it with the stone left slightly rough from the saw — the Gauforum's style was unmistakable, and though the hotel's plain stuccoed front wasn't nearly so scary, its hallways and public rooms were. Smooth marble walls, groups of rigorously angled brass-studded leather chairs, burnished metal balustrades, a dining room in black lacquer—the Elephant was a perfectly preserved piece of sleek Art Deco design, but it was also the point at which Radio City shakes hands with Albert Speer.

And this is where Weimar—where traveling in Germany—cracks open in a way that makes it impossible to maintain the light ironic tone in which I've so far described it. I can't go on inconsequentially quoting from the accounts of earlier visitors, using the long history of touristic commentary as a lens through which to focus my own response. I can't continue to treat its history as though it were merely picturesque, a cabinet of curiosities in which it's a pleasure to dabble. I can't describe Weimar as though it were a place in France or Italy, some Chenonceaux or Siena in whose past one might take an amused if admittedly simplistic interest. Not because I think we should we should turn away from monuments to concentrate, as Stendhal suggests, on contemporary life; not because our interest in the Weimar that changes with each decade should supersede our fascination with the city everlasting. That's not always the case, and if it were, one might simply evade the problem of Weimar by noting the details of its present: the smell of coal fires, always odd for an American; or the fact that during my visit the city was full of dust, with half its sidewalks and streets torn up, in the process of being replaced in preparation for the city's role as a cultural capital of the European Union; or that almost a decade after unification, the restaurants and cafes remained cheaper here, in the former East Germany, than they were in similarly sized cities in the West.

No, the problem is more stubborn than that, more intractable—even, perhaps, unsolvable. For the city doesn't mean what it used to, and speaks now of something more and other than Goethe's time, its meaning complicated, altered, made multiple and troubling in a way that Eliot and Thackeray could never have imagined. Weimar is often called both the best and the worst place in German history, but people sometimes skip over the worst, and the day after I got back to Hamburg I heard a TV commentator describe the town as the capital of the German spirit. It made me shudder because his words *weren't* ironic or double-edged, because he was indeed thinking only of Anna Amalia and her friends. Yet to describe Weimar in that way is to risk forgetting that, in the beech woods on the nearby Ettersberg hills, the Nazis had found the site for a small enclosure: though even they tried sometimes to forget what they were doing, or at least to hide it from themselves. Party members in Weimar decided to call the place after the trees, rather than use the one by which it had always been known, for Ettersberg was a name too fondly associated with the memory of Goethe himself, a place where his plays had been acted in the open air.

"Gedenkstätte Buchenwald." It is the strangest direction I have ever given to a cab driver. But I didn't need the word *Gedenkstätte*—memorial—even though it is now a part of the place's name. Was there some other Buchenwald? And in retrospect my insistence on the full name seems absurd, a bit of pedantry produced by my sense that there was something wrong, something entirely too comfortable, in arriving at a concentration camp by taxi; something I could make right by the formality with which I over-specified my destination. Of course, the pony-tailed cabbie found nothing strange about it, and he didn't bother with the qualifying term. "Buchenwald, Jawohl," and as we drove out of town the name appeared again on road signs next to those of nearby villages and towns, a matter-of-fact directional listing: turn here.

We went north through the hills, and each curve in the road seemed to open up a pastoral landscape, with distant fields gone yellow in flower. The woods here are full of beech trees still, though most of them now look young, and as we drove I thought about the place I was going to see. Buchenwald speaks, in Saul Friedländer's words, of a history that is both "too massive to be forgotten, and too repellent to be integrated into the 'normal' narrative of memory." It is no longer a part of the city's daily life, of the Weimar that, to borrow Goethe's words about Rome, "is replaced by another every decade." One balks, however, at seeing the place as a part of the city "everlasting," even as one knows that in some sense that's precisely what it is, a weight the city must eternally bear. Few critics would argue that the world of the *Weimarer Klassik* has been vitiated, invalidated, by the region's later history, though that might be true of a place like Bayreuth, whose custodians, Wagner's heirs, called Hitler their uncle. Nevertheless the Nazis did try to claim Goethe's legacy. Or maybe just to neutralize it. "What better way," as James Young has written, "to commemorate the obliteration of Weimar culture than to seal it in barbed wire, to turn it into its own prison?" And while Young's words point specifically to the Weimar Republic and the culture of the 1920s, they do still evoke the Nazis' attempt to control the memory of that older city as well. So today Weimar carries a double meaning, one elegantly summarized by Timothy Garton Ash as the problem of the "Goethe Oak . . . the ancient . . . tree . . . under which Goethe had supposedly written his sublime 'Wanderer's Night Song,' but which was then enclosed on the grounds of the Buchenwald concentration camp." In fact the tree made it until near the end of the war, the nightmare's mocking — or sustaining? — bit of greenery, before catching fire in an air raid; now all that's left is its ruined stump, halfway between the disinfection chambers and the crematorium.

Any student of German culture must learn to negotiate the contradictions and connections that the Goethe Oak implies; must worry at the question of how one might get from the poet to the prison, and back again; must worry at the question of their coincidence in something more than space. Even my own trouble in moving from a description of Weimar into an account of a visit to Buchenwald is a version of that problem. Down the hill I could take a Stendhalian pleasure in thinking about the past. Here I couldn't, and indeed there seemed a kind of injunction against thinking of it as being, in fact, the past. Never forget. As we drove I thought of Primo Levi and Paul Celan, the camp survivors who many years later had killed themselves, and also of Faulkner, for whose characters the past is not even past, who live on as their own ghosts in the long aftermath of the moments that have determined their being. Something similar seemed to be happening here. There may always, as Eric Hobsbawm has written, be "a twilight zone . . . between the past as a generalized record which is open to relatively dispassionate inspection and the past as part of, or background to, one's own life." But Buchenwald's resistance to anything like a "'normal' narrative" pointed to something more than that accustomed tension between history and memory. It suggested a past that had so outlived its own time that it seemed even now to tingle with the pain that an amputee feels where his arm used to be.

Paul Fussell has argued that travel narratives always draw an implicit comparison between the writer's own freedom — his freedom of movement, his freedom of thought — and the more circumscribed lives of the people through whose land he wanders. But here? How, I wondered, as I paid my cab and bought a guidebook at the guards' barracks that nows serves as a visitor's center, how could I possibly graph that model onto this place? Today everybody who arrives at Buchenwald comes either as a visitor or to serve them. Nobody — I hesitate to use the word "lived," and yet it's the only one — nobody now lived at Buchenwald, but that only underlined the difficulty of describing it. Even if I hadn't arrived in a taxi I would still have been ludicrously, painfully free to come and go in comparison to the many thousands who suffered here, to the Jews and homosexuals and Communists and Gypsies and Jehovah's Witnesses and political prisoners and Russian POWs who had been imprisoned or executed here. And though I was certainly a visitor, only the cruelest of definitions would describe each of those thousands as the visitor's binary opposite: the resident, the inhabitant, the native. That term might apply with justice only to the SS guards. The prisoners were precisely not natives; neither had they been in any sense visitors.

Such chopping of terms demonstrates the moral limits of the assumptions on which most travel writing depends. None of the ways in which I customarily described a place seemed as if they could apply to a concentration camp. The site beggared them and yet in doing so produced a decorum of its own, one that makes it impossible to quote from the memoirs Buchenwald's survivors have left behind in the way that I have from the touristic impressions of Weimar's Victorian visitors. I can't treat the narratives of Bruno Bettelheim or Jorge Semprun as though they were a form of cultivated table-talk; let me leave them instead as a kind of gap in my text, a gesture toward what is here, at any rate, unsayable. Of course, that sense of language failing has in itself become one of the standard features of the rhetoric with which we try to describe our reaction to the Holocaust. So too is our awareness of the gap between that time and this one, the victim's experience and our own. "I tried," Ian Buruma has written of Auschwitz, "to imagine what it had been like inside . . . I found it impossible. It was like trying to imagine extreme hunger or having your fingernails ripped out. I knew about the suffering, but could not imagine it. . . . The idea that visiting the relics of history brings the past closer is usually an illusion. The opposite is more often true." Even at the camps we fall back upon the conventional formulae of description and sentiment, though that does not necessarily mean such conventions are in themselves untrue.

Still, an awareness of that conventionality does suggest why some of the most sensitive accounts of visiting Buchenwald, such as those by Buruma and Young, stress the mediated quality of the experience: the way in which the choice of what to preserve and what to display, the terms in which the camp's victims are defined, the nature of its monuments, all serve to organize our memory of what happened here. To me the camp tells two fundamentally different stories, a difference best defined as that between the largest and grandest of its memorial sites, on the one hand, and the camp enclosure, on the other. They lie some distance away from each other, and on opposite sides of the hill; neither offers a view of the other. The memorial is the more familiar image. A walkway sweeps down the slope toward a broad terrace that's known as the "Road of Nations," a road marked by eighteen black pillars, one for each country whose citizens died here. Look out over the pillars and you'll see a patchwork of fields and forest, Thuringia's countryside at its prettiest. Turn around and you'll find that something else shares your view, a set of eleven enormous bronze figures. The group commemorates the prisoners who in April 1945 rose up against their guards and — as some versions have it — liberated themselves in advance of the American Third Army's arrival. A few of the figures wave and point, as if beckoning the future, others brandish weapons, and yet another holds up a flag; only one of these giants is depicted in the act of falling. Behind them rises a bell tower, and the ensemble as a whole has some of the triumphant spirit of the Iwo Jima memorial, however differently its statuary is modeled — in Young's words, "a spreading victory wedge of dignified fighting figures unbent by their travails."

Two things seem especially important in understanding the story this *Gedenkstätte* tells. The first is that, while the Nazis did murder over 50,000 people here, Buchenwald was not an extermination camp like Auschwitz. It began as a camp for political prisoners, and only near the end of the war did the persecution and killing of Jews become one of its primary tasks. The second is that Weimar lies in the region that after the war became East Germany. So Buchenwald, in which many of that short-lived country's rulers had been imprisoned, became a central feature in the DDR's founding myth, one in which the inmates' Communist-led underground became identified with the officially antifascist nation itself. In consequence, as Young writes, "the state museum and memorial at Buchenwald were not intended to mark the loss of life so much as to illustrate the glories of resistance—and to celebrate the socialist victory over fascism." If the monumental "Road of Nations" honored the victims in terms of their national origin it did not identify them in other ways; so far as the DDR was concerned, the Jews who died here died not as Jews but as political prisoners of French or Dutch or Polish or—often—German origin. Perhaps that emphasis is just as well, for with its heroic statuary and self-conscious grandeur the monument's guiding aesthetic seems so close to that of Weimar's Gauforum as to make you understand why Hitler and Stalin thought their nonaggression pact might work. But then Stalin saw Buchenwald itself as a good idea, he had his own need for such places, and until 1950 went on using the camp for his own purposes. After the *Wende* or "turn"—the term that has come to denote the opening of the Berlin Wall—the exhibits at Buchenwald began to note both the East German omissions and the Soviet crimes. I suspect that with time this particular memorial will come to seem less and less important, consigned to school groups and students of totalitarian sculpture, the relic of a discarded historiography.

The enclosure offers a different and more enduring narrative, precisely because it is the more painful, because it depends, in Lawrence Langer's words, not on "the redemptive [but on] the grievous power of memory." Yet even as one walks through its gate and begins to experience the camp as a physical place, a piece of land, a set of rooms—even here one cannot escape the question of mediation, of the way in which the camp has been presented, the story it has been made to tell. Buchenwald covered a lot of territory—work areas, railroad siding, mass graves, the SS quarters, the commandant's riding stable—but the central enclosure, the barbed wire area in which the prisoners' barracks were located, looks considerably smaller than the area taken up by the *Gedenkstätte*. My guidebook speaks of 48,000 people living in a space of about 40 hectares—100 acres—on the side of the Ettersberg hill, but the ground before me was not anywhere near so large. Twenty acres, thirty? Maybe bigger, but still small enough so that when I stood at the entry gates I could see it all at once.

What I saw resembled nothing so much as the landscape that Auden described in "The Shield of Achilles":

> A plain without a feature, bare and brown,
>   No blade of grass, no sign of neighbourhood,
> Nothing to eat and nowhere to sit down,
>   Yet, congregated on its blankness, stood
>   An unintelligible multitude.

"Barbed wire," Auden adds, "enclosed an arbitrary spot," and when I first saw the place it looked to me as if that was the only detail he'd gotten wrong. The spot had not been arbitrary at all. On one side the wire is in fact still up and has indeed been renewed, though it runs for only a hundred yards and encloses nothing. I stood beneath the camp's main gate, whose roof line seemed like a parody of the Belvedere on the other side of the city, and looked out at a blasted plain. No, not a plain, for it sloped away from me. But it was indeed flat and even, with "no blade of grass . . . and nowhere to sit down," a slope covered with stones, a surface that you could walk over only with difficulty, slowly, carefully—a place in which it would be impossible to run and impossible to hide. Utterly featureless it was for the first few hundred feet; this had been the "Mustering Ground," on which that multitude had shivered for hours at the whim of their guards in the cold and the rain. Then beyond were the places where the prisoners' barracks had stood, with the location of each one marked out in the stones.

Had stood. For the landscape I saw, the arduous ground over which I worked my way, was not the one in which the prisoners had lived, and the desolation that made me think of Auden's poem was, in some sense at least, a postwar creation. Almost all of Buchenwald's many dozen buildings have been razed. When the camp was in use it would have been impossible to see from one end of the enclosure to the other, and though the crowds and the noise and the smells, the shouts and the shots of the guards, might have made it seem like hell, it would not have looked so null and bleakly empty. Yet what if the East German authorities in charge of landscaping the place had decided differently? One recognizes the dilemma they faced: what to do with a place so evil that you want to destroy it utterly, yet also a place of such human suffering that you simultaneously need to preserve it in commemoration? And their solution makes sense: demolish the buildings, or most of them, but note exactly where they stood. Suppose, however, that the buildings had been left standing? Or that the people who planned this memorial had done what the custodians of so many New World battlefields have and turned the camp into a park, planted grass and trees, installed benches? Gettysburg and Quebec now contrive to look peaceful; so too do many military cemeteries. Buchenwald does not. This wounded land has not been allowed to heal, and because the ground itself looks as though it has not forgotten, because that plain of stones looks like a place in which the barking orders could start again at any moment, we find it that much harder to forget ourselves.

The DDR's citizens were, of course, meant to see this scarred land in dialogue with that overblown *Gedenkstätte,* to see their juxtaposition in terms of a single meaning: look at what our liberation has saved us from. But in comparing the two, and even leaving East Germany's own peculiarities aside, it seemed impossible to believe that many people would have seen the redemptive vision of the one as an adequate answer to the other. They told fundamentally different stories, the monument and the enclosure, and the latter was by far the more powerful. Still, I wonder: the decision must at some point have been made that Buchenwald's atrocities would be best memorialized by this kind of landscape. And while allowing for the *Gedenkstätte's* celebration of resistance, the ground within the enclosure itself has nevertheless been made to reflect a particular interpretation of the Holocaust, of the kind Friedländer has offered and on which I've relied myself.

By now, however, it is in itself one of that interpretation's chief constituents, a memory carved in the soil, a memory defined by the decision to leave this building standing and to knock that one down, to keep some of the wire up, to plant stones and not grass — decisions that in themselves now shape the terms in which we see the past. What if that land had been differently modeled? We might well have come to see the Holocaust in other terms, might have found ourselves — perhaps for good, perhaps for ill — with a rather different sense of its wounds and of its relation to our present lives.

For me the most affecting part of the camp was its small crematorium. I didn't count its separate bays or ovens — four, six? — but it could not have handled many bodies at once, maybe no more than a funeral complex in a large city. Even so it represented an enormous increase in the scale of death at Buchenwald: at first the camp had simply used Weimar's municipal crematorium. The building I saw went up in 1941, and its ovens, made by the Erfurt firm of Topf und Söhne, provided the prototype for those that would later be used at Auschwitz. But it wasn't just a place to burn bodies — the courtyard outside was regularly used for executions, and so was the basement, where corpses were stacked while waiting their turn for the incinerator. It must have been convenient, to kill on site that way, a thousand people and more in that basement room, with an elevator to take the cadavers to the fire upstairs. The ovens themselves were roughly cylindrical and nothing about them announced their purpose. They looked industrial and inscrutable, and if I hadn't known otherwise I might have thought they were used for making charcoal or firing a steamship, for any factory process that required flames and a chimney.

Two teenagers came in, a boy and a girl with their hands in each other's pockets, and stuck their heads inside one of the ovens, calling out to test its echo. I flinched and stepped away from them into the room next door, and then flinched again, for there was nothing inscrutable here. Old yellow tiles on the wall; a display case of rusty surgical instruments and a faucet over a large deep sink; a table, also covered in tiles, that sloped in from the sides to a central channel, and that sloped as well from the head to the drain at the foot. My throat felt as though it were shrinking inside me, shriveling tight and parchment dry. I have never been in a morgue; I know them only from televised detective shows. But I could recognize a dissecting table, and I knew what kinds of things had been done in this room. It was called the "Pathology Department," but it didn't look as though complicated medical tests could be performed here, and there weren't the refrigerated lockers I'd seen on TV, in which a corpse might be stored until the coroner was ready. Here there had been no need for either tests or cold storage. The doctors who worked at Buchenwald already knew what their subjects had died of, and they knew as well that there was no need to preserve any particular body for long. There would always be another one ready.

✹ TWO

The Peculiarities of German Travel

All that came later, long months after we had settled into our lives on Hamburg's Rothenbaumchaussee, months in which I'd both gotten used to Germany and then begun to find it strange again. We had arrived in early August, and on those first days, as we unpacked our boxes and began to learn our way around the large high-ceilinged apartment that came with Brigitte's job, as we admired its stuccoed moldings and looked skeptically at the furniture her predecessors had chosen, a few sentences from one of my favorite novels kept coming into my mind. "I am a camera with its shutter open, quite passive, recording, not thinking. Recording the man shaving at the window opposite and the woman in the kimono washing her hair. Some day, all this will have to be developed, carefully printed, fixed." That's the second paragraph of Christopher Isherwood's *Goodbye to Berlin*, the book that became *Cabaret*. As I read those sentences, I know, of course, that Isherwood's narration is hardly the neutral medium it claims to be, that it wouldn't be neutral even if he were a camera in fact; that the camera — or rather the photographer — selects the objects he shows us, if only by deciding at which second to snap open the shutter. I know too that Isherwood's first paragraph, which precedes the one I've quoted, contains a judgement that's anything but passive, a summation of the Berlin he sees out his window as that of "a bankrupt middle class." Yet when a week after our arrival, I sat down to write a letter and looked at the chestnut trees outside my window tossing in a sudden peal of wind and rain, at the umbrellas popping open on the sidewalk below and the bicyclists dodging the raindrops, at the wipers going on the Mercedes taxis that are here the color of Jersey cream—at that moment I was indeed willing to see myself as a kind of camera, "recording, not thinking," letting the details of this place wash over me, details that would later have to be printed and fixed, made coherent, made sense of. It wasn't quite a feeling of sensory overload, I've known that in Italy and India, and it was different here. My eyes weren't delirious, I wasn't standing slack-jawed with delight at the color and clang of the streets. Rather it's that I felt bombarded by bits and pieces of experience that I didn't know what to do with, that looked as though they ought to mean something—but what?

The watcher in the window, the wanderer in the fog. One thing, at least, did soon become clear: we were living in a neighborhood we couldn't afford, not on our own, not even in an apartment half the size of the one we'd been given. The Rotherbaum district lies just outside what had been Hamburg's old defenses, a nineteenth-century quarter of semidetached villas that's an easy twenty-minute stroll from the city's stock exchange. It was solidly bourgeois then and even more so today. With the exception of the Rothenbaumchaussee itself, its streets are leafily quiet, some of them laid with paving stones instead of asphalt, and their curbs seem a solid line of black BMWs. Judging by the number of bells on the door many of its houses look to be real houses still, unbroken into apartments. They vary considerably in their façades— brick, a few of them, occasionally a bit of rusticated stone—but most come plastered in either white or a soft pastel, and topped with a slate mansard roof. Some of them have oriel windows that have been blown up into sunrooms, airy porches that might go up for two or more stories and extend themselves into a gable. Here and there a lilac leans over a gate and offers the promise of a garden behind.

It is Hamburg's Upper East Side, but with buildings on a Brooklyn brownstone scale, its Knightsbridge and its 6eme. Real estate here and in the adjoining neighborhood of Harvestehude comes as high as it does anywhere in the city, and when I give my address to a friend I always feel like an imposter. Of course, not all its buildings are private houses still. The Rothenbaumchaussee itself looks to have been built mostly as *Mietshäuser* — literally, rent-houses or apartment buildings — and our own building has also done time as a hotel. There are restaurants and an occasional row of small shops — greengrocer, newspapers, bakery. The University has taken over many houses: the program in Near Eastern studies has its offices in the building next door and a weightily porticoed mansion houses an institute for the study of maritime law. Otherwise it's a neighborhood of smooth professional services: dentists, tax advisors, consulates, architects. And though I'm sure they all work hard enough, the district's low arboreal buildings give it a quality of hushed leisure, as though the whole place were taking a long lunch.

A few hundred yards to the east is the Alster, an artificial lake that dates from the thirteenth century, when somebody I'll call Müller or Miller threw a dam across a little local stream just before it joined the Elbe. It's Hamburg's central feature, a couple of miles from one end to the other, and roughly the shape of a veal chop. Bridges nip off a small piece near the bottom to form the Binnenalster, a pond in the center of the city's commercial district, a reflecting pool in which, on good days, you can see the spires of the city's churches. I prefer the much larger Aussenalster, its surface littered with sailboats, its willowy shore dotted with benches and — odd, this — white Adirondack chairs. A bicyclist dodges an inattentive unleashed schnauzer, a child strays too close to a swan, two elegant elderly women stroll arm in arm, a man leans on a railing to watch an eight from one of the city's rowing clubs slip by. It is Hamburg's favorite *passegiata*, and on a Sunday afternoon can seem as crowded as a train station.

Yet though we walk toward the Alster for pleasure, necessity tends to take us in the other direction. Just to the west of our street is the university district, the campus itself a cobblestoned plain, with the mesas and buttes of its buildings jutting skyward, its buildings as ugly and barely functional as those of its American urban equivalents. We walk through it to get to the shops on Grindelhof and Grindelallee, the main roads in what was once Hamburg's middle-class Jewish district. Butcher, café, cheese, bookstores both new and used, an art house cinema, hairdressers, an "American" diner, a trio of Italian restaurants with wood-burning ovens. And it was, in fact, after a mid-August meal of pizza and Chianti that we came out into the evening light and instead of turning home walked north, into streets we hadn't yet discovered. At Hallerstrasse the neighborhood changed, the commercial buildings vanished, and we crossed into Harvestehude, where the houses seemed even grander than those in Rotherbaum. Some looked closed up for the August vacation, but through the window of one I could see a family still sitting at dinner in a large and richly decorated room, its walls a soft blue and with Chinese figurines — a mandarin, a dog — in the window. In the house next door, a man rose in a room lined with books and pulled the curtains shut, as if he knew we were outside.

Brigitte is an art historian and though her field is medieval manuscripts she can read a modern urban landscape. "This street is newer than the ones near us," she said. "It's all Jugendstil." She pointed to a house. Thin lines of plaster molding ran down from a plain medallion, as though it were dripping, and the doors and window frames were cut in curls and swoops. On another a pediment was supported by two caryatids with faces out of Klimt, and under the eaves I saw a pair of dolphins flirting with one another. Straight lines seemed impossible; the houses themselves looked as though they wanted to swell and ripple. "Or it would be," she added, "except for the war. You can really see the bomb damage." I knew from my reading that much of Hamburg had been flattened, that particularly in its working-class districts the British firebombs had burned a clear horrific path. But I could find no such devastation here and looked for the shell-pocked walls I'd seen in Budapest, or the bullet-dented façades I'd noticed on the Pergamon Museum in what had been East Berlin. This damage was different, for it wasn't precisely damage, not any more, and I had to be taught to notice it. Brigitte gestured at a building across the street, an apartment house in a smooth faceless international style, toward two old buildings sandwiching one from the fifties, to the new top story of a third, the simplified lines of its roof and windows. To my untrained eye it all looked entirely normal, the kind of architectural hodgepodge one might find in any American city. But either end of the block we stood on was anchored by an intact Jugendstil mansion and so I took the point when she said, "There's no other reason for the street to have had its unity broken up." That, in this neighborhood, was what one could most readily see of the Second World War. And in looking at the way the holes had been plugged, at an urban fabric expensively though not invisibly mended, I couldn't help but think of the opening lines of James Fenton's sardonic "German Requiem": "It is not what they built. It is what they knocked down./ It is not the houses. It is the space between the houses." There no longer seemed to be any spaces here.

Like a camera with its shutter open. One hot and uncharacteristically sunny afternoon we turn left out the door of our building and head toward the Innenstadt for a bit of shopping — "downtown," that is, and not the "inner city" of a literal translation. Down the Rothenbaumchaussee and then across to cut through Dammtor station; up and over the flying bridge and past the Livotto Eis *gelateria* and then the opera house, where we've not yet been; through the Gänsemarkt and along Jungfernstieg, the city's fifth Avenue promenade; past the Alster Pavilion cafe, in whose band Brahms' father had played the horn. We've been here a week and we're looking for sheets, and perhaps predictably we end up not at Karstadt's or the Alsterhaus—not at the German stores—but at Habitat. Half the staff seems to be twenty-something Brits speaking German; the others are Germans speaking English. We don't find what we're looking for but there's something that will do, and once outside with our shopping bags we drop down at a canal-side café for a beer.

What, I ask, with a cool pilsner tingle in my mouth, what constitutes a meaningful cultural difference? At Habitat the German sales clerk had taken my two hundred mark notes and laid 19.50 in change on the counter, leaving it for me to scoop up myself instead of dropping it in my hand. That made me remember a newspaper article I'd read just before we left the States. The reporter had asked the counter staff at Manhattan espresso bars what they found most aggravating about their clients, and discovered that they especially hated those customers who simply put their money on the counter instead of placing it into the server's hand. It dehumanized the transaction, the *baristas* claimed, it made them feel as if they were being treated like a serving machine and not a person. Now that had been done to me—and how should I interpret it?

Brigitte herself hadn't noticed it; she's Swiss and moves from one set of manners to another as easily as she slips between languages. Yet perhaps, she suggested, it's a different attitude toward money—or maybe a different sense of the relations between customers and salespeople. Over the next few weeks, I found that in many stores there's a little tray on the counter and that the norm, the proper thing, is for the customer to put his money into that tray, for the sales clerk then to pick it up, and to drop the change there in turn. That's especially true in shops that handle a great many small transactions, like bakeries and newsstands, and also at registers run by older people. Neither of you should touch each other's hand, a notion that I can well imagine growing out of a rigid distinction between server and served. How much weight, I wondered, could I or should I place on this—how much could it tell me about the country in which we were now living?

That was the kind of question my camera-eye saw, and if thinking about it over the next few weeks didn't produce answers, it did at least help me develop a sense of the terms on which those answers might be found. The traveler—and still more the travel writer—approaches such moments as though he were a forensic scientist, trying to piece together a culture out of a fragment or two of evidence, extrapolating from a bit of bone or a scrap of language. What those extrapolations require above all is that we compare one scrap, one culture, to another. We may share the Herderian dream of taking each land on and only on its own terms, but though we may want to see a culture as it really is in itself, the only way in which we can make sense of a new place is to locate it in relation to those that we've known before. You come to understand a country not only through what it is but also through what it isn't, defining each new experience through its difference from those to which we are already accustomed. Such comparisons now have a bad name. Earlier travelers—and soldiers, and administrators—too often transformed those differences into a hierarchy of values. A country or a culture might be condemned, laughed at, ruled over, according to the degree that it departed from the traveler's own imported norms, seen not in itself but only as the obverse of some other, an "abroad" defined as "not home." Yet Herder's belief that countries are indeed different does in fact require us to make such comparisons; the mistake comes only when we try to assimilate them to a single criterion of value, when we forget, as Isaiah Berlin puts it, that "cultures are comparable but not commensurable."

So think not of norms but of the Rosetta Stone. There the unknown language finds itself matched not against an absolute standard but rather to its equivalent in a different tongue, and yet again in a different alphabet, matched to a range of other places and possibilities. There the process of comparison and clarification makes all terms relative, defined through each other. Hamburg's streets are cleaner than Amsterdam's but dirtier than Copenhagen's. It is proportionately less multiracial than London but much more so than Milan; quieter than Berlin, more bustling than Munich. And if young people here have more pierced tongues and noses and eyebrows and, for all I know, nipples than they do in Venice, they still wear less stuff on their faces than they do in my home town of Northampton, Massachusetts. Pizzas in Germany are a bit soupier than they are in the States, though they're not served with a bottle of oil on the side, as they sometimes are in France; and in none of those countries do they much resemble the stuff one eats in Naples. The Germans like plates of plain white porcelain. The English prefer them painted.

Yet what do such differences mean? A rectangular American pillow is for me the comfortable norm. Older hotels in the French provinces tend to have hard cylindrical pillows on the bed, like the ones you see on a Recamier sofa, with "normal" ones stowed away in the closet; yet though the cylinder is traditional, Brigitte says she's never seen one used in a French home. In Germany the normal pillow is square, 90 cm a side, a shape that for months seemed strange to me, as though I had either to scrunch it up or risk having my head drown in all that unaccustomed upholstery. I got used to it, though, and I'm willing to say that as a difference in cultural practice, this one doesn't amount to much. Some differences in taste point to nothing beyond themselves. The rest of the bed linen, however, is a different matter. Our apartment doesn't have a double bed—rather it has two single mattresses placed next to each other on a platform, each with its own sheets and comforter. None of the hotels we've stayed in has offered a double or a queen, and though I have seen double beds in shops, they're intended for people who live alone. You can tell because they're covered with a single duvet. Each person in Germany is meant to sleep under his own covers—and that does seem to me a meaningful cultural difference. No snuggling under a common blanket. Here the space between us not only has a crack down the middle but is also much more likely than the outer edges to be the place where there's no cover at all. It's as if the bedding itself were conspiring to keep us each in our appointed place, to prevent any meeting in the chilly middle ground. At times the temptation to see this as an emblem of German life is over-whelming.

Now it happens that most of the early travel books I've looked at talk about bedding. For as it is one of the most intimate of things, so too it is among the questions on which different lands do, for whatever reason, differ, as they differ in their sexual and sanitary practices or even in the way they make coffee. The seventeenth-century traveler Fynes Moryson writes that "throughout all Germany they lodge betweene two fetherbeds," and in *A Tramp Abroad*, Mark Twain describes the "narrow . . . German bed's ineradicable habit of spilling the blankets on the floor every time you forgot yourself and went to sleep." They notice the bedding not just because they come in nightly contact with it but because it's different from what they're used to: something peculiar to the place, that characterizes it as it does not another land. And if there is a danger in the traveler's reliance upon a comparison to some assumed norm, it's not the simplistic one I've mentioned above, in which that norm becomes a hierarchy. It has instead to do with our willingness to note and maybe even to revel in the particularities of each new place, a danger that lies in that word "peculiar."

The term comes from a brief 1889 memoir in which the British publisher John Murray III described the development of his eponymous handbooks, the compact little volumes that led generations of Anglo-American tourists across Europe and which, with the competing series published by the German firm of Karl Baedeker, stand as the first modern guidebooks. Murray writes that he began his project when "on landing at Hamburg, I found myself destitute" of advice about what to see and where to stay. In consequence he "set to work to collect for myself all the facts

. . . which an English tourist would be likely to require." Yet rather than "cram in everything . . . I made it my aim to point out things *peculiar* to the spot, or which might be better seen there than elsewhere" [italics in original]. So in Hamburg he notes the damage done by the great fire of 1842, the local habit of hiring professional mourners for funerals, and the hour at which the prettiest of the market flower girls may be found around the Bourse; while his 1854 *Southern Germany* not only offers advice about rates of exchange and the roads between Salzburg and Munich, but also includes charming little essays on Austrian salt mines, Alpine sports, and the way mountain inns fatten trout for the table. That later volume, however, included as well a room-by-room list of the paintings in Vienna's Imperial Picture Gallery, and as time went on, both Murray and Baedeker concentrated more and more heavily on providing inventories of museums and churches. For while trout can be eaten almost anywhere, an original masterpiece—the Sistine Madonna in Dresden or Dürer's self-portrait in Munich—is by definition peculiar to the spot, can best be seen in one place and one place only.

But it's not just guidebooks that emphasize the peculiar. All writing about travel does that. Flaubert in Egypt, Sybille Bedford trying to drive through Mexico—they need, they stress, the peculiar as much or more as Murray does, whether it lies in the particularities of the prostitute's trade or the details of local history. For travel is a form of digression, a digression from daily life. We travel for difference, and so we concentrate on those things—the buildings, the food, the people—that distinguish this place from that, and not on what they have in common. On the one hand, that lets us see what the inhabitants themselves no longer can, the things they take for granted, like bedding or ways of giving change. On the other, it ensures that we not only highlight but that we even exaggerate the differences between places, for what most strikes us are the exceptions to the normal run of our lives. And in consequence nearly all travel writing depends upon metonymy. Or perhaps upon cliché. It identifies those aspects of a country or a culture that differ — or are believed to differ — from other countries, other cultures, and then identifies that part with the whole. Nobody writes about Italy, for example, and notes that many telephones *do* work, except against a background assumption that most of them won't and maybe even shouldn't, not if they're proper, pre-cellular Italian telephones. No, the writer concentrates on those that *don't* work because that's what tells him that he is indeed in Italy and not Illinois. *Weisswurst* is typical of Germany because it isn't found in Thailand, and in Germany it's typical of Bavaria because it didn't originate in Schleswig-Holstein. In fact Bavaria *is* a *Weisswurst*, unless it's also *Lederhosen*.

When I learned we would be spending a year in Germany, I began looking for things to read, some history certainly, a few novels, studies of postwar and post-Wall society. But I also thought I would hunt down some travel books, as I had in preparation for visiting other countries. I knew of one already — Patrick Leigh Fermor's *A Time of Gifts*. My local bookstore gave me guides to national character: Gordon Craig's indispensable *The Germans* and John Ardagh's detailed social anatomy, *Germany and the Germans*. I returned to Isherwood — not only the *Berlin Stories* but also the more explicitly autobiographical *Christopher and His Kind* — and found many shrewd books of political reportage, like Mark Fisher's *After the Wall* and Jane Kramer's *The Politics of Memory*. Ian Buruma's *The Wages of Guilt* compared the way in which Germany and Japan have dealt with the memory of the Second World War, while Tina Rosenberg's *The Haunted Land* described eastern Germany's exit from Communism. Yet Leigh Fermor found no companions: my shelves stayed empty when I went looking for some Teutonic equivalent of Mary McCarthy's *Venice Observed* or V. S. Naipaul's *An Area of Darkness*.

The library helped me some, of course. There was Twain's *A Tramp Abroad*, a poor country cousin to *The Innocents Abroad* but redeemed by its account of Heidelberg's student dueling corps and its extraordinary appendix on "The Awful German Language": "In German, a young lady has no sex, while a turnip has. Think what overwrought reverence that shows for the turnip, and what callous disrespect for the girl." Jerome K. Jerome's *Three Men on the Bummel* described a late Victorian bicycle tour in the Black Forest, and though it isn't nearly as funny as it thinks, its concluding chapter on "The German from the Anglo-Saxon's point of view" does provide a useful crystallization of fair-minded British prejudice: "The German citizen is a soldier, and the policeman is his officer," while the quality of German tobacco is a "national sin." A few pages in the Greville diaries, James Fenimore Cooper's account of his trip up the Rhine — it wasn't an extensive record, though I did find Eliot's charming little essay on Weimar and two sketches of Hesse by the young Henry James. Boswell on his Grand Tour professed a "prodigious veneration" for Frederick the Great, to whom he hoped to be presented; after he wasn't, he wrote that he "hated the barbarous hero." A century later, the French poet Jules Laforgue lived at the court in Berlin, where his job was to read French aloud to the empress Augusta, a woman who had "received, as was the custom in her youth, all the education needed to preside over a Dresden tea service." And there were some books that I would have liked to have read, if only my German were good enough. Heine's *Harz Journey* may be readily available in English, but his letters from Berlin are not, and if the many volumes of Theodor Fontane's *Wanderungen durch die Mark Brandenburg* have ever been translated, no library computer that I've consulted seems to know about it.

Then there were the shelves of books on how contemporary Germany had dealt with its own history — on what is called *Vergangenheitsbewältigung*, the process of engaging with and, ideally, overpowering the past. Especially valuable here was

Charles Maier's *The Unmasterable Past*, an account of the battles that German historians have waged among themselves, their suspicion that what Hobsbawm calls a "dispassionate inspection" of their own recent history might, in some hands, amount to an apologia for the Nazi regime. I learned what the issues were—for the Germans. But I found nothing that might help me understand how I, as a traveler and a temporary resident, might deal with that history myself.

So I went back to Leigh Fermor. I'd read it years before, prepping for a trip to Vienna, but had moved quickly through its chapters on Germany itself and had little memory of them beyond the pleasure I'd taken in the writer's store of odd knowledge. That, and of his having "recklessly drained" the last bottles "of a fabulously rare and wonderful vintage" that one of his hosts had been saving, a "treasured Spätlese from the banks of the upper Mosel," something I remembered because they are among my own favorite wines as well. Now I opened it again—and found it a rich and most peculiar travel narrative indeed. The Anglo-Irish Leigh Fermor is an amateur of classical scholarship who spent the Second World War as a partisan leader in Crete. His band's successful kidnapping of a German general provided the basis for the Michael Powell film *Ill Met by Moonlight*, with Dirk Bogarde in the lead as "Paddy." *A Time of Gifts* records his attempt, at eighteen and recently expelled from his public school, to walk across Europe, "from the Hook of Holland" to the city that the Byzantinist in him calls Constantinople; though this volume, at least, takes him only so far as the Hungarian border. He wanders south along the Rhine, spending a night in the Düsseldorf workhouse, and chopping wood in the morning in exchange for his bed and breakfast. Later he hitches a ride on a barge bound toward Karlsruhe with a load of cement and tries to learn German by reading Shakespeare in translation. His circumstances change from day to day; more than once a phone call puts him inside a *Schloss* for the night, drinking coffee under the "snowy convolutions" of an eighteenth-century ceiling, listening to his host attack "the Waldstein Sonata with authority and verve." And with every step he recites the historic names for which each place is remembered, spins theories, learns folk songs, and even embroiders an explanation for "the whole feeling and character of pre-baroque German towns," with their *Fachwerk* carvings, their "florid finials . . . and armorial glass."

Page by page it's lovely. What gives the book its point, though, is its date, or rather the difference between the date of the journey itself and that of its writing. For while Leigh Fermor set out on his walk in December 1933 and draws upon the journals he kept at the time, the book itself wasn't put together until the 1970s; the older man writes it, and in full knowledge of what was to come. Yet it is knowledge of a special kind. Now and then he allows himself a retrospective moment: recording, in a footnote, his attempt to learn what later happened to some of his German acquaintances, or flashing forward to wartime Crete. What he does not do, however, is to foreshadow in a way that would destroy his memories of his own naivete, his own pleasure and excitement in his voyage, his uncomplicated affection for many of the people he meets. On his first day, he passes through a town "hung with National Socialist banners" and sees a haberdasher's window full of "arm-bands [and] brown shirts." In Munich "the proportion of Storm Troopers . . . in the streets was unusually high . . . and the Nazi salute flickered about the pavement like a *tic doloreaux*." He quickly realizes that "appalling things had happened since Hitler had come into power," but he also notes that many of the people he met were disgusted by it all. If he is never taken in by the German state, neither does he lose sight of those "high points of recollection that failed to succumb to the obliterating mood of war": his excited and ever-growing appreciation for medieval architecture, "two marvellous swans" of girls in Stuttgart, the kindness of the Bavarian "farm people and foresters and woodcutters," with whom he spent the evenings on his walk from Munich to the Austrian border.

As one reads, one fills in the gap of years, juxtaposing the warmth and the generosity shown to him by so many, with what one knows is to come. The effect is to separate Leigh Fermor's private memory of Germany from his, from our, historical knowledge. He does not treat his experience "as the harbinger of an already determined future," to borrow Michael André Bernstein's language in *Foregone Conclusions*, his study of Holocaust narratology. For "each present, and each separate life," in Bernstein's words, "has its own distinct value that later events cannot wholly take away, and we must . . . believe this in order to continue to have any conviction about our own actions and plans." We may read Leigh Fermor's tale ironically. But he could not have given a faithful portrait of the young man he was if he had chosen to discount or deny the pleasure of his journey, had he written it as though that self-described "sleep-walking" young man should have known what would happen.

The very terms of Leigh Fermor's success do, however, suggest the difficulty of writing a travel book about Germany. If his memories are largely pleasant ones, most people recall that period in a different way, and it is their memories that determine our image of the country. It is an image still dominated by the blinding darkness of the Nazi period, that neutron star into whose bitter gravity all German history seems to fall. So, in the fall of 1997, the *International Herald Tribune* ran articles with such headlines as: "Germany Wants to be Normal, but History Keeps Getting in the Way," "Cologne Faces Reality of Nazi Past," and "At 95, Hitler's Favored Director Still Provokes." And the paper even offered a bit of backpage filler that names Hugo Boss as the designer of the Nazis' uniforms. Well, that one brings a sour smile: they *were* better cut than the Allies'. My friend Walter, a journalist with the German magazine *Stern*, tends to dismiss such pieces as non-stories, arguing that they show up every time an American newspaper sends over a new correspondent. They're what the reporter knows before he gets here, and so he writes those first columns out of the prejudices and expectations he's packed along with his laptop. Moreover, it's what the editors back home know their audience wants to read. I take the point. Growing up after the Great War, Leigh Fermor may have "confused Germans with germs and [known] that both were bad." But in remembering my own childhood, I'm tempted to push the metaphor and to say that in the 1960s even those of us who hadn't yet learned about Auschwitz thought of the country as something like the Black Death.

The rationale for such stories does, however, seem a bit more complicated than my friend might allow. Recall John Murray's statement that his handbooks concentrate on "things *peculiar* to the spot, or which might be better seen there than elsewhere." In a German context that italicized word acquires an unintended but particular referent: the *Sonderweg* that many historians in both Germany and abroad have insisted on, a "special path" that kept nineteenth-century German society from the "normal" bourgeois development of France or Britain. For some, of course, that *Sonderweg* was Germany's particular glory and inseparable, in Thomas Mann's skeptical and yet oddly admiring description, from its "depth . . . the musicality of the German soul, that which we call its inwardness," its *Innerlichkeit*. Yet Mann believed that "such musicality of soul is paid for dearly in another sphere" and that the *Sonderweg* had led to the Third Reich. Other writers dispute that historiographical model. The British historians David Blackbourn and Geoff Eley have argued in their *Peculiarities of German History* (1984) that there was no special path, not if by that one means an inevitable road to Auschwitz. Nineteenth-century Germany was *not* all that different from its European neighbors, and Blackbourn and Eley insist on replacing a teleological reading of German history with an appreciation for the role of contingency in all human affairs. Things might have turned out differently. Might have—but didn't. For whatever Germany may have been in the nineteenth-century, it has most surely been peculiar in the one that has just now ended. If in traveling we are to follow Murray and concentrate on those "things *peculiar* to the spot," if we think of a country in terms of those things that mark it out it from others, then Germany's most easily discernible distinguishing features assume the shape not of architecture or cuisine or manners but of history. The metonymy with which it is still most surely identified is that of the Third Reich.

Whether after more than fifty years of the *Bundesrepublik* and NATO and the *Wirtschaftswunder*, after the European Union and the Wall and Willy Brandt and the Greens and the *Wende*; whether now that we all use German-made countertop coffee machines and wish that we could afford to drive German cars — whether that's *fair* is, of course, a different question. But it's also moot; I suspect that such a metonymy will hold for as long as any of us have a living memory of those for whom the war was a living memory. It is surely a superficial judgment, and as with Leigh Fermor it may not — I hope it does not — affect our, my, relations with individual men and women. Still, there it is, and that peculiarity presents the traveler with a curious problem. It ought in one sense to be simple to write about Germany. In a country where the young and well-educated often use the adjective "German" pejoratively, one can have an easy conscience in drawing on national stereotypes, the travel writer's old and now discredited stock-in-trade. Yet in another sense it's very hard. Think of the reasons for travel that Stendhal and Goethe suggested. The observation of manners and mores, yes, and monuments, and ruins as well, and sometimes even the country's "secret, inner life," which is not at all the same thing as what Mann meant by *Innerlichkeit*. There's Goethe's statement that "I am not here simply to have a good time, but . . . to educate myself." To educate myself above all about that which can be better seen here than elsewhere. Learning about such peculiarities does, however, seem as though it ought to undercut one's ability to have "a good time," and where does that leave Stendhal's belief that one should travel for "pure pleasure?"

I find Hamburg as attractive and easy a city to live in as any I know, and I have been as happy sitting in its cafés and walking along its streets as I have been at any point in my life. But there seems to me something risible, even something scandalous, in that sentence as I write it. For what role should we give to pleasure here? Or to put it another way, can one write about Germany without also writing about, concentrating on, and worrying away at The German Problem?

Blackbourn and Eley speak of the country's peculiarities in the plural, suggesting that there was not one *Sonderweg* but many: many separate strands of history, of regional and local identities, whose particularities have been buried by German's twentieth-century singularity. In an earlier age, what was perhaps most peculiar about Germany was its maze of local exceptions to a rule so vague it could hardly be called general. Most of the people living within the borders of the nation-state that Bismarck put together in 1871 would not, as the historian Michael Stürmer argues, "have described themselves . . . as Germans but . . . Bavarians, Prussian, Badeners," a diversity rooted in the differences of "bread and beer, in custom, language, and the local law." And, of course, Hamburg had—has—its own peculiarities. It is an Anglophiliac port city, where even now people speak English with a British accent; Bavarians tend, in contrast, to have an American one. Though it lies eighty miles up the Elbe, it turns out toward the Atlantic, rather than in upon Germany itself, and has always taken pride in its openness to the world outside; so open, in fact, that to many nineteenth-century observers it hardly seemed a part of Germany at all.

Stürmer writes that the Hamburger—the name itself offers a spurious provenance for American fast food—would instead identify himself as "*Hanseaten*, referring to the medieval glories of the Hanse," the trading confederation that linked Hamburg not only to Frankfurt and Cologne but also to Riga, Amsterdam, and that provincial capital called Berlin. Such self-descriptions, he adds, "always had an undertone, and still have, setting those using them apart from the German nation at large." You claim a regional identity as a way of dodging a national one, and in the early nineteenth century the memory of the Hanseatic League was revived as a mercantile alternative to other forms of German unification, an assertion of North German independence in the face of Prussia's ever-increasing territory. Some commercial treaties still obtained between the independent city-states of Hamburg, Lübeck, and Bremen, and so they set to work inventing tradition, referring to themselves once more as the "Hanseatic towns," and managed to keep a measure of autonomy even after they signed on with Bismarck's Germany. Hamburg still maintained a Berlin embassy in 1902, and even now newspapers will use "Hanse-stadt" as a synonym for the city itself, and without the sense of slang with which an America tabloid mentions Beantown or Gotham.

And it shows up as an adjective in daily life — in real estate ads, for example, where an apartment in our neighborhood can be described as offering "*höchste hanseatische Wohnkultur.*" The accompanying picture shows a gracious room of wooden floors and bookshelf-flanked windows, with good pictures on the walls, making the high Hanseatic style a rough equivalent for the New Yorker's "Prewar." Though in another ad the word makes me pause, for there I'm offered two balconies suitable for the most "*anspruchvollen*" — hard-to-please — of Hanseatens, as though the one entailed the other. Perhaps indeed it does: in Mann's *Buddenbrooks*, at any rate, the Lübeck-born Tony marries a Bavarian but can never quite reconcile herself to easy-going Munich, to the southerners whom she sees as "without dignity, morals, energy, ambition, self-respect, or good manners." It is a "stupid and shallow" place, where "they eat cake with a knife, and the very princes speak bad grammar." In the North, however, "people work and get things accomplished and have a purpose in life." The Hansa virtues of hard-headed industry and drive are precisely those which Max Weber associated with the rise of capitalism itself: Protestant virtues as opposed to Munich's Catholic vices. Hanseatic manners are accordingly self-possessed and tight-lipped and austere — and certainly far less forgiving of my fractured German than a Parisian waiter is of bad French. It is a style with which as a New Englander I am neither unfamiliar nor entirely uncomfortable, and though brusque it is always *korrekt*. The Hansa towns are unusually formal even by German standards — places where shopgirls in their twenties are apt to *Siezen* each other — and so in the Hansestadt itself I have heard *hanseatische* used as an exact equivalent for "stuffy."

That's of course a simplification. Hamburg has its *alternative* neighborhoods of vegetarian restaurants and piercing salons, its Turkish street markets and pockets of bluff good humor. Still, the set of behaviors that I call Hanseatic has nevertheless left its mark on the face of the city, and I don't mean on the way people look. Or maybe I do, for it is a place of tall and severely handsome people, who pace its streets as with a consciousness of their own rectitude, just a bit too aware of looking well. And perhaps that fits a city where opulence has always been a private matter. Hamburg was historically ruled by a self-selecting Senate in the interests of a merchant class every bit as proud as a clan of Pomeranian *Junkers*, men interested above all in the getting of money, not in spending it on the civic display associated with either the Church or a court. Even now the city's architecture is marked by a relative absence of grand public buildings. Its cathedral fell into disuse after the Reformation and in 1802 the Senate had it pulled down, using its stones and statuary, as the historian Richard J. Evans writes, "to reinforce the sea defenses along the Elbe. . . . [and] in the reconstruction of the city's rudimentary sewage system." Other medieval churches were sent to the knacker's yard as well, and much of what remained was destroyed in the city's great fire of 1842.

Lübeck makes a good comparison. It was a significantly richer city in the middle ages, but over the centuries its population fell and it never grew beyond its medieval core. Long before German unification Lübeck knew it was living on its past, and clung tight to what Mann's Thomas Buddenbrook calls "the old monuments out of our great period," monuments lovingly maintained and restored. But for nineteenth-century Hamburg the great period was now. Its harbor was swelled by the steamship, by the emigrants carried on the Hamburg-America Line, and by the trade in such "colonial wares" as tea and tobacco and spices. And so, as my 1900 Baedeker notes, the city's public face was marked by "the almost entire disappearance of relics of the past." Its one imposing—indeed bombastic—architectural gesture was a new Rathaus, whose hundred-meter tower stands in for that of the city's absent cathedral. It sits on a cobbled square that is bordered on one side by a canal. Steps run down to the water, where the lock periodically drains to let a tour boat pass; there are pedestrian bridges and a colonnade and a row of cafes, while the square itself is often filled by a fair, a Christmas market or a celebration of Swabian wine. It is a gracious space, one that almost makes it easy to forget that the building's back door opens directly on to the city's stock exchange.

In *Death in Hamburg*, his finely detailed study of "the world the merchants made," Evans writes that, given the city's paucity of "public monuments, the authors of guidebooks" suggested that visitors "gain a graphic impression of the city's commercial and industrial power" by taking a tour of the harbor. That's what the guidebooks still suggest today, and yet it isn't quite right to say that Hamburg lacks monuments. Instead of churches or palaces or opera houses, what nineteenth-century Hamburg built was its port, dredging the river's bottom so that even the largest ships could approach at low tide, cutting so many slips out of the Elbe's banks that they now look serrated. The port itself is in its way a monument, a celebration of the prosperity of which it was the cause. Certainly my old Baedeker treats it as one, offering not only suggestions about the finest views but also details of its construction, much as it does for Dresden's Zwinger or the cathedral in Cologne. Nor is that comparison misplaced. People here do indeed take the same kind of pride in their port and their river that a Kölner might in his church. They walk in groups on the esplanade that fronts the industrial Elbe, they talk knowingly of ro-ro ships and turnaround time and sit on benches above the river at Altona to watch the red and green bricks of forty-foot cargo containers swing through the air; they step out of a quay-side fishhouse and stop to see a tanker turn down a waterway, like a bus taking the corner. And in a very real sense what they are watching is Hamburg itself.

Yet if even a Hamburger is apt to agree with the guidebooks in seeing the port as an emblem for his city, he's not apt to find much relevance to his own daily life in the other place by which outsiders know it. The Reeperbahn was the port's rope-walk in the days when it needed one, parallel to the Elbe and a few hundred yards in, one of the main streets in the old working-class suburb of St. Pauli. Every port city needs someplace to sin, and even in the nineteenth century this district was known for its saloons and brothels; some biographers still claim that the teenaged Brahms had to support himself by playing the piano in one neighborhood whorehouse after another. A more recent bit of musical history carries a more certain provenance: the Beatles got their first big break in a bar just off the Reeperbahn, at Grosse Freiheit 36.

At night the neon pops and the crowds surge and the touts outside the theaters cry their wares, a goblin's market of voices. Most of the prostitutes work the side streets and wear an entirely unerotic uniform of leotards and sweats; solicitations come every few yards and as often as not in English. Though not everyone goes to the Reeperbahn for sex. The live shows still draw their crowds, but there are couples here who've come to see *Cats*, to dance or visit the wax museum or watch a movie—even an ordinary movie—to play the slot machines and drink beer and eat kebabs, or even to sing old songs in a piano bar. But I'm not shopping and so I find the street more interesting by day, when it's empty enough to look at. Nobody on the Reeperbahn in the middle of the afternoon looks as though they have a legitimate reason for being there, not even — especially not — the few men in suits. Nobody, that is, except the police; the ones I pass all wear shoulder flashes that identify them as members of the border patrol. There aren't many women about, and none of those who are proposes anything at all. A couple of barkers try half-heartedly to get me into a club; they have soup-strainer moustaches gone nicotine-yellow. I pass a gun store and a pawn shop and then step down a sidestreet for a look at Herbertstrasse, a single block barricaded at either end, with no women and children allowed. Red lights wink in the sunshine, and beyond the barrier the prostitutes sit unclothed in their windows. Or so I'm told, for I lack the heart to stroll down it, and so instead I watch as a man comes out around the barrier and walks away, going through what looks like a woman's wallet.

Almost any large European city now has a match for this district, and much of Hamburg's own prostitution has moved to other neighborhoods. Nevertheless the name "Sankt Pauli" still helps to sell any number of downmarket sex magazines, and the Reeperbahn remains the one thing, the only thing, that everyone from out of town knows about Hamburg already. The traveler presumes that the spirit of a place lies in such details, in the ways it which it differs from other lands: the club where the Beatles once played, the waterside warehouse that holds *Mitteleuropa's* entire stock of bananas. Yet that reliance on metonymy — on that which seems typical precisely because it's so peculiar — ensures that the visitor will see and value different things than do that place's inhabitants. Some of that difference may even be enforced by one's guidebook. Henry James wrote that in Italy the "streets and inns . . . are the vehicles of half one's knowledge," but his contemporaries would never have known it from reading Murray. In Germany, Murray's nineteenth-century handbooks allow that one might be interested in Alpine scenery or even such aspects of present-day life as, well, the Hamburg harbor. That, however, is not what Italy was for, and most of the period's guides to that country suggest that an Italian journey is almost exclusively a matter of ancient monuments, an inventory of the past, of marbles, mosaics, churches, pictures, palazzi, the relics of saints and of empire.

In consequence, as James Buzard has written, such guidebooks work to naturalize "the separation of 'tourist attractions'" from the details "of an ongoing quotidian life." They suggest — they require — that one's interest remains fundamentally different from that of the local populace. Barthes puts it well in one of his mythologies, writing that in the Blue Guide "the human life of a country disappears to the exclusive benefit of its monuments." Or so at least the traveler might wish. Take, for instance, this passage from Ruskin's *The Stones of Venice*, in which he excoriates the nineteenth-century city for having allowed its inhabitants to open shops around the doors to San Marco: "up to the very recesses of the porches, the meanest tradesmen of the city push their counters . . . vendors of toys and caricatures . . . a continuous line of cafes, where the idle . . . lounge, and read empty journals." The Venetian need to make a living conflicts with his own desire to see the church as it might once have been, and so he sweeps the moneylenders from the temple. For the present they embody is an imposition on the past, a degradation, an encumbrance. It is in his way, this ongoing everyday life, and indeed Ruskin suggests that his own freedom from such quotidian details is in itself enough to make him the place's proper custodian. The city is too important to be left in the hands of those who live there. Venice would be better off if it contained no Venetians, no one whose pesky private concerns might conflict with the value the visitor wishes to place upon it.

Though let me offer a more mundane example of the way a visitor's interests differ from those of an inhabitant. In Berlin I meet my friend Karin in a long narrow restaurant off Savignyplatz. She's an agent and I'm a hack, and so mostly we talk books, what we're reading, the things I've reviewed, the German novels she's lately sold to American publishers. But we talk about Berlin as well, and she gives me a tip, something I should look into, something about Berlin that's both new and not obvious. Golf courses. West Berliners weren't really the kind of people who played golf, not before the *Wende,* and anyway, there wasn't all that much land. But now, with the capital moving to Berlin, with more international companies opening shop, with the pretty Brandenburg farmland lying open all around—now, she said, developers were carving one golf course after another into the soil of the former German Democratic Republic.

I'm not a golfer, and though I couldn't summon up a Ruskinian sneer, I didn't see why I should be any more interested in a German fairway than I am in an American one. Yet clearly Karin found them a new and curious feature in the landscape of her home city. It might be a salutary development or an appalling one—nevertheless it was worth noticing, commenting on, a mark not only of change but of *the* change, and therefore interesting. To me, however, the presence of suburban golf courses made Berlin appear as though it might be less interesting, because less different, than it had been before. They might make the city seem to differ from itself, but they also made it more closely resemble other large cities, American ones in particular. That had an curiosity of its own, but it wasn't what I wanted from this city. Golf courses were not *peculiar.* They weren't the Pergamon Museum or Sanssouci or the food halls at the KaDeWe department store. For all I know, there may be ten million German golfers, but I couldn't see the eighteenth hole as a metonymy for Germany in the way that it is for Florida.

Of course, having written that sentence I'm afraid I won't be able to get those golf courses out of my mind, that without my ever actually laying eyes on them they'll become my emblem of post-unification Berlin. Our image of a place is composed of such things. Sometimes they're nothing more than the assumptions we've brought along, and if a place doesn't conform to our expectations we may, in fact, be disappointed in it. Others we pick up along the way, a late addition to our carry-on baggage. And often we construct that image by adding those metonymic bits together, which we take as coextensive with the country itself. Germany equals the sum total of the ways in which it differs from France or Denmark or even Burkina Faso. Yet that's not enough. We not only want those pieces to add up, to aggregate, we want them to add up to an already determined sum, neither more nor less. We want them to fit, we want those peculiar bits to make a whole, to go together like a puzzle, one tongue sliding neatly into one groove. Like the bits and pieces of bone that the physical anthropologist pieces together into our ancestor's skull. No empty spots, no pieces left over at the end. No contradictions.

And no chance at all that that might really be so. "Anybody ever tries to tell you," says the German-Jewish refugee Otto Cone in Salman Rushdie's *The Satanic Verses*, "how this most beautiful and most evil of planets is somehow homogenous, composed only of reconcilable elements . . . you get on the phone to the straightjacket tailor . . . The world is incompatible, just never forget it: gaga." It is an equation without an answer, in which every term is a variable, a human circle that cannot be squared. I take Rushdie's words as a gloss on Isaiah Berlin's passionate attack on the belief that "all genuine questions must have one true answer and one only," his argument that the facts of a culture are not "necessarily commensurable, either within a culture or (still less) as between cultures." I know — I believe — that that must be true. In Germany, however, I resist that belief even as I'm drawn to it, and resist it with something more than the usual traveler's strategy of resolving contradictions through the simple act of noting them. That's what one does in India — takes contradiction as providing in itself the norm. In Madras the conjunction of a bookstore with a computerized inventory and a painted cow loitering by the door becomes an emblem for the postcolonial nation, for the collision or at any rate the coexistence of Western technology and traditional life. Here, however, I seem to shy away from such resolutions. As perhaps do the Germans themselves, at least insofar as they accept the Herderian notion that, to quote once more from Berlin, "the ways in which a people . . . speak or move, eat or drink, their handwriting, their laws, their music, their social outlook, their dance forms, their theology, have patterns and qualities in common . . . belongs to a cluster which must be grasped as a whole."

I want this country to add up, want some way of making it all cohere. And yet one typically German thing belies another. The small bow with which many men, even young ones, seem to shake your hand? Can that be compatible with the sharp elbows of the old ladies pushing their way through a department store, banging their walking sticks down on your instep — the only Germans left who still believe in *Lebensraum*? The long green bottles of the Mosel, full of a wine so light and elegant that it seems not a liquid but the airy essence of flavor itself — how can that fit with the stodge of Bavarian liver dumplings? And how do those dumplings match themselves to the buoyant creamy stucco of an equally Bavarian rococo? It's tempting to rationalize all this away, and I could try to claim that while liver dumplings and a Mosel riesling might seem opposed, each nevertheless represents a kind of extreme. Each within its category pushes the envelope of the possible, and this too is metonymic of Germany as a whole, in everything from the rigor of its philosophy to contemporary kitchen design. I could make that case — but I wouldn't believe my own argument, and it makes more sense to ask myself why this issue nags at me so. Why does one even bother trying to make these bits and pieces of the typical, these epiphenomena of a culture, fit so tightly together? What are the stakes in accepting — or rejecting — contradiction?

The belief that Germany does not add up, that it remains incommensurate with itself — such a belief may be tremendously reassuring. It tells us that the past is not a monolith. But it is also frightening and for some of us it is perhaps unbearable, for it entails as well the belief that the past is or rather was contingent, that it wasn't all inevitable. That it could have been avoided.

✸ THREE

Visible Cities

A drone on sabbatical, I've called myself, my hours only as regular as I cared to keep them, shaped now and then by a newspaper's deadline, but much more often by groceries. Oh, I can make myself sound busy, even a routine measured out by errands and lunch can be made to seem full, and I was often enough at my desk, with my computer open to the files that have eventually become this book itself. But I also seemed to spend a lot of time reading in cafes. On winter afternoons I liked to go to the Sternschanze, an edge neighborhood that seemed half-Turkish and half-tattooed *Alternative*, and hole up in the Unter den Linden with a mystery and a piece of plum cake. Once spring came, I would bicycle up along the Alster canals to sit on the Leinpfad's riverfront terrace, stretching out a beer through the last hundred pages of *The Devils*. Well, reading novels is a part of what I'm paid for, but still, I could have done it in less pleasant surroundings. Brigitte, however, had a far more regular work day, arranging schedules and tutors and internships, managing an office and a budget and occasionally the lives of the students whose program she was directing. I'm not going to explore the running of a Junior Year Abroad or turn our thirteen students into characters. From our point of view, their year was largely and thankfully without event: no crises, no arrests or crack-ups or drugged-out walkabouts. So I'll skip over the time we spent with them. But I can't so easily pass by Brigitte herself, even though her presence in these pages has so far been almost entirely, and indeed literally, nominal.

Some travel narratives are buddy acts—Bill Bryson's *A Walk in the Woods* or, more classically, Robert Byron's *The Road to Oxiana*, in which the relation between the writer and his companion is in itself one of the book's subjects. Others fly solo—people flit across the radar of Paul Theroux or Jonathan Raban, but they're never in range for long. One's own spouse is another matter. She's the person on the other end of the late-night, if undescribed, phone call from Weimar, and never quite far from one's mind— always present, even when she's not. D. H. Lawrence referred to Frieda in *Sea and Sardinia* as the "q-b" or Queen Bee; the nickname seems almost a defense against what every record suggests was a formidable character. Eric Newby's wife Wanda appears in such books as *Round Ireland in Low Gear* as the straight-faced voice of a skeptical common-sense, someone always trying to rein him in, and always just barely failing. Both women are full partners in the narrative, their presence detailed and particularized: characters. I might characterize Brigitte, at least in part, by saying that I don't think she'd like to be depicted in that way. Oh, she's skeptical enough, this quadrilingual *Annales*-trained medievalist, who claims that panel painting is now a dead art and likes Bach and Webern but not Brahms. She is skeptical enough about my own slipping and sliding between the personal and semi-scholarly that she might prefer not to appear in this book at all. Still, to leave her out entirely would seem something less, or other, than an act of marital tact. I can't treat her as V. S. Naipaul does his own wife in *An Area of Darkness*, where Patricia Naipaul figures in but a single sentence, as an unnamed "companion" who, suffering from the heat, "slumped forward on her chair, hung her head between her knees, and fainted." The next two hundred and fifty pages pass without his mentioning her presence, and she makes no other appearance in his work.

Such an omission falsifies the writer's experience of travel, though in Naipaul's case it may also point to some deeper truth: a mark of the imaginative weight, or lack of it, that he accords to other people. For me a better solution is that which Anthony Powell, through his narrator Nicholas Jenkins, suggests in *A Dance to the Music of Time*. Jenkins writes that "to think at all objectively about one's own marriage is impossible . . . Its forms are at once so varied, yet so constant, providing a kaleidoscope, the colors of which are always changing, always the same." One can, he adds, chart "the moods of a love affair [or] the contradictions of friendship," but marriage, with its thousand "dual antagonisms and participations, finally defies definition." These thoughts come to him on his way to the nursing home where his wife Isobel is recovering from a miscarriage. He does not, however, explore either her response to the lost pregnancy, or his own, and concentrates instead on a chance meeting with a friend in the building's hallway. His wife appears, but she is only rarely the subject of his narrative, and over the marriage itself he draws a kind of curtain — flicking it back now and then, but not for long and never all the way. And that's how it will be here as well.

Yet Brigitte and her interests nevertheless provided the motive force for much of what I saw in Germany, even leaving aside the fact that I wouldn't have been there at all without her. I knew enough to get myself to Munich and Berlin, Weimar and Lübeck. But many of the other places I've been, not only in Germany but in France and Italy as well, aren't ones that I would have visited on my own. The monuments and relics of medieval Europe lie often in unobvious and isolated places, for all that many of them once lay along the active routes of pilgrimage. So, in France, Brigitte has taken me to look at church capitals in the Poitou and to bow before Ste. Foy in Conques, to Fontenay and Fontevrault. In Italy we've driven through a blinding winter rain in the hills north of Lake Garda to reach a series of glorious wall paintings in Trento, a cycle of the year that decorates a room in the bishop's castle; and spent a hot and dusty summer Sunday visiting Monza, for its cathedral's hoard of early Lombard metalwork. Sometimes it feels as though we're ticking our way down the UNESCO heritage list, like mountaineers bagging another peak. But the trip has almost always been worthwhile; except maybe for Monza, which is now best known as the site of the Italian Grand Prix, and looks it.

A last meeting, a rush to pick up our Volkswagen rental, and then we start to follow the road signs we've never noticed on the streets we walk every day, picking our way toward the autobahn. And then south. Brigitte drives; I try to navigate and sometimes succeed. It was a Thursday in early October, the start of a long weekend, and coming back on Sunday we would be caught near Hannover in one of those ten-mile traffic jams that German speed and its consequent smash-ups can all too readily produce. For now, though, our way was clear, almost two hundred kilometers of it to our first night's stop in Hildesheim, a finger-tip of Catholicism curving east from Westphalia into the Protestant lands of Lower Saxony. On the following days, we would follow that finger down toward its base, heading, though with any number of secondary stops, toward the cathedral cities of Paderborn and Münster. It wasn't a weekend of research but it could count as one of study: Brigitte had no plans to write about these places, but a few slides from each of them had already shown up in her lectures. She knew them from images — as images — but photos are never enough and your own eyes still matter. Physical presence counts. You stand must before a tympanum or a door to see its details of texture and relief, must walk the length of a nave and step between the columns to understand the exact relation of one part of the building to another. There are worse ways to get a tax deduction.

She doesn't think of herself as an architectural historian, but Brigitte has to teach the stuff anyway. If she's not precisely part of what Philip Larkin describes in "Church-Going" as "the crew/ That tap and jot and know what rood-screens are," she does nevertheless know, and usually jots. Tapping she leaves to her colleagues, and her own interest lies more in a church's fittings than in its articulation of space. So she's particularly drawn to cathedral treasuries, those storehouses of what Larkin calls "parchment, plate and pyx," and moves through them with a quick eye for the odd, the ancient cameos used as gemstones on a cross, the reliquaries made out of exotic materials like ostrich eggs or coconut shells. And by now she's been in so many treasuries that she can skim them, mentally strip-mine or gut them; while I dawdle through a cathedral complex, taking twice as long to see less, my eyes going everywhere and nowhere. Oh, I've gotten better at it. I even have my own preferences in reliquaries—how indecent that sounds!—though I'm always in danger of not knowing what I'm seeing, and especially of not knowing anything at all about the history of the places to which I've been brought. Hildesheim? Brigitte expresses surprise at my modernist—or maybe it's my American—ignorance, and I counter by asking if she knows Larkin's poem; a draw. But not really, not even close. Hildesheim trumps "Church-Going," even though it suffers from the usual story in this part of Germany: blown to bits in the spring of 1945.

Not that the city had had much industrial importance. That was why it had remained intact for so long. With under 100,000 inhabitants, it hadn't been a target for strategic bombing, like Hamburg or Berlin, nor was it chosen for a revenge attack, as the German raid on Coventry had been answered by one on Lübeck. Still, I was continually surprised, in visiting not only Hildesheim but other small cities as well, by how late the bombs had fallen, so late it almost seemed as though they might have been avoided. Bombing here had been strictly tactical; I imagined a couple of American generals in a villa on the Rhine, standing over a map and saying, "All right, this is where we want to be in a few days, let's take it out now." What they took out here were the sixteenth-century wooden buildings on the Marktplatz; my 1900 Baedeker describes one of them, built as the butcher's guildhall, as "probably . . . the finest timber building in Germany." It's back up now, an exact copy, steep-roofed and high and with each floor staggering out a bit from the one below, so that its whole intricately carved façade appears to sway. We had a drink in the woodsy anonymous bar on the ground floor, and at night both the building and the square itself are convincing enough. They look as though they might be old: a cobbled space surrounded by elaborately stepped and gabled buildings, with a pedestrian zone's hush, untouched by even the sound of cars. By day, however, you can see that the wood is uncracked and the paint so even and shiny and new that the *Fachwerk* carving seems as lively as a cartoon. Unreal city, in which nothing has faded; it will need a century to stop looking like Disney.

Other parts of Hildesheim did better. On some of the unbombed streets, the buildings have slumped with the centuries, their timbers bent into a picturesque and entirely functional dilapidation. The churches had their roofs burned off and their windows shattered; their blackened stone still owes more to 1945 than it does to auto exhaust. A bulletin board in one of the cathedral's aisles shows pictures of a ruined choir; almost every major church in Western Germany has such a display, with postcards of rubble to match. But bricks and stones seem to come back better than wood, and the cathedral has been convincingly restored; indeed some people prefer the rebuilt version, as being in a way closer to its spare eleventh-century original. "Entirely disfigured in the interior in 1712–30," my old Baedeker says, and a picture of 1890 shows its interior all covered by stucco, with Tiepolo knock-offs on the ceiling. The bombing stripped out such encrustations; the rebuilding did not replace them.

And the bronzes for which we'd really come here had been kept safe and intact. One of the things I like about traveling in

Germany is the sense it so frequently offers — far more so than England or France, maybe even more than Italy — that some now quiet place was once important; was even once, however briefly, at the center of its world. Any number of cities have housed the German emperor, whether Charlemagne or his successors; Paderborn was one, our next day's stop, where in 799 the great Charles himself had met the Pope to prepare for his assumption of the imperial crown. Many centuries later, the dispersal of power in the German-speaking lands, the hundreds of ambitious and competitive princes with their capital cities that needed to be built and decorated and administered — all this meant that small places might hold large talents. Goethe had no London or Paris in which to make his career, and went to Weimar instead.

Hildesheim had had its own importance, and an enduring one. Emperors moved around. States merged, or fell apart. Monasteries stayed put, and a thousand years ago, when the city was on the margin of what was then called Christendom, a man called Bernward was appointed bishop here. He had traveled to Rome, he had been the emperor's own tutor, and in Hildesheim he built — perhaps even himself designed — the church of St. Michael, which established the principles of Romanesque architecture in Germany. A powerful bishop, later canonized, and at the head of a powerful foundation, one from which other monasteries sprang, missions to the pagans in the north and the east. Such daughter houses — colonies, really — were a means toward political influence and strength. Nor was colonization limited to the Church: the young men of a town near Hildesheim marched away to new lands in the east, and today we still talk about the Pied Piper of Hamelin.

A thousand years ago, but Bernward left much behind, buildings and a memory and so many artifacts that on my desk as I write is a two-volume catalog, almost twelve hundred pages, of a recent museum show on his time. Nobody knows who made the objects by which he is best remembered, the names of those who carved the molds and cast the bronzes that are now described as

Bernward's own, statuary that first rested in St. Michael's, but was later moved to the cathedral. One of the pieces Brigittte had brought us here to see is a triumphal column, twelve feet high, carved around with a procession of scenes from the life of Christ, with his birth at the bottom and the Palm Sunday entrance into Jerusalem at the crown. The piece makes one of those clever gestures by which Christian art appropriates that of the classical world: Trajan's column, the pagan triumph here echoed and yet also defanged, the history of miracles substituted for that of martial glory. Though maybe, I thought, as I walked around that tall trunk of bronze and traced the arboreal motifs that divided some scenes from others, maybe there was also a reference to the world-supporting tree of Germanic mythology. For those, after all, would have been the pagans Bernward was really worried about.

What most held our attention were the church's inside doors, a pair of them made in 1015, fifteen feet tall and each cast in a single piece. On the left, the fall of man, eight panels stacked one upon another, from creation to expulsion; matched on the right by the appropriate New Testament moment. Some figures stand in high relief, as though wresting themselves out of the deep-olive bronze itself: the three Magi lean forward as if to listen to what Mary, bending out over the child in her lap, might say. And God, in casting Adam and Eve out of the Garden, seems to rise on his toes and lean his whole nonexistent weight upon one perfectly straight finger. Not the lazy curl of Michelango's God, with which he summons Adam into being—this is the prosecutor pointing an accusatory digit at those whom he knows he will convict. They know it, too, and the pair seem to shrivel away, their bodies' edges melting back into the door. These were the first such monumental doors since ancient Rome, and in their sense of human drama they wouldn't really be matched for four hundred years more, when Ghiberti cast the Gates of Paradise in Florence. Or so my reading would later tell me. At the moment, and on the spot, all I could do was wonder whether or not Ghiberti had known these doors — one of those idle moments when the amateur thinks he's made a connection. I turned to ask Brigitte, but she was bent over her notebook, writing quickly, her eyes now and then darting up to catch another detail, and I decided my question could wait.

Nothing we saw on the rest of that trip made a comparable impression, and perhaps there's no need to describe the other stops we made: coffee in handsome, half-timbered Einbeck (home of bock beer); lunch in the spa town of Bad Gandersheim (two boys kicking a soccer ball against the door of a Romanesque church); an hour at a moated castle called Burg Vischering that made gentry life seem faded and narrow and poor. Yet making this list, and allowing this itinerary to stand for the trip itself, has brought the whole of our drive back to me, so that I see once more the wrong turns my map-reading made us take, or the way in which, on that Sunday, the flat watery land around Münster changed into one of wooded hills and ravines and roads that seemed to wind back into time. Münster itself does linger in my mind, though not primarily because it too was once at the center of things: in 1648 the Peace of Westphalia, which put a stop to the Thirty Years' War, was signed in its Rathaus. No, a sharper memory is that of the iron cages hung from the tower of St. Lamberti, in which the tortured bodies of three Anabaptist leaders had been exposed in 1536. The Anabaptists had been a vicious sect, violently suppressed. They probably deserved it, but still, this continued reminder seemed grotesque, as though centuries from now the bones of the Branch Dravidians were to lie in the lobby of the Bureau of Alcohol, Tobacco, and Firearms. Yet once seen, I can't forget them: those cages, and not the cathedral treasury or the prosperous pleasant streets or even the dozen kinds of dark bread our hotel offered at breakfast will provide the metonymy by which I recall this place.

A few weeks before, I had spent a morning in Hannover, walking through the gardens at Herrenhausen. Hannover, as in "House of": the German state from which in 1714 the Protestant George I had been called to the English throne. His successors had reigned over both Britain and a large stretch of Germany, though the crowns had been split in 1837: under Salic law women were excluded from succession, and the young Victoria had to turn the place over to an uncle. The palace of Herrenhausen from which the Electors of Hannover had ruled no longer stands — the family connections did not, in the early 1940s, extend so far as Bomber Command. But the gardens that surrounded it continue to flower, the main aesthetic attraction of a city otherwise devoted to trade fairs and industry.

The park comes first, an attempt at Englishness, with bridges and temples scattered about and four rows of limes running away into the distance, dead straight for a mile and more, and flat, so that you can see your goal from the start, a small domed building that marks the entrance to the now-absent palace. The gardens themselves, at the end of that *Lindenallee*, look rather severely French, a geometrical arrangement of parterres and flowerbeds, of straight paths with their intersections marked by fountains. They had been laid out at the end of the seventeenth century by the Kurfürstin Sophie, the patron of Liebniz and granddaughter of England's James I, and were meant to evoke Versailles. But how disappointing they are in comparison! So small as to make their dreams of grandeur seem hollow. Herrenhausen didn't look as though it had ever reached the heights to which it aspired, and I had to remind myself that something more, or rather less, had contributed to what seemed, today, its failure. For these gardens were never intended as a self-sufficient piece of landscape design, and everywhere I went I felt the lack of a proper perspective from which to view them. In one spot there was a little manmade cascade, from the top of which you could look down on an arrangement of box hedges. But it wasn't high enough, not quite, and with more elevation the plantings would have been more legible;

if, that is, one had been able to see them from the upper window of that now-vanished palace.

The garden's fountains were scheduled to go on at eleven that morning, and so a few minutes before, I settled onto a bench near the largest of them, a jet of water that climbs eighty meters into the sky. The missing *Schloss* had put me in a Gibbonesque mood, and I remembered the historian's claim to have conceived his book as he "sat musing in the ruins of the Capitol, while the barefooted friars were singing vespers in the temple of Jupiter." But I couldn't match his emotion—my bench wasn't the steps of Santa Maria Ara Coeli, and musing over the vanished glory of the House of Hannover could stand as a definition of bathos. Still, that absence of an appropriate perspective was, I thought, rather like the difficulty I had with German history as a whole: the war had knocked the center out, making it hard to interpret the much that was left behind. Then the fountains started, the noise of water filled the soft September air, and the *Grosse Fontäne* began first to bubble and then to spout. The water climbed and fell and then feathered its way up higher, a cloud of vapor that shone prismatically in the sun, and the wind blew and the water fell again, the first drops of mist came toward me, and then more, and still more, so that by the time the spout had reached its full height the bench where I'd been sitting was soaked by an artificial rain, and I'd run around to the fountain's other side. And then, with Gibbon still in my mind, I began to grow fanciful, and I told myself that this was what the absolutism of the *ancien régime* had been able do. It could make it rain, it could even create the conditions for a rainbow. But it could not control the wind and the sun and it could not determine just where that rain would fall.

In Münster I had taken those cages as a metonymy for the place, and it would be easy enough to see Herrenhausen itself as one for Hannover and its history. Yet that wasn't precisely what I had been doing on that bench. My comparison of the difficulty I had in viewing the gardens to the difficulty I had in understanding German history was easier to see as a metaphor; while I had certainly been making a metaphor in turning the fountain's overtopping of itself into an image of the nature and limitations of absolutism. And once back home in Hamburg, I began to think more carefully about the relation between these two different kinds of figurative language and the different ways in which they bore on the experience of travel.

The classic distinction between them is Roman Jakobson's 1956 "Two Aspects of Language and Two Types of Aphasic Disturbance." Some aphasics, Jakobson writes, put a metonymy in the place of the words they can't say; others substitute a metaphor, and he identifies the one form of figuration with prose and the other with poetry. Prose narrative "metonymically digresses" from one thing to another, from the part to the whole it suggests, so that the narrative itself is "forwarded essentially by contiguity." It moves from one object or scene to the next because they are either spatially or chronologically contiguous, and in that movement attempts to evoke a world, as indeed I've tried to do in listing our own itinerary. A different law governs poetry: that of metaphor, which works not through contiguity but through a "similarity" in which one term is "substituted" for another. So lips become rubies, hair silk, and eyes variously cornflowers or coal. Metaphor relies on the comparison and resemblance of apparently dissimilar things; it allows the mind to juxtapose the disparate fragments of the world and reveal their hidden correspondence.

The travel narrative as a form is essentially metonymic, not only in the ways I've already described but in Jakobson's terms as well. It "digresses" from one thing to another, moves from spot to spot and subject to contiguous subject as new sights or people or thoughts stray across one's path. Travel narratives do, however, rely on metaphor as well and, as many critics have noted, the very idea of metaphor stands in itself as a kind of travel. The word's Greek etymology tells us that its original meaning is "a change of place," and equivalent to the Latin *translatio,* a "bearing across," a movement of meaning from one spot to another. So Ernst Robert Curtius opens his account of metaphor in *European Literature and the Latin Middle Ages* by quoting a Latin phrase, "*pratum ridet*" or "the meadow laughs." A human quality is "transferred" into nature and, however momentarily, the borders between the one and the other blur.

Yet such figuration is often more complex, and sometimes politically loaded as well. Metaphor turns a place—or a person—into something other than itself. Think of the Nazi equation of Jews with vermin, or for that matter of Leigh Fermor's childhood link between Germans and germs. Or take Conrad's primitivist account, in *Heart of Darkness*, of the way in which "going up that river was like travelling back to the earliest beginnings of the world"; the phrase twists a whole continent into something like the Land Before Time. In fact Eric Cheyfitz has suggested, in his *Poetics of Imperialism*, that rhetoric itself makes possible the habit of mind we call colonialism, arguing that the very idea of metaphor "seems to find its ground in a kind of territorial imperative . . . *transporting* a term from a *familiar* to a *foreign* place, from . . . its so-called 'proper' signification to a 'figurative' sense." Metaphor opposes the familiar and the foreign, the self and the other, while simultaneously collapsing the difference between them. A good example is Greene's *Journey Without Maps,* in which the writer transforms the West African forest into a figurative version—a substitute, an externalization—of the psychic terrors of his own childhood. Yet in the process neither the child's experience nor Africa itself can maintain a fully independent existence, and our postcolonial moment has tended toward a suspicion of all such figuration, of any language that threatens to assimilate one thing—one culture, one place, one set of values—into another. My playing around with Herrenhausen hadn't done much damage. Still, I had to admit that to the degree I saw the *Grosse Fontäne* as a political system I had stopped seeing it as water.

Then there are the buried or rather inverted metaphors on which all travel writing depends, in which the description of abroad becomes a tacit description of home, the one standing as the other's obverse image. James's famous catalogue, in his book on Hawthorne, of all that America lacks—"no aristocracy, no church . . . no castles, nor manors. . . . nor ivied ruins, no cathedrals"—provides an inventory of everything that Europe so picturesquely has. Goethe offers something similar in his account of an Italian street, in which "the people shout, throw things, scuffle, laugh and sing all day long," their lives made easy by the "mild climate and cheap food." No wonder this self-described "Cimmerian" believes that "though I am still always myself" he has nevertheless been "changed to the . . . marrow." And those words serve in themselves to give metaphor its best succinct definition. He is the same, only different. One place invokes another, and the sum of their metonymic differences provides in itself a metaphor for all that divides them. Indeed the travel narrative as a genre threatens always to turn a place into its metaphoric other, a dialectic in which difference seems to dissolve precisely because it has been so clearly noted.

If metonymy tends to underline the difference between home and abroad, then metaphor works to erase it. Certainly that erasure characterizes the most thoroughly metaphoric of all travel texts, Italo Calvino's *Invisible Cities*, a book of marvels that calls itself a novel but which nevertheless says more about the conceptualization of place than does almost any travel narrative proper. "Irene is the city visible when you lean out from the edge of the plateau at the hour when the lights come on": so begins the description of one of the fifty-five "forms of possible cities," each of them named for a woman, that Calvino imagines Marco Polo describing to Kublai Khan. Irene *is*—the verb itself substitutes one apposite term for another. And yet if it is, it also is not, for "Irene is a name for a city in the distance," unattainable, and "if you approach, it changes." The city you enter is one place, the city you leave another, and "each deserves a different name."

Marco's words suggest that these cities—which remain, after

all, invisible — aren't places so much as experiences. In fact in one of them, Zemrude, "it is the mood of the beholder which gives the city . . . its form . . . [and] you cannot say that one aspect of [it] is truer than the other." So Tamara is where "the eye does not see things but images of things that mean other things," while Valdrada embodies the Zen awareness that each of our "actions is, at once, that action and its mirror-image." In Chloe "strangers . . . imagine a thousand things about one another . . . conversations, surprises, caresses, bites. But no one greets anyone." Though that could be any city, and the more one reads, the more one realizes that Calvino's many names might all refer to different aspects of the same place, that what the book does best is to evoke the many-angled experience of urbanism, like those Renaissance paintings of an ideal city, with their unimaginable conjunction of one perfect building to another.

"Perhaps," Marco tells the Khan, "I have already spoken of Irene under other names; perhaps I have spoken only of Irene." Or of Venice. For after listening to his servant describe some thirty of his imperial possessions, the Khan tells Marco that there remains one place of which he never speaks, the Serenissima of his birth. Marco replies, however, that "every time I describe a city I am saying something about Venice," and indeed he can't help doing so, for "to distinguish the other cities' qualities, I must speak of a first city that remains implicit. For me it is Venice," the norm from which all others depart. Yet in traveling such departures, such differences, may quickly seem "lost: each city takes to resembling all cities, places exchange their form."

I often ask the students with whom I read Calvino to describe a real place as though it were a dream, or a desire, or a mood — a metaphor that tells you about a place, a place that tells you about a metaphor. The results are always a bit precious — none of us have Calvino's airy touch — but what's more interesting is the fact that the places they describe are never recognizable. A hometown, a favorite café, even the campus I cross each morning — they seem to drown in a lake of significance, impossible to visualize. Moreover the same thing happens, if at a much higher level, with the most relentlessly metaphoric account of an actual city that I know, Eleanor Clark's splendidly overwrought *Rome and a Villa*. Clark describes the shadows at Hadrian's Villa as so deep that they "allow you to go past the dismal surfaces, slowly, as you would enter a long poem," and the thought seems as lovely as it is impenetrable. But Calvino's Marco reminds us that a "city must never be confused with the words that describe it." Each of his places — Olivia or Sophronia or Eudoxia — seems to shimmer away into its own evanescence, subsumed or erased by the very language in which it has been described, impossible to hold in one's mind. They vanish. Or perhaps they escape, for if they can't be confused with the words that describe them, then we must also "give up any thought of knowing and understanding them," of ever fully owning them. Metaphors may, as Cheyfitz suggests, exercise a kind of control, but their superfluity can also provide release, an antidote to their own ills, and if Marco discovers in the "negative mirror" of "elsewhere . . . the much he has not had and will never have" then that lesson about the impossibility of any final possession is meant for the Great Khan as well.

John Updike has suggested that "perhaps only an Italian could have written this delicate epic of urbanity," someone from a land of towns so "vividly individual" that they "seem each to embody a different principle." Perhaps. Certainly I can't think of another writer, and in particular a German writer, who offers Calvino's combination of rigorous system and play. Nevertheless *Invisible Cities* reminds me not only of Italy but of Germany, too, and in fact my discussion of figurative language here stands, above all, as an attempt to find a way in which to talk about German regionalism, an attempt to define its plenitude. And where that attempt seems most necessary is in trying to understand those places like Hildesheim or Münster that speak of an older Germany, the Germany of the Holy Roman Empire.

In the late eighteenth century that empire, to quote from Nicholas Boyle's biography of Goethe, was comprised of "nine

Electors . . . 94 spiritual and temporal princes, 103 counts, 40 prelates, and 51 free cities. . . . all equally sovereign rulers over their own territories"—territories as large as Prussia, or as small as the Bavarian town of Weissenberg, with a population of less than four thousand. "The resultant complexity of frontiers, customs dues, and transport," Boyle writes, "may be left to the imagination," and yet, he adds, it would "be a mistake to regard the Holy Roman Empire as a hollow sham simply because it did not have the characteristics of a modern nation-state." Neither holy nor Roman nor an empire, the old joke goes, and yet it did provide "a historical, emotional, and juridical framework" within which to balance the powers of its competitive and increasingly ambitious states, a framework that tended to preserve small polities like Weimar and even such large free cities as Hamburg from the greedy mouths of Vienna and Berlin.

"Germany? but where is it? I cannot find the country." So Goethe and Schiller had written in a broadside of 1796, and in doing so defined a split between its "educated territory," which they saw in terms of that old empire, and its "political territory," which with some prescience they fixed in Prussia. For there was no German state as such, and the lands in which its language and culture held sway were without the natural borders that gave some coherence to Italy, despite its political fragmentation. Germany was an overflowing cup. It offered no identity, however fictitious, between a people and a territory; and doubtless that's why such thinkers as Herder became the principal theorists of the idea of nationality itself. Where is Germany—or when? I've tried to number the one-time polities in which we've slept, but their ever-shifting borders mean that most places would count double at least, and I'm not certain just what name to use for some of them. Take Heidelberg—is it in the Palatinate, or Baden-Württemburg? It all depends on which period you choose, and of course Berlin itself has been the capital of half a dozen regimes, from the old Mark Brandenburg to the post-*Wende* republic. I gave up counting once the episcopal states alone had hit double digits; and yet for me one of the great pleasures of our German life was the antiquarian delight of learning my way around this historical maze.

Germans like to think that they are like nobody else, special, unique, original, and in this the national imaginary can even now attach a positive meaning to the idea of a *Sonderweg*. At the same time, they often think that their own beliefs and attitudes — their very specialness — are somehow also universal. And this peculiar Teutonic exceptionalism, this "provincial . . . cosmopolitanism," in Mann's words, seems perfectly in keeping with the mental habits of the empire, which did indeed claim to be universal while simultaneously allowing for the peculiar histories and particular customs of its member states. How, in fact, could the empire fail of that universality, when it included examples of almost every political arrangement the mind could conceive? Or at least the German mind.

The Saxon duchies, Boyle writes, had been so "fragmented by inheritance and recombined by intermarriage" that in Goethe's time Saxe-Weimar-Eisenach consisted of four separate and non-contiguous territories. The Elector of Brandenburg had in 1701 made himself king in though not of Prussia, which was in any case a Slavonic territory outside the boundaries of the empire. Osnabrück was alternately ruled by a Protestant prince and a Roman Catholic bishop. The Elector of Saxony — I am mixing my dates shamelessly — was the elected king of Poland and the Elector of Hannover the hereditary king of England, which he ruled as a constitutional monarch while retaining absolute power in Hannover itself. Though absolutism wasn't itself absolute, it knew degree: few rulers went so far as the Landgrave of Hesse-Kassel, who paid for his palaces by selling his subjects off as soldiers. The Schönborn family, which still owns fine Rheingau vineyards, managed for two centuries to maintain the bishoprics along the Rhine and Main as heritable property, with the family sees passing smoothly from uncle to nephew to cousin. In the free city of Hamburg, political careers were open to talent, or rather to mercantile wealth; in the equally free city of Nürnberg, such careers were reserved for a closed hereditary patriciate. Still, the cities did tend toward some form of representative government, even if they also used their liberty to operate as cartels, hanging so many regulations on trade and industry that a talented outsider usually found more freedom in the employ of an absolute ruler.

"Imperial institutions," as James Sheehan writes, "were a labyrinth of overlapping jurisdictions and special privileges. They had no well-defined centre, just as the Reich itself had neither a capital nor a single source of sovereignty." It was a hermeneutic circle of a polity, its whole incomprehensible without a knowledge of its constituent parts, and those parts inconceivable without their whole. Or as the nineteenth-century social geographer Wilhelm Heinrich Riehl put it, "The whole only achieves greatness through a differentiated cultivation of its constituent parts." Riehl is perhaps best known as a theorist of the division between community and society, *Gemeinschaft* and *Gesellschaft*, but he also merits a special footnote in the history of the English novel: reading his *Natural History of the German People* gave George Eliot a model for the "stealthy convergence of human lots," the slow intertwining of one social group with another, that became *Middlemarch*. Writing in the decades between the Napoleonic end of one Reich, and the Bismarckian birth of another, what Riehl especially values is the diversity of German institutions and society, a diversity that he locates above all in the "individualized country" of Germany's riverine middle, caught between the kingdoms of north and south. Even after Napoleon this remained a region of small states. Bavaria and Prussia had swallowed the prince-bishoprics between them, but Weimar remained, and Baden, and two dozen or so others, a belt loosely girt around a vanishing waist. To Riehl, this region stands as an emblem of the German whole, for in its combination of "admirable diversity and . . . lamentable fragmentation" it best illustrates the "paradox of a land and people at once homogenous and unified and also polymorphic and disparate."

They are particular and universal at once, these pocket principalities, as indeed were their smaller eighteenth-century predecessors. Universal because particular: because in their local variations, in the exceptions and peculiarities through which they depart from the rule of a nonnormative non-state, each fragment of what would become Germany seems to suggest its entirety. One quirk speaks for another, even if those others are as different as Lübeck and Munich, both of which got going under the same twelfth-century Saxon duke. One part may substitute itself—metaphorically, metonymically—for the whole, and in describing Weimar or Hildesheim or even Berlin, I will perhaps be speaking of Hamburg under other names; perhaps I have spoken only of Hamburg.

"What I want to see is the Everlasting Rome, not the Rome which is replaced by another every decade." Goethe's stance isn't one that a traveler in Germany can maintain, not when the pastiche antiquity of Hildesheim or the reconstruction of Berlin perpetually remind you that nothing here is everlasting. And it isn't a good attitude anyway: too many echoes of the twelve years of the Thousand Year Reich. Still, the remains of the First Reich, of the millenium between Charlemagne and Napoleon—those run sempiternally everywhere, a riverbed that still shapes the land even though the stream has changed its course. The Holy Roman Empire isn't a spectre haunting the contemporary world, like the Nazis or Stalin, but it does nevertheless have a kind of presence, one that now seems pebble-smooth and picturesque, if only because so much that's more painful has followed. It's there in statues and architecture, in the palaces become government agencies, in local accents and a sense of regional identity. Regional kitsch, too — the bookshops I browsed through in Dresden were filled with historical romances about the many mistresses of Augustus the Strong. It lingers even in Germany's present constitution. If the Federal Republic scattered its institutions — the central bank in Frankfurt, the High Court in Karlsruhe — as a way to avoid a concentration of power, if even now many Germans look suspiciously at the idea of a single capital in Berlin, it isn't a simple reaction against the *Hitlerzeit*, but speaks instead of something like a formal nostalgia for the decentered world of that old empire.

Our own wanderings through that empire seemed to conform to a particular type. One of the oldest kinds of travelers' tale is the pilgrimage narrative, those medieval accounts of a visit to the Holy Land or Santiago del Compostela, records of such marvels as the Church of the Holy Sepulchre and the curative powers of the bones of St. James. And ever since, as Donald R. Howard has written, the pilgrimage has "remained a favored *image* of travel" into which all kinds of trips are conflated, "the voyage of exploration, the chivalric quest, the sojourn, even the prodigal's return," let alone that Bunyanesque passage through life in which the "goal is growth in character." Even the most colloquial or indeed ironic use of the word still suggests a devotional end. The pilgrim travels in a spirit of witness, hoping to reach some site "worthy of reverence." He has both a purpose and a definite goal, and in the Middle Ages was often warned against letting himself get distracted. "The ideal pilgrim," Howard writes, "would have travelled, as St. Bernard of Clairvaux is said to have done along the shores of Lake Léman, with his eyes upon the ground to shut out the glories of the world."

Few of them did so, and yet that sense of resolve was still in Goethe's day a model, and indeed for long after: travel as in *travail* as in work. We see it today in the Blue Guides, with their relentless inventories of one church or museum after another — guides in which, as Barthes writes, the "human life of a country disappears," leaving only its monuments behind. The nature of his worship might be different, but the Grand Tour-ist neverthe-less slips on a pilgrim's mask, and in doing so might seem to have elected history's physical remnants over an often bothersome con-temporary world. Certainly our own travels could from the out-side have looked that way: a steady budget of cathedrals and pictures and palaces, of destinations chosen more for what they once were than for what they are now. Yet the past has never stood still, and if you go looking for Goethe's Everlasting you may sometimes bump into the present instead, may encounter an ever-changing human life in a way that you otherwise wouldn't.

Years ago in Provence we stopped in the blister-bluster of sun and wind to look at the triple portal of a twelfth-century church in the small town of St. Gilles. "Squalid little lanes," my own Blue Guide says, before going on to detail the carvings on the door and the vaulting of the crypt. But what we found was some-thing more, or other, than squalor. What we found was the world of the North African unemployed, of men and only men, sitting empty-eyed on benches or standing in listless groups, together and yet somehow alone. It was a scene of almost cinematic sad-ness that made us feel out of place, intruders, even as the church itself served to remind those men that they too remained dis-placed in what had become their home. That moment in St. Gilles taught me almost everything I know about the world of France's Arab immigrants, and we wouldn't have had it if we hadn't been ruin-bibbers, in Larkin's words, and "randy for antique."

So it was in Germany as well. We were in Essen, the center of what had once been the German armaments industry, a place that looked impressive still, and still grim, with our train gliding past mile-long factories on the way to the city's center; though that's the wrong word for what's now a form of emptiness. Bombed flat, as I expect it should have been—and as I write that sentence I catch myself and shudder, but sometimes one should say it. Flat-tened and then rebuilt, as bad a job of 1950s city planning as any in Europe. We're here for the cathedral's Madonna: late tenth-century, hammered gold over a wooden core, Byzantine face, gleaming toddler on her lap, gemstones for eyes. The oldest in the West, all the guidebooks say, and my atheist wife lights a candle before it, while an Indian man prays fervently beside us. A thousand years ago, this was a convent for royal nuns, with the town growing up around it—a small place, until the Krupps learned how to cast cannon. Now reconstruction has funneled all the foot traffic in this new-built Altstadt into one single jostling street, down which we've walked to reach what is, in effect, the old city's only attraction. No visitor's insulated bubble. A skinhead hands out leaflets; young men move tight-packed, gangs of a kind I've never seen in Hamburg's central shopping district. Old people with bad teeth and faces by Bosch, many of them with canes, and canes that look needed—not carried for effect, as they so often are, the swagger-stick of age. More women than men, of course, a war-made surplus. And as we turn to enter a café I hear a lip-curling voice in my ear say "Ausländer."

I don't know why, but such moments seemed to happen only when we were out looking at churches. Maybe my antennae switched off in Hamburg, which I'd come to think of as home; maybe we simply lived in the wrong neighborhood, or rather in the right one. So almost every echo I heard of those appalling twelve years, every skin-crawling second, came when we'd gone on the road in search of a more distant past. I spun toward that voice and found it belonged to an old woman; while she herself was turned away just enough for me to tell that I wasn't the *Ausländer*, the foreigner, she was speaking of. Indeed I couldn't tell whom she was talking about. Maybe it was the huddle of young men drinking a dozen yards back—when we passed I had heard them speaking Russian. But it made me nervous, that voice, because for a visitor here every casual unpleasantness seems even now to carry the past as a penumbra. It is a land in which no behavior can be, not so much innocent, as innocently seen. And a word in the street, which would pass unnoticed in Paris or New York, can be enough to make you shiver.

Yet our forays into the past also produced a more complicated sense of the immediate present. Once a month Frau Schulze cut my hair at the shop a few doors down from our apartment building. She was from Dresden, blonde and fifty and jolly, with a grown son, and came West in 1990, almost as soon as the Wall was down. She did a good job: that is, my hair looked fine, and she was always patient with my attempts to speak German. So one day in early April I told her about our latest trip. We'd been to the Harz, the country's northernmost range of significant hills: a kind of Teutonic Berkshires, in whose woods and valleys the Brothers Grimm had gone prospecting for stories. The Harz runs east-west, or rather East-West, and we stayed just over what had been the border, posing for pictures on that now imaginary line, and passing a disused barracks on the way to our hotel. Wessies come here now: Spain and Tuscany are overrun and the real pastoral is to be found in the rural east, where there was never any money to modernize anything. It is an idyll found on bumpily prewar roads whose every turn makes one expect a gingerbread cottage, in farming villages that at sunset look abandoned, their barns huge and weatherworn. Though by now the money has in some sense arrived, and in towns like Quedlinburg or Wernigerode new plaster fills the gaps between the beams of one patched half-timbered house after another, with their details picked out in a rainbow of fresh paint, of blues and greens and yellows.

I told all this to Frau Schulze, proud that I could manage a description, and she laughed and said, "*Ah, es ist nicht mehr so braun?*" And I knew what she meant, because the barns in those empty villages were indeed still brown, it's what old wood looks like when the paint has gone. That night, however, we went to one of Brigitte's friends for dinner, a party of art historians in a loft apartment. Brigitte left the account of the trip to me, and so I told them about the reconstruction, somehow managing *auf Deutsch*, and ended with what Frau Schulze had said. No longer so brown. And our hostess Monika stopped her normal mischief and with sudden seriousness asked, "What did she mean by that?" Just the paint-job, I say. She shook her head. "Here we say 'brown' when we're talking about fascists." Brownshirts. A brown neighborhood. Some people have brown politics, others are red or green. But I still think Frau Schulze meant the paint. One country, now, yet still divided by a common language.

Or is it indeed one country? For the more I thought about Monika's words the more they seemed to point to something, though not precisely to what she'd intended. Germany's regional fault line used to lie between a Protestant north and a Catholic south; a centuries' old distinction that continued to hold so long as the Wall did too. In electoral politics that division still holds, with the Protestants mostly liberal and the Catholics largely conservative. But the regional difference that matters more today is that between East and West, and over a dozen years after the *Wende*, most Westerners still know the East only as tourists or bosses. The Eastern experience of the West runs a bit deeper, since so many people, like Frau Schulze, have come across the old border to work. Even today many Wessies see the East as a mix of unrepentant Communists and immigrant-bashing crypto-fascists, while Ossies think of the West as a land of soulless and arrogant interlopers. And there's just enough truth in either caricature to make them bite.

For our last stop in the Harz, we had driven down out of the hills, heading north to Magdeburg along the Elbe. We'd come—of course—for the cathedral, but I don't recall much of it. Not even my notebooks will bring back the Magdeburger Dom, and all I remember is profusion, an elaboration of one sculpted form after another, on the portals, in the chapels, a building huge even by ecclesiastical standards, and its surfaces all busy. Outside the Domplatz was lined in yellow baroque; occupied now by the Landtag, the legislature for the new state of Sachsen-Anhalt. I hadn't wanted to come here. Magdeburg had been one of East Germany's centers of industry, but the factories were gone now, leaving behind unemployment and one high-rise housing project after another, the DDR's equivalent of Chicago's Cabrini-Green.

It was the worst city in Germany so far as antiforeigner violence was concerned, and it didn't reassure me when my friend Walter pointed out that, with blue eyes and once-blonde hair, I wasn't the kind of foreigner who needed to worry.

We finished at the cathedral and ate lunch at an Italian place, new and spacious and anonymous, the kind of restaurant that in its pastel décor and warehouse-issue menu could be found in every German city. Even Magdeburg had caught up enough to have one. Brigitte ordered for us, in Italian, and our waiter grew expansive. Bread and wine appeared more quickly than they might have, and Brigitte asked him where he was from, how long he'd been here, whether or not he liked it. *Va bene*, he said, and his voice shrank a little. You make good money and it's okay if you keep to yourself. But what does that mean, she asked. He grew circumspect. Any problems? He grew distant, and when it was time to pay the bill, they both spoke in German.

And why should he talk, not knowing who we were? All the same, his hesitation said that the problem was real. We ourselves had no personal encounters with one of Germany's principal present-day ills, the growth in xenophobia that is both a part of the rise in right-wing nativism across Europe and a particular response to the country's straightened, post-unification economy. We knew it only secondhand, and I soon came to see even such exposure as I did have as a kind of odd collateral benefit of traveling with a medievalist. Barthes writes that the tourist of his day—his essay on the Blue Guide dates from the mid-1950s— had lost interest in monuments and instead made "everyday life . . . the main object of travel . . . social geography, town-planning, sociology, economics." That's an overstatement, though it's true enough for some people, at least if the "everyday" extends to shopping. Nevertheless the easy opposition of past and present has become one of the most conventional of all the tropes—the traps—to which travel writing is subject. We all know places where history has been turned into a bubble in which the tourist can hide, places in which it seems there's nothing that's *not* for tourists: the old city of Quebec, Rothenburg ob der Tauber, any number of chateaux and country houses. But in most places the bubble pops and a sense of the past—even a picturesque past—remains fully imbricated with an ongoing everyday world. Without Magdeburg's cathedral we wouldn't have had the chance to ask that waiter even such questions as we did.

We left the restaurant to walk back to our car, and had spread a map out on the hood, charting our road back to Hamburg, when a Volkswagen with Cologne plates pulled into the empty space across the way. A couple got out, chunky and sixty, the woman with a fanny pack slung across her belly. Dressed like an American, but German all right. Her husband walked over to the ticket machine next to me and tried to punch in a couple of hours worth of parking. I'd had no problems with it earlier, but something was wrong now. The clock didn't register, the little screen stayed blank; he put some coins in and watched them come back, he stuck them through again but the machine wouldn't swallow, it wouldn't let him pay. He stood there unhappily, with his hands on his hips, a reluctant scofflaw, and unsure if he was risking a ticket. His wife shook her head and shrugged. "Come on," she said, "*Wir sind jetzt im Ossieland.*" We're in Ossieland now—what else can you expect? And she walked cheerfully off, as though pleased that things weren't working. We would not see so much of the present if we were not first interested in the past.

✱ FOUR

The Dentist's House

A few weeks after we'd arrived in Hamburg, a small, preprinted form appeared in the mail. One of the dozen large boxes of books and clothing that we'd posted from Massachusetts had been damaged in transit; someone would have to go to the customs office and claim it. I got out the fragile contraption I'd found in our apartment's back room, a frame mounted with wheels and bungee cords that looked halfway between a handtruck and a luggage rack, and set off. I was a bit nervous, because I hadn't yet tried my German out on anything more challenging than friends and groceries, but also for that reason pleased. It was a ten minute walk along the familiar path — through Dammtor station, up and over the flying bridge that comes down by the Holocaust memorial, past the *gelateria*, and then, instead of going straight on for the opera house, turn right down a long blank street. Customs was halfway along, its public face a large room, almost empty, with benches in the middle and counters on two sides. I went to one of them, showed my form, and was given another one that asked for my name and address, the same information that had been on the first one. I filled it out and handed it in and took a number and sat down. There was just one other person waiting, but behind its various counters the office had a dozen people at work, or perhaps just employed. When my number came up, I went to the counter where I'd handed in my form, only to be sent over to the other one: this desk received requests, that one answered them. My box appeared. I identified it as being indeed my box, packed by me and sent from my home address. It had been squashed a little in shipping, burst along a part of one seam, but not badly so. I was given a knife and asked to open it. Books. And on top, the very first volume that both the customs official and I saw, was *Hitler's Willing Executioners*.

I got a laugh out of that story when a few days later I told it, *auf Deutsch*, in my German conversation class—*Hitlers willige Vollstrecker*. My Greens-voting teacher laughed and so did my fellow-students, a Polish doctor and a French *au pair*. A good story: how, in my first encounter with the German state, such issues were already present. Of course, there's nothing more to the anecdote. I said that yes, they were my books, the droopily mustached official helped me tape the box back up, and I wheeled the thing home to unpack it. Daniel Jonah Goldhagen's book had spent months on the German bestseller list. He had enjoyed a triumphant author's tour, and German publishers had already begun to release books about his work. I'd seen newspaper pictures of him walking on the resort island of Sylt with Rudolf Augstein, publisher of *Der Spiegel*. Still, I felt vaguely embarrassed about it, as if the book's appearance at the top of the box had confirmed the German stereotype about the American stereotype of Germans.

It was Christmas before I settled down at last to read it, knowing I had to, knowing I didn't want to—to read both Goldhagen and Saul Friedländer's *Nazi Germany and the Jews*. It seemed to me that I'd read far more about German attempts to come to terms with the fact of the Holocaust than I had about the thing itself. I had read *around* it, in books like Jane Kramer's *The Politics of Memory* or Charles Maier's *The Unmasterable Past*. Then, on the afternoon of Christmas day, at Brigitte's parents' house on the Swiss-Italian border, I started to read the book that, whatever its strengths and limitations — perhaps indeed because of its limitations — seemed to have changed the debate. I read it in Lugano and in the breakfast rooms of hotels in Parma and Mantua, and in our sleeper compartment on the train back from Switzerland to Hamburg. I put it aside as we returned to Germany and became busy with our lives once more, and then grabbed it again and stayed up late one night to finish it, reading on even though the terms of its argument had long since become clear.

It is vulgar in the extreme. I mean that as a compliment — well, half a compliment. I remember being asked, in eighth grade, to identify the chief cause of the Civil War. That's easy, I said, it's slavery. Wrong. It was about sectionalism, the teacher said, or the conflict between agriculture and industry, or states' rights. Yet as a child knows that the only states' right anybody was willing to die for was the right to hold slaves, so too we all at bottom know that the Holocaust happened because a great many Germans hated the Jews. We know that, even if such an explanation has never seemed enough. And, of course, that hatred was not in itself enough. It needed the addition of Hitler and the Nazis, it needed the years of fascist legislation before the mass killings began, years in which, as Goldhagen says, an "eliminationist antisemitism" became institutionalized in German life. It needed the conquest of Poland and the invasion of Russia, it needed the chaotic years of the Weimar Republic and the myth of the stab in the back, it needed the inflation and the slump. But that hatred was the most necessary of all the necessary causes. Without it the Holocaust would not have happened. Without, that is, many ordinary Germans' "willingness to kill and to brutalize Jews." And Goldhagen's great merit lies in the relentlessness with which he rubs that fact in our faces.

The book is, however, limited by that same vulgarity. Having found his necessary cause, Goldhagen proceeds, after some opening disclaimers, to treat it as sufficient. In some places he seems a strict social constructionist. Even those Germans who were not Nazis shared an ideological hatred of Jews that allowed them to kill and, indeed, he argues that it would have been hard for them *not* to share that hatred: "During the Nazi period . . . most Germans could no more emerge with cognitive models foreign to their society . . . than they could speak fluent Romanian without ever having been exposed to it." In other places, however, Goldhagen emphasizes the killers' status as "moral beings capable of making moral choices" and argues that the perpetrators acted freely. And acted freely in something other than a moral sense, for he also insists that in many cases these killers were given the choice as to whether or not to participate in a given massacre. On the one hand, individual Germans chose evil; on the other, their social construction ineluctably led them to make that choice.

This tension — this contradiction — in his work becomes particularly acute in his account of the death marches of spring 1945, in which columns of Jews were paraded endlessly, aimlessly, around the countryside, with the guards beating and starving and shooting their prisoners, even though they might at any moment meet an Allied unit and Himmler himself had ordered them to stop. "To the very end," Goldhagen writes, "the ordinary Germans who perpetrated the Holocaust willfully, faithfully, and zealously slaughtered Jews . . . even when they had received a command . . . that they desist from their killing." Goldhagen suggests that this continued killing was motivated by the guards' hatred for their prisoners as Jews — that the guards chose it, despite everything that might have made them choose not to. He also claims, however, that "the Germans' treatment of Jews was autistic," arguing that their "actions can in no sense be seen as being the consequence of any set of rational, reasonable considerations." It is a tactless choice of words, but let it stand: his use of the term "autistic" undercuts his argument in a way that makes anti-Semitism in itself seem an unconvincing explanation. For such a word suggests that cruelty can take on a life of its own, that atrocity can become a reflex, unwilled, uncontrolled by conscious volition. Could it not be that the guards simply went on doing what they were used to doing, what they were trained to do, what they no longer had the emotional resources *not* to do? Reading Goldhagen's account of the death marches made me want to know what these actions might look like to an historian who had studied atrocities in other contexts. But *Hitler's Willing Executioners* will give its readers no help in finding that historian, for implicit in Goldhagen's work is a belief in the noncomparability of the Holocaust that extends even to the level of bibliography.

Most readers troubled by Goldhagen's work — troubled, that is, not only by his powerful descriptions of horror but by his interpretation of that horror — have fastened on one thing above all. For Goldhagen elides the difference between the Germans and the Nazis, he in effect denies the myth of the Good German. Some younger Germans admire that. If each new generation deals with the past by announcing that the past has not been dealt with, then reading Goldhagen is for the German equivalent of Generation X a rough match for the student strikes of 1968. Many older readers, however, and in particular German liberals of the war generation, have been disturbed by that identification of the Nazis with Germany as a whole. That generation needed to believe that there were indeed good Germans, a belief absolutely essential to the country's reconstruction, to the establishment of its democracy and its reintegration into European society. Perhaps they willed more good Germans into being than the facts would warrant, and perhaps in doing so they have made too much of the German resistance to Hitler. Nevertheless the idea of the good German; the myth and the memory of the Officers' Plot of 1944; the transformation of the Bendlerblock in Berlin, where that plot's leading figures were executed, into something like a secular shrine — such things provided postwar West Germany with a belief, with a narrative, around which its identify could cluster. It is no wonder that those readers whose polity — whose very lives — have been founded on the distinction between the Nazis and the Germans, would see Goldhagen's work as simplistic and crudely essentialist. Yet such myths have now perhaps served their purpose. It would be uncharitable to suggest that an emphasis on the guilt of ordinary Germans has come into vogue now that most of the guilty are dead. Better to say that the Federal Republic is now so well established that it can afford to remember what it once tried so hard to forget. One sign of that, however small, is a plaque put up in 1994 outside the Johanniskirche, a few minutes walk from my Hamburg apartment. A menorah burns in its lower right-hand corner; the inscription begs forgiveness for the church's indifference during the destruction of Hamburg's synagogues, its silence during the murder of Hamburg's Jewish citizens.

How much should a traveler let such horror weigh on him? It seems easy enough to agree with Walter Benjamin that "there is no document of civilization which is not at the same time a document of barbarism," to acknowledge that the "cultural treasures" of the past "owe their existence not only to the efforts of the great minds and talents who have created them, but also to the anonymous toil of their contemporaries." We are now encouraged to remember the slaves who made the bricks for Monticello, the Flemish weavers going blind over their tapestries and lace; we visit Versailles and recall the poverty of the French peasantry. And so we should, allowing their shadow to flicker across the sunlight of the past, maintaining an awareness both of what the picturesque has cost and of the aestheticizing distance on which our own pleasure depends. That awareness has, however, become so routine as to approach banality, so familiar that it makes me want to argue with it, to insist that it only qualifies the sun, it doesn't send it into eclipse. Not if that barbarism represents what one might — crudely, cruelly — call ordinary human suffering. Doubtless the poor in Weimar had their faces ground from time to time, for all that Karl August was what one calls an enlightened despot. Nevertheless their suffering was not unique or even especially noticeable; it was not, in Murray's sense, peculiar to the place, peculiar as Bernward's doors are to Hildesheim or the Goethe House to Weimar itself. Yet the trauma of Buchenwald, or Mauthausen, or Sobibor—that is indeed peculiar, a kind of suffering that not only defines those particular places but that also marks them out from other places. It remains qualitatively different from the barbarism of daily life that is for Benjamin inseparable from the record of civilization. It is, in fact, a part of the great defining peculiarity of Germany's history, one of the most powerful of all the metonymies through which we distinguish it from other lands.

And in trying to respond to that metonymy I find myself thrown up against the borders and boundaries of the travel narrative as a genre. Most contemporary travel writing is neither here nor there, to borrow a phrase that has served Bill Bryson for a title. His words point to the sense of footloose freedom that so often makes both the writing and the journey itself seem a diversion from one's actual life, inconsequential, neither here nor there even as they are very much about being either here or there. That hasn't always been so. The "literary representation of the foreign," as Nigel Leask has written, once stood on the outer edge "of emergent discourses both of the self and of scientific knowledge." Botanists, geologists, the first ethnographers—they all found the traveler's tale an appropriate form in which to present their research. The great chronicles of exploration, from the nineteenth century and earlier, often do carry a conviction of their own importance, their own consequence, a conviction that is perhaps inseparable from their imperial purpose. The contemporary travel book, in contrast, most often describes a journey that in some sense did not have to be made. And I don't just mean books about the good life abroad by writers like Peter Mayle and Frances Mayes. That's also true—maybe more true—of the adventure travel of someone like Redmond O'Hanlon or John Krakauer. In writing about Germany, however, that sense of inconsequentiality seems impossible to maintain. In her introduction to *The Politics of Memory*, Kramer notes that once, after a reading in Hamburg, "a nice man raised his hand and asked, in a rather discouraged voice, 'Why don't you ever write something funny . . . about Germany?'" as she so often does about Italy or France. Why not indeed? Such stories do exist. The national debate over the morality of shopping on Sunday might be a good one, and so would the troubles of the country's university system, which everybody agrees is broken, but that nobody really knows how to fix. Yet turning Germans into funny foreigners doesn't quite seem adequate. At Buchenwald you may meet various ghosts, but you are not apt to have an amusing human encounter of the sort that can elsewhere yield an anecdote—at least you hope you won't. Nor do most foreign visitors want to melt into the local life. It's not just the weather that makes it unlikely the bestseller list will ever feature a volume called *A Year in Schleswig-Holstein* or *Under the Nordrhein-Westfälische Sun*.

At its best, however, travel writing can offer something more than the picturesque, something more than the clever anecdote. Jonathan Raban calls it "a notoriously raffish open house where very different genres are likely to end up in the same bed," and Colin Thubron adds that the form allows one to juxtapose "landscape and history . . . incident and encounter, domestic detail, stray thoughts . . . the apparently trivial alongside the apparently important. It flouts conventional categories and crosses disciplines at will." It can be as miscellaneous as the contents of the writer's own mind, and can encompass everything from the purely linear, one train, one town, after another of Theroux's *Great Railway Bazaar* to the set of learned historical digressions that make up Claudio Magris's *Danube*. It may offer an account of the natives' manners and mores, it may concentrate on the scenery or turn itself into nature writing, and it may even fuse the two into a work of cultural geography, like Raban's own elegiac *Bad Land*. Paul Fussell underlines that mongrel quality in noting that whenever "we cannot satisfactorily designate a kind of work with a single word (*epic . . . romance . . . sonnet*) but must invoke two (*war memoir . . . first novel . . . travel book*)" we are crossing into "complicated territory, where description, let alone definition, is hazardous." Though the danger isn't enough to keep him from risking that definition: the travel book is "a sub-species of memoir . . . [that] arises from the speaker's encounter with distant or unfamiliar data, and in which the narrative . . . claims literal validity by constant reference to actuality." Fussell adds that such narratives often take the form of a quest, a quest whose goal, one might add, isn't so much an actual place as it is the answer to a question. The writer—Robert Byron in *The Road to Oxiana*, Peter Matthiessen in *The Snow Leopard*—sets off in search of knowledge, a search that serves in itself to give the narrative its motion. Which brings us back to Goethe, his desire in Rome to "discover myself in the objects I see." The physical journey coalesces with an intellectual one, and the writer discovers not only a place but the meaning of his own experience.

That emphasis does, however, ask the reader to maintain an interest in the writer's own sensibility—and as I write that sentence, I note the distance at which my own diction clumsily tries to place it, as if to deny that this is precisely what these pages have begged of you. For in relation to Germany that emphasis is bound to be troubling. To ask you to read about Germany as though it were Italy, to relax into a record of the impressions that the country has made on one's sensibility—that does indeed seem neither here nor there, a distraction from the peculiarities of its history, a butterfly that might well deserve to be broken upon a wheel. Yet that very sense of disproportion isn't only intrinsic to the travel narrative, it is also one of its chief attractions. As Thubron suggests, its very inconsequentiality invite serious questions instead of precluding them, in the same way that a leisurely walk down the street may set you musing, may spark ideas, or make you notice connections that you hadn't seen before. Nevertheless both those questions and their answers remain those of a *flâneur*—occasional, provisional, piecemeal. They are the questions of an amateur. So let me rephrase an issue I posed a few chapters ago. If one really cannot avoid concentrating on The

German Problem, what effect does that have on the way one writes?

In the preface to his *Little Tour in France*, James writes that once a traveler goes beyond "the delight of the eyes" he has no choice but to pursue "the inner springs of the subject—springs and connections social, economic, historic." That's precisely what James himself refuses in that volume to do, concentrating instead on the pageant of French history and architecture, the intrigues of the sixteenth century as they played themselves out in the chateaux of the Loire, the visual feast of the Romanesque. In Germany, however, in this land of ghosts and echoes where the very churches proclaim their own sins, even those of us who might prefer to "write something funny" find ourselves drawn toward those "inner springs." Drawn, that is, toward a different kind of rhetoric—a rhetoric best defined by Stephen Greenblatt in *Marvelous Possessions*. Writing of Montaigne's "On the Cannibals," that great and early attempt to comprehend the wonder of the Americas, Greenblatt stresses the importance of the essayist's decision to put the piece in the voice of his servant, "'a simple, crude fellow,'" and therefore "a reliable observer." For with clever people, Montaigne suggests, sensibility intrudes itself; they "never show you things as they are, but bend and disguise them according to the way they have seen them." Yet his servant doesn't have the verbal dexterity to lie or exaggerate, and Greenblatt uses that fact to make the servant's report into the very type of the rhetoric of exploration. In Renaissance travel literature "by those who claim to have seen the new lands for themselves, it is style that plays the authenticating and legitimating role played by Montaigne's servant . . . [a] style . . . humble, unimaginative, uninventive, and hence by implication reliable . . . [an] unfigured language of perception." In contrast to poetry, where style was "frequently understood as an elegant garment," what the literature of exploration claimed to offer was "an accurate account of the other, a clear view of the naked truth," a text in which style functioned as a "trustworthy" but above all unobtrusive servant, "the agent of simple reporting."

Most nonfictional writing about Germany has tended, since the Second World War, toward the rhetorical model that Greenblatt uses Montaigne's servant to define, and not toward the impressionistic record of a sensibility on tour that one associates with Stendhal or James. It has allied itself with the literature of exploration, stressing its own reportorial quality, its own reliability — about this country we still want the news. As Montaigne held his servant to be a "reliable witness," so the writer on postwar Germany has seen him or herself as bearing witness to the kind of large questions we don't usually ask about other countries. Part of taking The German Problem's temperature is the desire to be up to date, to provide the latest bulletin; a desire that rests upon the paradoxical belief that the country is in a state of perpetual crisis, at once constantly changing and yet somehow also unaltered. *Are they still . . . do you think they are going to try it again?* Such questions aren't often asked directly, but they lie nevertheless behind every newspaper story one reads about the problems of unification or the decision to send troops anywhere beyond the country's borders. "Germany Wants to Be Normal," as the headline in the *Herald Tribune* puts it, "but History Keeps Getting in the Way." And it is because history keeps on getting in the way that nearly all travel books about Germany date from before the war, when the country was still presumed to be "normal." If travel writing is in some sense the province of amateurs, then Germany has been a place for professionals. They are called journalists, and the skilled political coverage they provide bears about as much relation to the travel book as a professional kitchen does to that of a good home cook.

Genres like states are defined by their borders, and the critics of travel books have been as active as post–Cold War mapmakers in charting its territory. For Dennis Porter, it may at one edge touch political witness, while at another, though not necessarily polar, limit it will approach ethnography. So Lévi-Strauss manages in

Tristes Tropiques to make anthropological fieldwork masquerade as a travel narrative—or maybe it's the other way around. Tzvetan Todorov suggests that such writing oscillates between observer and observed, autobiography and science. His own boundary is reached with *Democracy in America,* which "leans too heavily toward the description of its object to be considered a travel narrative, even if Tocqueville sporadically refers to the circumstances under which he gained a certain piece of information." But as Raban's description of that "notoriously raffish open house" would suggest, such borders are above all porous. Some narratives tend toward the reportorial, while others seem pure mood and atmosphere, yet nothing is contraband, nothing is interdicted, and no passports are required. That's especially true for the frontier between reporting and travel writing, which looks as permeable as that between Bavaria and Thuringia, between the old and new *Länder* of the German Federal Republic. Nevertheless that border is there. It may take a few miles, but you can usually tell which one you're in—the pavement might change, or the accent, and after a bit you know you've crossed over.

A single sentence of Kramer's can serve to illustrate both the difference between travel writing and reporting, and the difficulty of fixing the smudged line between them: "One morning in Berlin this spring, on my way to an interview with a city planner, I stopped at the new Galeries Lafayette, in the east of the city on Friedrichstrasse, to pick up a croissant at the basement supermarket." The sentence slips smoothly from one gear to another. It's the travel writer who buys the croissant, and who in fact gets so distracted by the shopping that she's late for her appointment. But it's the journalist who finally does meet the city planner and who stitches that interview together with many others in presenting a masterful account of Berlin's post-*Wende* reconstruction. And that croissant aside, the article's gaze seems entirely directed outward. Kramer exists in her own text only as a lens through which to focus, and not a sensibility to explore: however much her personal crotchets and assumptions may tacitly have shaped her reporting, she never says, with Goethe, that she discovers herself in the objects she sees.

Would her work be richer if she did? If she were more fully a *flâneur*, if in walking over a building site, she did not invariably do so with someone who can tell her about it? Clearly travel was involved in the writing of such wonderfully informative books as *The Politics of Memory* or Marc Fisher's *After the Wall*. But they emphasize neither the writer's own individual experience nor a sense of place and motion, the peculiarities of the local and the sometimes bumpy business of getting there. Travel in such books seems as utilitarian and transparent as the reportorial eye itself is often alleged to be: something one has to do to get from city to city, interview to interview. It almost never figures as its own end, and in the writing the accidents and the discoveries — the serendipity — of a journey seem almost entirely edited out.

My own sense is that the stranger a country seems to one's assumed audience, the more possible it is to avoid the choice of one rhetorical mode over another. A fluent integration of reporting with the chances of the road seems more likely in writing about Siberia or Central Asia, as Thubron himself has done, than in an account of Western Europe — more likely, that is, for someone writing about a region from which news is scarce and about which an eyewitness account maintains its primary, illustrative, and exploratory value. Yet in practice, most writers must choose. Only the greatest have fully alloyed serious political writing — that taking of a nation's temperature — with an account of their own temperament: V. S. Naipaul, perhaps, in *An Area of Darkness,* or Rebecca West in *Black Lamb and Grey Falcon,* in which her odd ironic sincerity persuades us that what she learns in the Balkans matters to her own individual destiny, that somehow her reporting can save her. No contemporary Anglo-American writer on Germany has matched their achievement: the place denies us their self-absorption, that necessary ability to balance the fate of nations in the scales of one's own idiosyncrasies.

Still, Kramer's sentence does in the end remain a single sentence, and that very fact means that the distinction between the travel writer and the reporter seems far from absolute. The one may rely on chance and the other on contacts, but those too can easily blur together and may depend as much upon the writer's own frame of mind as they do on anything else. Most accounts of the language of colonialism, for example, have shown how close the conventions of travel writing are to the newspaper article and the government survey — or have shown, rather, that the rhetoric of a purportedly objective report is every bit as trope-ridden as that of a more consciously subjective work. Often that rhetoric seems accurate enough: Delhi's streets are indeed more pungent than London's, and Hamburg's manners considerably stiffer than those of New York. But it's perhaps less important to note that accuracy than to understand the way in which such a rhetoric serves to structure a discourse. As travel books about Rome once had their required scenes, their obligatory accounts of Carnival and the Colosseum, so any journalist writing about contemporary Germany has his or her own set-pieces to perform. Right now that discourse has a forked tongue: it speaks at once of the renascence of Berlin *and* of the continuing failures of the East to catch up. In the 1980s, however, almost everyone traveled to Bavaria, to talk in Passau with Anja Rosmus, a.k.a. "The Nasty Girl," who had earned death threats for her persistence in exposing the lies behind her hometown's claim to have resisted the Nazis. While after the *Wende* the reporters all went to interview the East German painter Bärbel Bohley — in Fisher's words, "the 'Mother' of the Revolution . . . who helped organize the revolt of 1989, and then found herself discarded by a people eager to leap into the inviting waters of the west." One visits a concentration camp, one walks along the course of the Wall, crosses what's no longer Checkpoint Charlie, and tries to relate the two great emblems of twentieth-century Germany, to trace a connection between the War and the Wall. The best example is Katie Hafner's *The House at the Bridge*, an account of a Jewish family's attempt to reclaim their expropriated Potsdam mansion, a house that in East Germany had become a daycare center.

And above all one broods about history, about what Garton Ash calls the "Goethe Oak" and the burdens of a memory that provides, as Kramer says, "the most loaded politics" of all in "the new, united German state"—a politics that affects everything from urban planning to the country's retrograde citizenship laws. It is exhausting. And monotonous. *Father/Land*, by the American journalist Frederick Kempe, includes a few chapters on the Nazi past of the author's own relatives, along with more conventional reporting on such topics as generational change and the German army's role in Yugoslavia. Kempe's subtitle, however, is "A Personal Search for the New Germany," and there's not a wafer's difference between that and Kramer's own "Looking for Germany in the New Germany." For if the rhetoric of Germany appears to discourage some kinds of writing, it seems to enforce others. One writes with (or perhaps against) the belief that that one must somehow "cover" the country: must go East to report on the internal borders that belie the absence of other boundaries, must worry about immigration and unemployment and their effect on the local elections. About everything, in short, that the Germans do themselves.

Most Anglo-Americans manage, in contrast, to treat Italy's internal problems as a form of local color: corruption and incompetence and even the Mafia can still be made to seem charming. But a discussion of Germany's national vices leads somewhere else, and insofar as its history makes you think that its problems are yours as well, the country effectively elides the distinction between the traveler and the native, as though its *Sonderweg* were universal after all. So we stress the difference Germany has made to our collective fate and continue to feel the reporter's need to stand as a "reliable witness." We make the assumption that—because of the Nazis and their war, because of the Cold War and its Wall—Germany not only mattered then but continues to matter now. Matters because it's a place to be afraid of. But does it, is it, still? Or does one now have the freedom to travel through the country and note not only those places in which you feel the sheer consequentiality of its recent history but also the pure Stendhalian pleasure of the ones where you don't? Yet as I write those words of negative definition, as I confess my interest in what, at times, Germany doesn't make me think or feel, I have to acknowledge that I've been caught once again by the peculiarities of its past.

One afternoon just after the New Year I went out to Eimsbüttel for lunch at my friend Helga's — "out," even though Eimsbüttel is well within central Hamburg. For my sense of geography wasn't yet secure, and the U-Bahn connections still made her apartment seem terribly far; later on I would learn the buses and extend my sense of the bicycle routes and find the city a more compact place than it looked. And I would find Eimsbüttel itself attractive. I liked the commercial activity of its long straight main roads, with their wide sidewalks and small shops: bakeries that weren't part of the city-wide chains, a place that sold only Rhône wines. The district had been developed later than Rotherbaum, and it was more densely built — no big office buildings or hotels but instead street after solid street of six-story apartment buildings. There were few detached houses: a more modest neighborhood than the one where we lived, and more diverse, busier, and more crowded, too. It was a place we ourselves would have been able to afford.

Most of the academics we knew lived there and Helga was one of them, the closest thing to a counterpart I had in the University's English department. She was as slight and steely as a jockey, and the only German I knew who spoke English with a touch of Cockney. We had met a few years before, on my first visit to Hamburg, and struck up a friendship over a discussion of British postmodernism. Now she was home for a term with a new baby.

I volunteered to bring lunch, and so, with a bag of sandwiches in my hand, I edged my way around little Moritz's stroller in the building's foyer and climbed the three flights up to her flat. When I arrived she was trying to trick the boy into eating, and miming delight at the taste of strained carrots. But he was eight months old and wasn't having any of it—the whole kitchen seemed flecked with orange.

I had finished Goldhagen the night before and wanted to talk about it, not about the events he describes but about his description itself, for I was beginning to think out the critique I've presented at the start of this chapter. Yet it's hard to separate these things, and once Moritz moved from carrots to milk we found ourselves working through one of Goldhagen's conclusions, indeed the conclusion of much recent work on the Holocaust: the absurdity of the claim that "we didn't know." The camps took too many people to build and to run, there were the railroad workers and the architects and the companies that made the equipment, and above all there were the many thousands of soldiers who had taken part in the earlier, massive, but not yet industrial killings in Poland and Russia. Not yet industrial because they involved bullets rather than gas; because the bodies were not burned but instead buried or simply left where they fell; because the killings were often directly personal, with the killers knowing which corpses they were responsible for. These were the kinds of atrocities that Goldhagen stresses, and part of his evidence came from the photos taken by the soldiers themselves, photos which might be posted on the regimental bulletin board or sometimes indeed sent home, a memento of one's service abroad. A souvenir: something memorable, but also something normal and acceptable.

Helga's own family had been far away from all that. Her grandfather had been a nationalist but not a Nazi, and he had what you might call a good war—that is, a clean one—commanding a garrison in the Channel Islands. And the curious thing, she added, was that he always spoke of his time there with nostalgia, in her childhood the whole family would grow sentimental at posters of Jersey in a travel agent's window. Moritz finished nursing and we moved into a book-lined living room, where we sat on futons and watched him grab at his blocks. His mother went on. There had, she said, been a prison camp on the island—not a concentration camp but one for captured airmen and soldiers. It wasn't a place her grandfather had been involved with himself, but things had happened there, and a part of her own growing up had been an attempt to parse out what responsibility he might have had for a unit outside his own line of command. Even now she wasn't sure. It wasn't something she agonized about, not now, but still the question was there: what had he known, and when? Then Moritz rolled over on a toy and began to cry, and she scooped up him and we slid into talking about day care.

Such moments, in which history is picked up and searched through, and then laid almost casually aside, came frequently in my conversations with our German friends. But they put that history down like a sponge or a handkerchief that they know they'll soon need again, and so I found myself replaying our conversation when I left an hour later. And our talk seemed all the more present because Goldhagen had devoted several chapters to an account of the atrocities committed by a unit from Hamburg itself, by men who had once stood at the same street lights where I was now waiting myself. Police Battalion 101: *Ordinary Men*, as Christopher Browning puts it in his own study of that same formation. But the two historians use the same set of facts to reach opposite conclusions. Less than a third of the battalion's personnel had joined the Nazi Party, and its commanding officer announced, in issuing the orders for the unit's first massacre, that any individual member might be excused from taking part. Only a dozen of its nearly three hundred men accepted that offer. Goldhagen argues that such facts demonstrate the degree to which "eliminationist antisemitism" was widespread even in Germany's non-Nazi population. Browning concentrates instead on a sense of group conformity. Refusing to kill meant "refusing one's share of an unpleasant collective obligation" and threatened to isolate one from one's comrades. Both writers note the revulsion that many of the battalion's members at first felt for their work, but Goldhagen argues that these men nevertheless killed "in good conscience," believing that the unpleasantness of their task, as measured in their victims' gore, was a necessary means to a desirable end. Browning, in contrast, depicts them as caught between "the demands of conscience on the one hand and the norms of the battalion on the other," and concludes that "if the men of Reserve Police Battalion 101 could become killers . . . what group of men cannot?"

Few surviving members of that unit would now be under ninety. And yet I do occasionally meet someone whose behavior strikes me as especially authoritarian and unpleasant: a clerk in a shop, a desk worker at one of the many government offices where one must register one's self. There are such people in all countries, only here there's a label to stick on them, and I sometimes catch myself thinking yes, yes indeed, that person would have been a Nazi. But he isn't. In another time he or someone like him — or even I myself — might have been and done appalling things, and yet the crucial word is indeed "another." Our own times *are* different, or at least they are here, and as I move through the city I find it difficult to connect the faces I see with the actions that both Goldhagen and Browning describe. Only once, in looking at a photo in *Hitler's Willing Executioners*, did such a connection come viscerally home to me. But it wasn't the photo of a massacre. It was the picture of a woman named Vera Wohlauf, an officer's wife. She is walking along the beach, in trousers and a halter-top, her midriff bare and her hair pulled back. She is long-limbed and slender, her face is open and smiling and pretty, and she does not look in that photo as though she belongs in that time. There is nothing period about the candid expression on her face, and she looks instead like my contemporary, like the young woman in a shearling coat whom my head turned to follow as I started down the steps to my train. Yet Vera

Wohlauf accompanied her husband to Poland—it was in effect their honeymoon—and occasionally went along on killing operations. Sometimes she carried a riding whip.

Seeing that picture made me more attentive to the marks that the Holocaust had left on Hamburg itself. Not the marks of the war, the new building sandwiched between two old ones, but those made by the absence—whether through murder or exile—of its Jewish population; a population that had shrunk, as the plaque at the Johanniskirche told me, from 20,000 in 1933 to 945 at the end of the war. So now, on a visit to the Hamburg historical museum, I learned that there had been three synagogues within an easy walk of our apartment. Two of them had been adjacent to the university itself, where 20% of the faculty had been Jewish before Jews were banned from teaching, and one of those, the Bornplatz synagogue, sat on a square through which I walk almost every day. It was pulled down after Kristallnacht, but no building has since gone up in its place, and its ground plan is now marked by metal strips set into the pavement. Part of its facilities have survived: the building that housed its Talmud-Tora-Realschule, and which now serves as a branch of the city's *Volkshochschule,* the German equivalent of a community college. Yet this section of Hamburg hadn't only been heavily Jewish, it had also been heavily Nazi. Richard F. Hamilton's *Who Voted for Hitler* estimates, in fact, that over 50% of the non-Jews in my neighborhood of Rotherbaum may have voted for the National Socialists in the elections of July 1932. It is a shocking figure, one of the highest in the city, and it effectively destroys the myth that the Nazis made their strongest appeal in small towns and to the lower middle class.

Crossing the street near my gym, I step into a small triangular park, a piece of pie maybe an acre or so in extent. But nobody walks their dog here or lies on its untended grass because in the middle there's a large mass of granite, rough-hewn so that one can see the marks of the chisel, several blocks fitted together to form a giant gravestone, massive and high but without inscription. There's a wreath at its base, evergreens and mums, but it looks to have been there a week and is now falling apart — a ribbon says it's from a church in the industrial suburb of Wandsbek. So: a memorial, but one that at first seems illegible. It takes a while to find the small sign at the park's edge that states that this piece of grass, convenient for the rail lines, was the collection point for Hamburg's Jews, the spot from where, in 1941, 3,000 of its citizens were deported to the ghettoes of Riga, Lodz, and Minsk. And that sign's obscurity seems typical of the places in this city that are associated with the Holocaust. They are so understated as to be almost unannounced. Certainly nothing marks the site that's closest of all to our apartment. It's right next door, unnoted except in my guidebooks, a three story building with gray plaster outside and some nice stucco at the windows. #38 Rothenbaumchaussee once housed a Jewish community organization. Then the Gestapo made the building into its local headquarters. Now my wife's dentist works there; I think as I pass of *Marathon Man*, and admire the black Porsche in his forecourt.

I don't know what to do with these facts, what I should feel about them, what I do feel about them. In *The Portrait of a Lady*, James writes that his heroine Isabel Osmond sees the ruins of Rome as an objectification of "the ruin of her happiness . . . She had grown to think of [the city] chiefly as the place where people had suffered . . . [and] gazed through the veil of her personal sadness at the splendid sadness of the scene." Her own misery gives her a sympathetic imagination of the suffering of centuries, and in "the starved churches . . . the marble columns . . . seemed to offer her a companionship in endurance." Isabel's imaginative leap, however, is one that in Hamburg I could neither make nor believe appropriate, and not only because I myself was not suffering here. I found myself shying away from envisioning the scenes that might have been played next door — was the building purely administrative, or did the basement have its special uses? What would it have been like at the square from which those 3,000 left? Yet to wonder about such things, to try to work up an experience of pain and dread: that seems less an exercise in historical empathy than a desire for the *frisson* of a horror movie. Nor did I ask the historians I knew at the university for help — what did in fact happen, what kinds of testimony are available? It seemed to me that once — and perhaps too lightly — having decided to spend a year in Hamburg, I could not afford to let it become such a movie. You might say I was afraid of the vividness of my own imagination, though you might also say I was afraid to know too much.

Nor am I alone in that fear. "Fully 29 percent of Americans," as Fisher notes in *After the Wall*, "tell researchers they would never set foot in" the country. For many of them that decision is a principled one, but some in that number are surely motivated by squeamishness, by a desire to avoid the unpleasant, to avoid thinking about Germany's history. Why spoil a vacation? And indeed it is better to stay home than to come here and shield yourself in ignorance, trying to notice only the castles and the beer. Of course, others in that 29 percent already know that unpleasantness too well. Cynthia Ozick will write admiringly about contemporary German fiction, but describes herself as doing so from a "non-visitor's distance." I have friends, most of them Jewish, but some of them black, who have come to Germany and found it so creepy, so marked by a past that seems at once omnipresent and yet impossibly distant, that they are unwilling to return. They too are right to stay away. The Holocaust is too much at the front of their minds for them to travel here comfortably. Yet even for those of us who can, keeping a sense of daily equilibrium is never really a matter of putting that history out of one's thoughts.

Or is it? Perhaps the best way to explore this question is to describe a particular place, and my reaction to it over time. At the start of this chapter, I mentioned walking past a Holocaust memorial on my way to the customs office — mentioned it casually but deliberately, dropping it into a sentence between a train station and an ice cream stand, a landmark on one of my regular walks. Alfred Hrdlicka's *The Hamburg Firestorm* is unlabeled: as with the monument commemorating the deportation, you have already to know what you're looking at, perhaps what you're looking for. Its main component is a tattered and broken wall of bronze, relieved — though that's not the word — by a figure that seems blasted into a frozen and yet molten immobility, a figure whose torso looks as if it were dissolving into the wall but whose head, a face turning into a skull, remains still free. So are his legs: he's wearing boots, and Hrdlicka has given them a tread. The monument has other parts as well: on the wall's reverse, a block of granite with some blackened stone figures on top, whose posture echoes a Last Judgement; some jutting bronze poles and girders; a free-standing block of stone in which a figure that recalls Rodin's *Thinker* looks on the verge of decapitation. The whole is horrific without being especially provocative, and what gives the piece its point is less Hrdlicka's actual modeling than its position in the landscape of Hamburg itself.

It sits on a strip of tree-shrouded grass between a busy street and a pedestrian way, on the edge of Hamburg's Botanical Gardens, where the city's walls used to be, a few minute's walk from one of its three major train stations, at the border between the Innenstadt and the nineteenth-century villa districts. Tens of thousands walk past it each day. But that isn't what matters. What matters is the other monument a few yards away, the one the Nazis left behind. It is a cube of blonde sandstone, with carved soldiers perpetually marching in rows around it, their legs and torsos in perfectly matched and staggered relief. One rank follows closely on another, and though their faces would never have been individualized — the contrast with St. Gaudens's Boston memorial to the 54th Massachusetts could not be greater — they have suffered some from erosion and also from vandalism, and now seem to be fading into each other.

This blocky mass went up in 1936, to commemorate the dead of Hamburg's second Hanseatic Infantry in both the Franco-Prussian and the first World War. A local monument, but standard-issue for the period. I found a virtually identical piece serving as the base for a fountain in the Rhineland city of Speyer: the same kind of stone, the same soldiers, even the same inscription. *"Deutschland muss leben, auch wenn wir sterben müssen"*: Germany must live, even if we have to die. Ten yards away from the Hamburg cube there is a long, low memorial stone set into the ground, and again engraved with the regiment's name and the dates: 1870–71, 1914–18. And there is another block as well, marked simply 1939–45. A second unit has also put a stone here, however, and this one isn't content with the bare dates. The 225th regiment has added a phrase, in raised Gothic script, in honor of their *gefallenen and vermissten Kameraden,* and on the December day that I visited these memorials with my notebook someone had left a wreath. It was tied with a ribbon in memory of those "Loved Comrades," a slogan to which, after a few inches of empty satin space, this word had been added: *Unvergessen,* unforgotten, the word single and alone as if in defiance.

Hrdlicka's sculpture was commissioned because the Hamburg authorities could not decide what to do with that sandstone block. It had been the only thing in the immediate area to survive the war unscathed, and in the years since, as James Young writes, it has "come under siege by demonstrators . . . [and] incited full-fledged rock-and-bottle riots." Its inscription has been especially troubling, with those words coming to stand as a "mockingly hollow . . . affront to the dead of all wars," and yet veterans' groups have resisted attempts to have the thing moved or destroyed. Eventually the city decided to build what Young calls "a contemporary countermonument right next to it," in the hopes that that would be enough to "neutralize [its] fascist charge." Yet just what, or who, does Hrdlicka's work memorialize? The dead of the camps, certainly, but also, as Young adds, "those killed in their beds during bombing raids, even soldiers killed on the battlefield" — and not only the dead of Warsaw and London. Through its dialogue with that earlier monument, the piece in effect adds the "war's makers . . . to the sum of war casualties." It is a remembrance of all the victims of fascism, which in this reading includes the city itself. For no one here will note its title without thinking, at least in part, of the Allied air raids of 1943, of the incendiary bombs that melted "the glass in the tram car windows" and made "stocks of sugar [boil] in the bakery cellars."

Those last quotations come from W. G. Sebald's *On the Natural History of Destruction,* an investigation of the occlusion, in Germany's own public memory, of the country's wartime suffering: the years of bombardment, the hundreds of thousands killed by Allied air strikes. Certainly the details Sebald resurrects are horrible enough, with the fire snatching "oxygen to itself so violently that the winds reached hurricane force . . . and drove human beings before it like living torches." Even so, a viewer may — should — find himself uneasy at the way Hrdlicka's monument elides the difference between the different groups of the dead: uneasy, though recognizing too the fundamental truth of the awful equivalence, in death, of what in life was not equal at all. *The Hamburg Firestorm* may neutralize that sandstone block, but while Young does treat it as a paradigmatic example of a countermonument, it is not a Holocaust memorial, or not quite, or not only. Call it an anti-fascist installation instead. Still, one has to admit that in purely formal terms it doesn't quite work. Of the two memorials, you're more apt to notice the Nazi one, which both faces the footpath squarely and makes a clear and legible statement. Hrdlicka's piece, in contrast, stands at an oblique angle to passersby and doesn't announce its purpose. Nevertheless they make a frightening pair — that sleepwalking lockstep juxtaposed with its consequences, a work of inhuman order set against a posthuman chaos.

Most people walk by *The Hamburg Firestorm* without stopping, without even turning their heads to look at it. And I'm usually one of them. Oh, I know it's there — unless I'm talking to someone I register the fact of its presence, and yet I do so without fully taking it in. I'm aware of it only as something in the background, and if I say to myself, "There's the memorial," it's in the same way as I note other landmarks on my walk, the entrance to the U-Bahn, the brick cupola on the post office, the line of blue neon on the cinema across the street. Passing it is a part of my daily routine, and as such it's too familiar to be seen with any regular degree of close attention. Despite its subject, I'm no more apt to notice a new detail in Hrdlicka's work than I am in any of the bits of bronze that dot my home campus in Massachusetts. And it is intolerable, this not seeing, I find it deeply troubling that I can walk past this site without being each time deeply troubled. I don't want it naturalized within the cityscape, I don't want to get used to it, I want to defamiliarize *The Hamburg Firestorm* so that I can each time see it as though I had never seen it before. I could say that the fact that I don't simply means that Hrdlicka's sculpture isn't very good—that it's just not strong enough to rouse me into perception. If it were better, I would think more about the suffering it represents; though if it were indeed more powerful, I might well be more troubled by its moral sleight-of-hand.

Still, your eyes can grow used even to Bernini or Henry Moore, and if living here has made this place a part of my daily landscape, so too has it made the Holocaust itself a feature of my mental one, as immovable as that fascist statue. Always there even if not always looked at. I walk past that memorial, and sometimes indeed I hurry past it, on my way to an appointment or because it's raining and cold. Because I live here I pass it so often that I can no longer always see it—because I have a set of habits and rhythms along whose path these statues happen to lie. The headline in the *Herald Tribune* says that Germany wants to be normal but hasn't quite been able to figure out how. The longer you stay here, though, the more normal it seems. Not, on a daily basis, the historical nightmare, but the line at the bakery, the bookstore windows, the bicycle ride around the Alster. Helga's little son rolls over, and the gears of conversation slip from past to present. It's easy to respond appropriately, or to feel that's what you're doing, when a place has been peculiarly devoted to suffering. It is much harder when the place is a palimpsest of other meanings and activities as well. As the months pass, you come to accept the utter banality, not of evil, but of buying sheets and pillows in a place where evil has happened. You accept it as in India you accept the perpetual presence of the poor, and if you don't, if you can't, then you will not be able to bear staying.

Even as I write those sentences, however, the very idea makes me squirm. It suggests that one's daily life is simply one's daily life, and much the same anywhere. And that, of course, was one of the things that fascism relied on: the ordinary citizen's willingness not to notice that things were horrible, because the horror had become normalized, because the Nazis had gotten people to accept their terms, their way of seeing. When you walk past a Holocaust memorial without pausing to look at it, you may feel for a moment as though you are evading the event itself, as though you were turning away from something that is happening now. But it's not the same thing, or so I tell myself as I walk from the Innenstadt to our apartment, and hope that I am right. The house next door is now only the dentist's, and in Germany the practice of everyday life is not today a matter of accepting the presence of horror but rather one of accepting its pastness, of coming to terms with what its present once irrevocably *was*.

In thinking about how our minds deal with such facts I often find myself remembering Faulkner, as I did on my cab ride to Buchenwald. I recall in particular his character Quentin Compson, whose consciousness is so dominated by memory — a family memory of the defeated South, a personal memory of both his sexual desire for his sister and his failure to defend her honor — that he cannot ever bring himself to embrace the present. Quentin wants always to stay in the moment in which the past was *not yet*, and though the time in which he wants to remain is hardly one that can sustain him, he cannot cope with the fact that it's over: neither that it happened nor the idea that he might one day accept the fact that it did. For him the horror goes on, in a flayed perpetual present — and so it has been for many Holocaust survivors. Yet how should it be for those of us who have no such firsthand experience? Should we too try always to hear that scream from the other side of silence? I don't think so. To have a keen vision of that suffering perpetually before us, to quiver always with the perception of historical pain — that, paradoxically, is to turn yourself into something like an aesthete of horror. So give thanks that dailiness numbs the consciousness, that it serves as memory's foe. The dry-cleaning has to be picked up, dinner needs to be cooked, and these mundanities are intolerable, and they are saving, and when I say that I don't know what to do with facts like the past of the house next door, what I really mean is that most of the time I ignore them.

In February Brigitte's friend Jean-Pierre came for a weekend from Paris, and over dinner one night he asked me what I thought about living in Germany. But I didn't understand the question, and after a moment he added that most Frenchmen still thought first about the war. So do most Americans, I answered. And then I said, as though realizing it for the first time, that I no longer thought much about either the war or the questions around it, that I was in fact surprised to realize how little I thought about them from day to day. Hamburg now felt like home, a place I took for granted, and asking me how I felt about it was like asking how I felt about my own life. Like home, he said. Like nowhere, or anywhere.

❀ FIVE

Fragments and Digressions

My favorite bookstore in Hamburg was a place called the Bücherstube Stolterfont, just up the street from our apartment: a small, free-standing building almost buried in the trees by the entrance to the local U-Bahn stop. Building? A shack, really, its walls flimsy and its roof askew, a structure whose plate-glass front made the whole shop look perilously open to the city's steady wind and rain. But the display behind that glass seemed always attractive: new biographies of Bismarck and Che; stylish paperback editions of Robert Walser and Ingeborg Bachmann; a pictorial history of Ellis Island and a boxed set of Günter Grass, including the author's own reading of *The Tin Drum* on twenty-three CDs. Inside were bookcases running around the room's three solid sides, with most of the stock double-shelved and inde-cipherably arranged, while the floor was so jammed with high-piled tables and revolving racks for paperbacks that gridlock started at two customers and a dog. No cash register, just an adding machine and a drawer, with receipts written out by hand. And no computer books or self-help manuals or investment guides. Fiction, poetry, a little art and music, biography, the com-plete works of Theodor Adorno—it was the kind of store that made me wish I could read every volume it contained.

Except I can't. I can't make it through anything more than the simpler of the children's books that line the wall by the door. The shop's dog-eared furnishings would in themselves be enough to make the place charming, but the fact that it reduces me to something close to illiteracy makes it irresistable. In Germany I go into more bookstores more often and with more pleasure than I do at home, and not just because Hamburg's are bigger and better than the ones in my small Massachusetts town. No, if I walk into every bookstore I pass, if I find them an endless temptation, if I spend so much time poking through their shelves without making a purchase that I must look like a shoplifter, it's precisely because I can't read anything. Bookstores at home are never so teasing. Even if their stock weren't almost always over-familiar, the thrills they offer are all too easily accessible. A foreign language, however, is enough to turn the shop into a realm of unattainable pleasure, where mocking eyes peep out from around a curtain, and every book-lined room here seems as though it might be a fabulous lost library, like that of Alexandria or the monastery in *The Name of the Rose*; a cabinet of wonders that maintains its bewitching power to the exact degree that it also remains inaccessible.

That's even true for those books that I *can* read, or rather those that I could and maybe even did, before they were translated into German from either English or what's called "Amerikanisch." Sometimes a volume I've passed up becomes suddenly attractive, as if Nicholson Baker's *Wie gross sind die Gedanken?* might be more compelling than his *The Size of Thoughts*. And however did Sebastian Faulks's First World War novel, *Birdsong*, get to be called *Gesang vom grossen Feuer*, song of the great fire? That's a book I know well, but seeing it in translation gives me a flicker of uncertainty: is it still the same story? The new title makes it seem as seductively labile as the dame in forties noir, the one the detective is no longer sure he recognizes. Though that's nothing compared to the attractions of the German books themselves, and sometimes it's simply too much. So I buy something, a volume of

E.T.A. Hoffmann or Theodor Storm, and look around for some-body to give it to. I struggle my way through a dustjacket and hope that back home I'll be able to find a translation of Adalbert Stifter. And yet I know that my sense of these writers will remain at best an approximation, while the real thing is kept behind closed doors. At times even literally closed, in the glass-fronted cases they use here for scholarly editions of the classics. Still, I'm somehow happy that the book in those cases I'd most like to read—the five volumes of the *Wanderungen durch die Mark Brandenburg*—has never had an edition in English. So long as I haven't gone through Theodor Fontane's account of his late nine-teenth-century wanderings in the countryside around Berlin, it can remain the object of a Proustian longing, forever out of reach and therefore incapable of disappointing me.

For years another book shared the *Wanderungen*'s status as a locus of desire and in a way shares it still, for though huge and now translated it does not, even so, quite exist. It has never ex-isted, and because of that been longed for even by those of us who aren't monoglots. Walter Benjamin's *Das Passagen-Werk* got its first full English translation in 1999, a year after we'd returned to the States. I had known about it for a long time, of course, about that unfinished and unfinishable project in which Benjamin had sought to define the experience of modern urbanity, the oper-ations of capital, the spectacle of the crowd. I knew that he had left an enormous pile of notes and manuscript behind in Paris when, in 1940, he had left the city just ahead of the Nazis' ar-rival, traveling toward what he hoped would be the safety of the Spanish border, a border he failed to cross and at which he killed himself. And I knew that in what is called *The Arcades Project* Benjamin had attempted not only to write a book that would contain the world but also to assemble that book out of quota-tions, cross-references, and fragments; almost as though the world were a kind of annotated index to itself.

A German edition was first assembled and published in 1982, but though Brigitte had it on our shelves at home, all I'd been able to read in Hamburg was an earlier translation of Benjamin's 1935 prospectus, "Paris, Capital of the Nineteenth Century." There he had located what he took as the characteristic features of the city's modernity, such as the panoramas, those huge and hugely profitable, crowd-pleasing pictures of the age just before photography — walls of pigment in which painting "begins to outgrow art . . . [and] the city dilates to become landscape." He had described the world exhibitions, "sites of pilgrimage to the commodity fetish," in which the accumulation of things becomes in itself an entertainment, "an enthronement of merchandise." I knew about his own fetishization of the *flâneur*, that walker in the city who "seeks refuge in the crowd," the bourgeois wanderer, connoisseur, and potential customer, in the throng but not quite of it. James had used the term as well, but in a way that suggests his own relaxed willingness to be amused. Benjamin lifts it from Baudelaire, and there is something almost frenzied in his sense of its purposeful purposelessness.

I had not only read about but had walked through and shopped in the structures that gave Benjamin his title: the arcades or *passages* of Paris, the urban malls that began to take shape in the 1820s — the midpoint, in the history of retail, between the bazaar and the department store. Eleanor Clark has written that in Rome the streets "do not constitute an *outside* in our sense, but a great rich withinness, an interior," a place that puts you *in* something rather than "outside of something." The arcades are just the same, or rather the exact opposite, a species of internal exterior. In origin they depend on new technologies in both glass-making and iron construction: materials that would come, as Benjamin argues, to define those spaces, such as exhibition halls or railway stations, through which one passes on the way to somewhere else. Yet though the arcade has some of the street's attractions — shops, cafes, intersections — it is neither quite street nor hallway either, neither fully inside nor out. Or perhaps it's a space like a church, one that remains public even though inside. The arcade penetrates, it runs from one exterior to another, it allows you to move almost surreptitiously between them. And sometimes in exiting, in stepping again into the open air, you'll find yourself someplace unexpected — you'll find that the twists and turns of that walk inside have brought you out where you didn't quite plan to be.

Benjamin struggled with the *Passagen-Werk* for the last dozen years of his life, sometimes abandoning it, but near the end spending almost all his days in the reading room of the Bibliothèque Nationale, just a few steps from some of the city's surviving arcades. He took notes, copied quotations, and arranged his materials into thirty-six folders, of wildly varying size, that his editors have called "Convolutes" — materials in a braid of his own German and the French of his sources. Yet he seems never to have actually begun to write. Susan Buck-Morss, the project's best American critic, has described the *Passagen-Werk* as a book that isn't really there, "not even a first page, let alone a draft of the whole . . . We are in a real sense confronting a void." And while its translators would like to see it as a "determinate literary form" they too acknowledge that it is usually regarded as "at best a 'torso,' a monumental fragment or ruin, and at worst a mere notebook." Possibly we even prefer it that way, prefer that sense of an achieved incompletion. It seems right that a book meant to be made out of fragments would remain in pieces, fitting that a work about urban fissures and interstices would be itself so full of them. Fitting, too, at least to anyone vulnerable to the romance of theory, that the great work of a life cut off should have remained unfinished, so that each loss serves to accentuate the other. But maybe we say that because we can't ourselves imagine how these inchoate pages might have been — inevitable word — *reduced* into form. We content ourselves with the wreckage of something never quite built, as though the ruins of a palace were one and the same with the stone and glass and iron out of which it has yet to be constructed.

And perhaps the book is something more than just unwritable. Benjamin refers time and again to a story by Poe called "The

Man of the Crowd," which he admires as one of the first descriptions of both an urban mass and of *flânerie* alike. But the tale begins by noting that "it was well said of a certain German book that 'er lasst sich nicht lesen' [*sic*] — it does not permit itself to be read" — and *The Arcades Project* itself might be that very book. Unreadable, at least page by consecutive page. So many sheets of disjoined paragraphs, so many bold-faced quotations, in which Benjamin's own commentary seems to drown: an active reading of *The Arcades Project* in its entirety would require something like the mental agility it takes to deal with that other work-in-progress of Paris between the wars, Joyce's *Finnegans Wake*. Stupefying. It's both more fun and more rewarding to skip around, to browse and to wander, to lose your way in the pursuit of some private and improvised itinerary. Read it as a *flâneur:*

> An intoxication comes over the man who walks long and aimlessly through the streets. With each step, the walk takes on greater momentum; ever weaker grow the temptations of shops, of bistros, of smiling women, ever more irresistible the magnetism of the next streetcorner, of a distant mass of foliage, of a street name. Then comes hunger. Our man wants nothing to do with the myriad possibilities offered to sate his appetite. Like an ascetic animal, he flits through unknown districts — until, utterly exhausted, he stumbles into his room, which receives him coldly and wears a strange air.

And that is exactly what it's like to read *The Arcades Project*. The more you walk, the less you notice, and with each block, each page, the sense of unabsorbed detail grows ever more overwhelming. For *flânerie* can be as numbing as it is beguiling, and this is not a book to read so much as to read in.

Though even then the same observations and quotations, the same conjunctions of facts, keep swimming up before my eyes. Benjamin may describe the city as phantasmagoric, but the word seems more appropriate to his text itself, insofar as reading it produces a dreamy and not entirely pleasant sense of repetition and recurrence. Is it simply that I'm constantly drawn to the same sections, so that in opening the thing I seem to turn always to the same few Convolutes, just as the city dweller has his established haunts and habits? Or is that replication a feature of the project as a whole? That would lead to a different urban metaphor, with the separate folders as neighborhoods, some of them bigger and more important than others, yet each with its fishmonger and shoe-repair shop, its bar and its baker. Another metaphor comes to me as well. Jonathan Raban has drawn an analogy between the memory theaters of the Renaissance and the modern department store. In the one, he writes, could be found "everything the mind had ever conceived," with each thought or idea assigned to its proper niche, carefully warehoused on one mental "gangway" or another, while in the other lay "a three-dimensional encyclopedia . . . [to] every rank and category of material object." And just as the adepts of memory could use such theaters as an aid to oratory, pulling the components of a speech out of the appropriate chambers and corridors, so "if you could hold Macy's in your head, with all its distinctions and discriminations, you would be close to possessing the key to the workings of America at large." The analogy stands even when you substitute the *Passage des Panoramas* for Herald Square, and the arcades provide an emblem for the convolutions of the human mind itself, a place in which thought has been spatialized into hallways and avenues, shops and stalls. The *Passagen-Werk* may have been meant as some verbal equivalent of the city itself, an index to urbanity, but it is perhaps best understood as nothing less — or nothing more? — than the inventory of Benjamin's own brain.

One of the most suggestive of all such inventories comes at the end of W. G. Sebald's *The Rings of Saturn* — yet another book that tantalized me at the Bücherstube Stolterfont, and for whose translation I also had to wait until we'd returned to the States. I had read *The Emigrants* when it first appeared in English, eight months before we left for Hamburg, and like so many readers had felt myself stirred, not only by Sebald's unforced moral gravity but also by the freedom with which he crossed generic boundaries. Fiction, memoir, biography, travel — it wasn't clear just where in his work the borders lay, or if they even existed at all. Now, in Germany, I found that there was more of him, and leafed through the pages of *Schwindel. Gefühle.* and *Die Ringe des Saturns* with a sense of anticipatory pleasure, anticipation that his own death a few years later would twist into a species of vertigo, making me feel as though my own stomach had been sucked out. *The Rings of Saturn* is one of the most unsettling of all contemporary travel narratives, and its German original carries a subtitle that the American edition lacks: *Eine Englische Wallfahrt.* A pilgrimage, though one that seems without any definite goal. In its pages Sebald, who lived in Britain from the mid-sixties on, describes how he "set off to walk the county of Suffolk, in the hope of dispelling the emptiness that takes hold of me whenever I have completed a long stint of work." That attempt to stroll his depression away only serves to deepen it, and "a year to the day after I began my tour, I was taken into hospital . . . in a state of almost total immobility." For in that quasi-pastoral landscape, this most Benjaminian of contemporary writers finds himself "preoccupied" with the "traces of destruction, reaching far back into the past, that were evident even in that remote place," such as the remains of the Allied air bases that once spotted the countryside, the now plowed-up runways down which the bombers roared toward the Rhine. Nor does he limit himself to physical traces. A television show leads him into a meditation on King Leopold's Congo, while in other moments he slips into thoughts of the naval battles fought off the Suffolk coast, of St. Catherine of Siena or the Taiping rebellion, the hurricane of 1987 and the natural history of the herring.

The particular inventory I have in mind comes in the book's last chapter, an evocation of the "miscellaneous papers" left behind by another melancholy East Anglian, the seventeenth-century physician Sir Thomas Browne, the author of *Religio Medici* and *Urn-Burial*: antiquarian, baroque stylist, sifter of rumor and legend. Browne's works, like those of Sebald or indeed *Das Passagen-Werk* itself, are best described as miscellanies, a verbal equivalent of the cabinets of curiosities — *Wunderkammern* — so popular among the learned of his day. So Browne's papers, as Sebald writes, treated "such diverse subjects as practical and ornamental horticulture . . . the Saxon tongue, the fishes eaten by our Saviour," and included as well the catalogue for a collection that seems to have "existed purely in his head and to which there is no access except through the letters on the page." This last "treasure house" contained works like "King Solomon's treatise on the shadow cast by our thoughts," fragments of ancient travel writing, pictures of "the worst inhumanities in torture," and such oddities as "a precious stone from a vulture's head."

The inventory that Sebald excerpts from Browne's own account runs on for three pages, and one doesn't have to read much to realize that it stands as an emblem of Sebald's own work, his own bringing together of disparate books, images, and fragments of history that have no necessary connection outside his pages. The list ends with a bamboo cane owned by the friars who brought the secrets of the silkworm from China to the West, and from there Sebald slips into an account of the whole history of European sericulture. Starting in Byzantium, he moves his readers along to the court of Henri IV and then to the Huguenot weavers who settled in England, and so on, with many twists and turns, until he reaches the Nazi attempt to make Germany self-sufficient in silk, a material of vital use "in the dawning era of aerial warfare and hence in the formation of a self-sufficient economy of national defense." It was even suggested, Sebald writes, that the cultivation of silk could be used as an "almost ideal object lesson for the classroom," with the worms "suitable for a variety of experiments . . . at every stage in their evolution," right up until the harvesting of their cocoons. "And when a batch is done, it is the next one's turn, and so on until the entire killing business is completed." For Sebald's departures bring him back always to the same place, the same set of facts: to the industrial killing of the Holocaust, that ghost on every page he writes. It is the history from which the people of *The Emigrants* have wandered out, hoping for an escape that, despite their physical survival, they will never quite achieve. So it is with Sebald's own narrative. It too enacts that attempt at flight, at making a detour into some different past. But no matter how far he digresses, he is always drawn back, never closer to that history than when he seems farthest away. And it is dazzling, this failure to escape, failure and success at once; for a lesser writer would find it easy enough to get away, would not discover the wisps of fact that suck him back always toward the land that was once his home.

Departure and return, as interdependent as the pulse and the pause of a beating heart. That motion serves, moreover, to characterize something other than just Sebald's own work. It is a central feature of the travel narrative as a genre, a form that is by nature digressive, and best suited to those given to circumlocution, to those who tend to wander, whether that wandering is across the earth or simply away from whatever point seems at issue. Though often, of course, it's both. "If this won't turn out something — another will — no matter — 'tis an assay upon human nature — I get my labour for my pains — 'tis enough." So writes Laurence Sterne in his *Sentimental Journey through France and Italy*, that masterpiece of dilation and delay, in which the "Sentimental Traveller" never quite manages to reach Italy itself. Almost any incident may turn out to be something, can be made to serve some narrative end; and what looks like digression might in fact offer the best moments in any writer's "assay upon human nature."

In this sense the travel book provides an example of what the critic Ross Chambers calls "loiterature." Chambers's book of that title attempts to offer a theory of digression, whose crux is his observation that "the literature of hanging out does not, and can't, stand still. But its art lies not in moving but in moving without going anywhere in particular," in a narrative *flânerie*, "an epistemology of the unsystematic" in which one seems to lounge upon the page. Loiterature perpetually steps out of line, it changes the subject, "it moves, but without advancing" — a literature of distraction, in which narrative "cohesion" is allowed to relax. Yet travel writing also implies that line out of which one steps — does more than imply it, marks it so strongly as to make digression itself possible. It lays down the narrative norm from which one departs, a coherence relaxed but not absent. Most such works allow themselves to be structured by the traveler's itinerary, a chain whose separate links are the stops along the journey, the progression of day after day after day. In less than expert hands that can make for a maddening linearity: the time of narration mimics that of the journey, and one damned thing perpetually succeeds another on the page, as it did in life itself.

But like the *flâneur* who knows when and how to indulge in a bit of creative loafing, the best travel writing will itself occasionally pause for a while and doodle. It's something like jazz: it makes a series of improvisatory riffs, measured out by a fixed itinerary. It discovers its form both within and against the standard time in which one city or meal follows another. Mark Twain provides a good example, in books like *Roughing It* or *A Tramp Abroad,* in which he will, as Larzer Ziff writes, typically manage "a sequence of events [by allowing] them to follow his mind's meanderings." He digresses from the place to the contiguous thought, inserting an account of the California blue jay into a description of Heidelberg, and in drifting by raft down the Neckar and the Rhine he constantly interrupts himself — though not the boat's own passage — to tell one tall tale after another. "Twain at his best always rambled," Ziff writes, "and to recognize this is to identify a fundamental connection between his mental and his physical wanderings," as though stepping across the landscape were a guarantee of the mind's free movement.

Though Twain himself puts it better: "the true charm of pedestrianism does not lie in the walking . . . but in the talking. The walking is good to time the movement of the tongue by."

Or perhaps a good walk is enough to make one sing.

Bruce Chatwin's *The Songlines* describes the writer's attempt to understand the dreamtracks of Australian Aboriginal cosmology, a "labyrinth of invisible pathways" winding across the continent, the mythic tracks of the "Ancestors" who long ago called out "the name of everything that crossed their path . . . and so [sang] the world into existence." From the Aboriginal point of view, as one of the Chatwin's people suggests, " 'the whole of bloody Australia is a sacred site,' " celebrated by songs in which the rise and fall of the notes becomes a description of the land itself, with each phrase of the music providing something like "a map reference." The songlines meander across the desert, their very existence unsuspected except by the initiate, and Chatwin's book looks at first to meander as well, with no apparent shape to its narrative, almost as though it were itself on walkabout. Its movements are, however, as purposeful as an Aboriginal's visits to one ancestral footprint after another, and *The Songlines* itself can be taken as the most paradigmatic of contemporary travel texts, a book about wandering and writing and the relation between them; in which the two are indeed as one.

In his opening pages, Chatwin writes that as a child he read from a poetry anthology called *The Open Road* and was told that his own last name derived from the Anglo-Saxon "Chettewynde," or "the winding path"; in consequence "the suggestion took root in my head that poetry, my own name, and the road were, all three, mysteriously connected." That detail suggests that his own interest lies somewhere other than in the literal truth of his Australian experience. Nothing *The Songlines* tells us about the place is false, but Chatwin has admitted that he "invented huge chunks of it in order to tell the story that I wanted to tell," and the book was in fact marketed as fiction. Though maybe "myth" would be better. One of his principal informants about Aboriginal life, for example, was a man called Toly Sawenko. But he has here been renamed "Arkady," and that signifies something more than the writer's desire to keep his source private. For Chatwin has massaged his material into the form of a pastoral romance, in which a city-bred sophisticate heads off to the Australian desert in search of a wisdom that he can no longer find in Europe. Of course, he must start by proving himself worthy, and the book's opening scene is one of initiation, in which Arkady seems to put him on trial, testing and probing to see if he should bother talking to this "Pom" at all. Not that there's any question of Chatwin's failing this ordeal of knowledge. He replies to his first taste of hidden learning by showing that he too has a store of recondite information; he passes the test and, like a folktale hero, is allowed to move on to a higher level, where both the questions and the answers become more difficult. Later, at a beautifully staged barbecue marked by "the smell of frangipani and sizzling meat," he encounters almost everyone he needs to know, the wizards of whom he may ask precisely the questions he wants answered, and he thus makes rapid progress. Yet just as he's about to be granted some crucial bit of information, there's the "noise of a jet" and his informant's voice is drowned out, the thread lost, the quest frustrated.

Those sources will soon vanish altogether, and force Chatwin to rely on his own devices. Halfway through *The Songlines*, he finds himself stuck in an isolated settlement, cut off by floods from his base in Alice Springs, and there he turns toward what's brought him to Australia in the first place. All his adult life he has been preoccupied by what he calls "the question of questions: the nature of human restlessness," and he reminds his readers of one of Pascal's "gloomier *pensées*," his judgment that all human misery stems from "our inability to remain quietly in a room." For years he has kept a set of notebooks, the raw material for a book about nomads that he long ago tried — "unsuccessfully" — to write, "a mishmash of nearly indecipherable jottings, 'thoughts', quotations, brief encounters . . ." Now he opens them up, determined to set down "a résumé of the ideas . . . which had amused and obsessed me." As one reads it's impossible not to think that, whatever its factual basis, the whole of the earlier narrative has been crafted to make this moment possible: the journey within that he can undertake only when he's forced at last to sit still.

What follows are a hundred pages of fragments drawn from those notebooks — quotations from Baudelaire, Rimbaud, *The Anatomy of Melancholy*; anecdotes of his travels in China, Mali, Afghanistan; meditations on hunting, monotheism, and archeology. It is a mental inventory that looks fit to rival that of the *Passagen-Werk* itself, and in fact Chatwin admired Benjamin, with his ambition to make a book out of quotations alone. Only the most naïve of readers would take these entries as an unshaped presence in the text. Chatwin did abandon the manuscript for a book called *The Nomadic Alternative*, and the notebooks do exist, containing ideas for that work along with much else. These volumes, eighty-five of them, bound in "black oilcloth," are now stored in the Bodleian, where they are embargoed from public examination until 2010. But their presence in *The Songlines* is carefully calculated and highly selective. Chatwin did not decide to use them until a late stage in the book's composition, and he did so in order to solve a formal problem: how to include his more speculative and grandiose ideas without making the book itself sound windy.

For why are we so restless? One passage wonders about the evolutionary origin of a baby's instinctive "demand to be walked"; another quotes Mandelstam's observation that Dante's prosody begins in "the human gait, the measure and rhythm" of our pace across the land. And the notebooks as a whole serve both to test and to entertain Chatwin's conjecture that "Natural Selection has designed us — from the structure of our brain-cells to the structure of our big toe — for a career of seasonal journeys *on foot* through a blistering land of thorn-scrub or desert." Nor does he stop with that unprovable proposition: the fossilized remains of the earliest humans lead him away from the thorn-scrub and into an exploration of our fear of the dark, our relations with the predators who stalked us before we learned to stalk them, our impulse toward violence and indeed the very beginnings of evil. In this whirl of ideas, the dreamtracks of Australia's Aboriginals come themselves to stand as a kind of metonymy, not only for the land they describe but also for some lost originary state of human life itself. They are the only surviving fragment of "the Songlines [once] stretching across the continents and ages . . . wherever men have trodden they have left a trail of song (of which we may, now and then, catch an echo)," some last remaining trace of that never-quite-forgotten union of the word and the world.

"Many works of the ancients have become fragments," Friedrich Schlegel wrote at the end of the eighteenth century, and then added that "many works of the moderns are fragments at the time of their origin." And his own statement is a good example, one of the 451 aphorisms and observations that comprise the *Atheneum Fragments*, that founding document in the history of German Romanticism. Sterne might provide another instance, and so would the carefully constructed ruins of eighteenth-century landscape architecture, in which a completed work is presented as fragmentary, its edges left deliberately rough or ragged. It's in this light that I want to consider Chatwin's decision to find the climax of his journey not in physical motion but in the intellectual process to which that motion has led him. For though Chatwin may have been searching for answers, he was also writing a book, which isn't quite the same thing. I see no reason to doubt that these bits and pieces had their origins in his notebooks, but while these fragments may be "authentic," they are nevertheless a literary construct that plays a determining role in the formal design of *The Songlines* itself. The reader of a travel narrative often assumes that the work has some basis in external reality simply because it offers a few reliable facts: an itinerary one can follow, a set of streets one can actually visit. Yet that assumption turns out to be circular. An appeal to "facts" allows the narrative to accommodate the very rhetorical devices the writer needs to establish that reality in the first place: such moments of narrative loitering as letters and diary entries, stray thoughts, quotations, anecdotes that don't seem to go anywhere. Such fragments — such digressions — serve to increase our illusion of access to an actual and unmediated world. Choppy and broken, apparently unpolished and therefore "real," they point toward that which the writer hasn't been able to assimilate, that which doesn't seem susceptible to the coherence of art. They point, that is, toward "life": a formal strategy that gestures toward a world unconstrained by the corset of form itself.

The raffish house of the travel book welcomes those fragments and digressions, in which the writer seems to step freely from one room to another, to depart from and return to some central hall of narrative. Chatwin's notebooks, for example, don't precisely conclude, but after both he and his readers have spent some considerable time going through them, Arkady shows up to rescue him from his own isolation, and we can move once more, out into the book's last chapters. *The Songlines* ends with a visit to some Aboriginal elders, lying on hospital bedsteads in a clearing, men who "knew where they were going, smiling at death in the shade of a ghost-gum." As Chatwin did himself, already suffering from the AIDS that would kill him just two years after the book's publication. His biographer Nicholas Shakespeare has suggested that Chatwin's decision to rely on his notebook fragments was determined by his illness, by a sense of ebbing time and strength. Necessity forced — no, *allowed* — him to find the formal solution that Benjamin never quite could, a way to *use* the products of his endless reading and research.

And maybe Benjamin would, like Chatwin, have had to be a novelist himself to reach that conclusion, or at any rate willing to treat his own investigating mind as a character within the text.

Chatwin made his work into the dramatization of an intellectual journey. He set the struggle for understanding within a narrative frame and in doing so found a way to shape an incoherent mass of material into a "determinate literary form." For his fragments at once ground the book's speculative quality and make it soar. They may suggest that this small volume is all that he's been able to wrestle into language, but they also point to something beyond, something larger than what's on the page. These chips and splinters of observation stand as a metonymy for the half-seen truth of which they form a part, just as the crumbled stone of a ruin implies the building that once stood firm, and they allow him to get away with a series of outrageous claims precisely because they aren't presented in the form of a finished text. Except, of course, that it is.

Late March, and we're in the Harz, a trip that I have already in part described. One morning I left our hotel before breakfast and walked out of town, going uphill through the woods alongside a many-channeled mountain stream. The trees were winter-bare and the ground a rug of dead leaves, but the sound of water made the place seem happy, a maze of sharp little hillocks and pocket-sized islands. Ilsenburg, the town was named. I was climbing, I knew, toward a mountain called the Brocken, though even its lower slopes were still a long way off: not a grand peak, but a mythic one. It was the legendary site of the witches' sabbath, and Goethe had set the *Walpurgisnacht* scene of *Faust* on its summit, with Mephistopheles complaining about the climb and wishing for a broomstick. More recently the Brocken had known a different kind of witchery — before 1989 it had been one of the East's major surveillance stations, its summit covered with radio masts and off-limits to tourists. And Ilsenburg, I now half-remembered, had a literary importance of its own. It was the town toward which Heine had walked on his own descent from the Brocken at the end of his *Harz Journey* of 1826, one of the most engaging books in all German literature.

Heine was still then in his twenties, but had already written some of his best poems; even so, he still had to work at avoiding the business career his family had planned for him. Back at the hotel, I checked the Penguin *Selected Prose* that I'd brought along, just in case. Heine doesn't mention where he stayed in Ilsenburg, or indeed if he stayed at all, though it could well have been at this very place, an old coaching inn called the Red Trout. Room and board from six marks — or at least it was in my 1900 Baedeker — and the inn's entrance arch and courtyard did still speak of its past. But inside everything had just been done over, and the sauna and pool and indeed every detail of our room were a lure for the weekending West; so was the drinks table where the bottles of grappa rose thick as stalagmites. Heine would have liked that, and as I turned the pages I found I'd been right. We'd been going in opposite directions, Heine down and me up, but our paths would have crossed if only there weren't 170 years between us. The river we'd walked along was called the Ilse, and Heine had been delighted by its fizz and foam, the way it "flows in pure curves from all manner of cracks in the rock, as though from mad watering-cans, and further down it trips lightly over the pebbles like a cheerful girl." For the "Ilse is a princess . . . How her silver ribbons flutter!" and standing on the "enormous granite" Ilse Rock he remembered a legend about some dalliance between "the old Saxon Emperor Heinrich" and the river herself, and suffered an attack of giddiness in which "the red slate roofs of Ilsenburg" below him "began to dance, and the green trees flew about in the blue air."

At that precise moment, however, Heine chooses to stop the narrative short. "*The Harz Journey* is and remains a fragment," he writes, "cut off, as though by the shears of inexorable Fate." Which is perhaps just another way of describing a whim that would be irritating if it weren't inseparable from his charm. Heine's narrative, with its interpolated poems and reluctance to take itself too seriously, has seemed as bubbly as the Ilse itself, so bright and sparkling that you want him to go on forever, to keep inventing such moments as those in which he defines the Bible as "God's memoirs" or describes sunrise on the Brocken as "nature's display of demagogy." And you especially want him to go on because, as he says, the Lower Harz into which he continued past Ilsenburg is the more "romantic and picturesque" part of the region. But that second and undescribed half of Heine's journey had included his only meeting with Goethe, for whom the young author of "Die Loreley" was just another tourist. Heine was hardly alone in being snubbed by that still-living monument— Schubert is said to have gotten his setting for the "Erlkönig" back unopened—yet he may still have felt that he could neither write about that encounter nor safely ignore it. Better to stop; and indeed there was no need to go on. *The Harz Journey* may be too brief to provide a complete inventory of Heine's mind, but it does display the whole range of his personality, his odd mixture of the sly, the tender, and the scabrous.

That, I think, is what he meant in writing that "individual works may remain fragments, so long as they form a whole when put together," so long as those picked-up pieces amount in the end to some full portrait of their creator. And full even though it must inevitably remain unfinished. If, in Schlegel's words, many literary works remain "fragments at the time of their origin," they do so precisely because, as he himself suggested in the most famous of his own fragments, "The Romantic type of poetry is still becoming; indeed, its peculiar essence is that it is always becoming and that it can never be completed." The Romanticism of which Heine was such a powerful if idiosyncratic voice longs for what is as yet unrealized, speaks always of something evermore about to be. Even Goethe had first published *Faust* as a fragment, and Wordsworth had once meant the *Prelude* to serve as the preface to something truly grand. Evermore—or sometimes nevermore. These were also the years when people looked at the wreck of Heidelberg Castle and discovered that it was beautiful, more beautiful than it could possibly have been when the place was whole; the years when Caspar David Friedrich found himself obsessively painting one weather-blasted oak after another. The Romantic fragment is an unfinished ruin, it simultaneously dreams of the past and the future, of the whole that may once have existed, or that might yet exist, someday. And perhaps it's no surprise that such a form would have had a particular appeal to German artists and intellectuals in the first decades of the nineteenth century: those, like Friedrich or Heine himself, who were living in the interregnum, with the old empire dead around them and a new nationalism struggling to be born.

But these thoughts smell of the lamp, and came only after our own Harz journey was long over. What I thought at the time, lying by the Red Trout's pool in a post-sauna daze and paging through my Penguin once more, was that I should try to duplicate Heine's walk. I could start in Göttingen, a place that "looks its best when you turn your back on it," find a silver mine to go down, visit Goslar where "the paving was as rough as Berlin hexameters." I could dream of ghosts and learn why "there is nothing more uncanny than unexpectedly glimpsing one's own face by moonlight in a mirror," could climb the Brocken and test Heine's claim that the mountain itself "is a German" in the "thoroughness" with which it turns the surrounding landscape into "a clearly drawn and distinctly coloured map." I might even continue on through the part of the journey he hadn't written up — no Goethe, of course, but the rest of his itinerary would be easy enough to follow.

That would have been the proper thing to do — or at least it's what more and more travel writers now seem to make themselves do, following out in minute detail the paces of some earlier wanderer. Marco Polo, Captain Cook, a famous writer, an obscure monk — any of them will serve as the peg on which to hang a trip or rather a narrative of one's own. Sometimes the result is wonderful, like Richard Holmes's record, in *Footsteps*, of his own young attempt to trace the path of Robert Louis Stevenson's

Travels With a Donkey in the Cevennes. Holmes omits the donkey, regarding the Scottish writer himself as companion enough, but he tries in almost every other respect to duplicate his predecessor's tour, taking the same number of days and sleeping when he can in the open; even worrying, at one point, that Stevenson has gotten "three or four hours ahead of me." As those words suggest, in writing some twenty years after the fact, Holmes has ironized his own romantic belief in the biographer's ability to recapture the past, and transformed the journey in search of another into one of self-discovery instead. Most writers aren't so skillful, and most attempts to follow in an earlier master's footprints seem all too predictably plodding. I could imagine Heine laughing at the idea of some pedant chasing him down the ages on foot; the best way to run after him in spirit would be dismiss the idea as silly.

Still, I can't leave him so easily behind. In his concluding paragraphs, Heine sets the scene of his writing in town, where on the first of May "the white foam of flowers hangs on the trees," the windows gleam, "brightly-clad girls" carry bunches of violets, and a procession of orphans marches "along the Jungfernstieg." He's in Hamburg, where his rich uncle Salomon ran a bank, and probably indeed looking out the window of Salomon's corner-lot house on the Jungfernstieg itself. He's in my landscape, or I'm in his, with the Binnenalster shining across the street—a walk I take on every second day. But I'll give him the view, I'll get off the street and out of his sight by ducking into—well, into the first arcade I can find. Except that the nearest one, the Hamburger Hof, is built on the very site of that uncle's house. A plaque by the entrance commemorates his efforts to help the city in 1842, when its Altstadt was destroyed by fire: Salomon Heine not only rescued the city financially but even had his own house blown up in an attempt to contain the spreading flames.

Now it's an imposing place in russet sandstone, with classicizing busts on its rusticated façade and a turret over the clothing shop on the corner—a bit out of step with the sobriety of Hamburg's prevailing brick. Inside there's an optician, baby gear, lingerie, flowers, tobacco, some cheapish chain clothing stores, a pastry shop, a bar. Escalators everywhere, three levels, an atrium — a hundred yards of shopping before it opens out at the far end into Poststrasse. It's bewildering, but what it isn't, at least at first, is the kind of structure to which it seems Benjamin might stand as a guide. Arcades are ubiquitous throughout Germany, in this rain-stricken city in particular, so common that they no longer speak of either new modes of construction or a new conception of merchandising. Most German cities have reconfigured their central shopping districts into pedestrian zones, in a way that makes the arcade seem merely an extension of the street itself, a space far less odd and magical than it had been for Benjamin, liminal only in the way it opens onto an underground parking garage. And though their number exploded only after the 1970s, they do have a full century and more of antecedents, which means that in our day they are a less original use of space than the suburban strip mall. Less objectionable, too, but still less original. The arcade no longer startles, no longer suggests the future in the way that the *Passagen* of Benjamin's Paris had.

Newness was not, however, the only thing about them that Benjamin found attractive. We need to remember that the arcades he described were already old, and that he saw them always with a certain doubleness, a sense of nostalgia for the novelties they once had been. They stand for him as the emblems of an already outmoded urbanism: relics, the ghosts of modernity's half-forgotten origins, the heralds of a world and a technology that in its continuous development had soon made them obsolete. They may have started as the repositories of luxury goods, but by the time he wrote they seemed mustily old-fashioned. That, indeed, was a part of their appeal. Their aura lay in their very obscurity, and if today some Parisian arcades are chic once more, others maintain that Benjaminian dimness, like the *Passage des Panoramas,* whose narrow winding corridors are badly lit and seem to specialize in bygone things like stamps or old photos. Hamburg's *Passagen*, in contrast, are utterly without that sense of mystery. They are too up-to-date and too predictable: entirely without idiosyncrasy. Those Parisian stamp dealers look as if they could only exist in an arcade, where a dozen of them can cluster together in a hidden world. But there's no such concentration in the Hamburger Hof, and no significant difference between what's for sale in a German arcade and what you might buy in the street outside. Inside you won't need an umbrella, that's all.

Nevertheless there is a strangeness here. I've haven't counted the arcades in Hamburg's Innenstadt and don't know how many there are. It seems a part of their — not mystery, but rather character, that they remain uncounted, that it's sometimes hard to tell where one begins and another ends. I step out of a boutique-lined corridor to walk along one of the city's canals, itself lined by shops, and sheltered here by an arcade in the Italian sense of the word: a colonnade open on one side to the air itself. Then it's in once more, past a place where I've bought shirts, and out and over a bridge to find myself, without having once stepped into the street, in the passage that leads to the bookstore I've been all along trying to reach. How many of the things have I walked through? A realtor could tell me, and yet the experience has seemed continuous, a single hole bored through the city's inner space. Hamburg's arcades may have no mystery, but they do have confusion. I often get lost in them, barely know one from another, and I constantly discover new ones. Nor can I ever quite tell, after I enter the Hansaviertel, the largest and most self-contained of the city's *Passagen,* just where inside it I actually am. Is this the corridor that leads to the stationery shop? That place with the tablecloths — down there? Is it even in this arcade at all?

Wandering from hall to hall, I am at first reluctant to take Benjamin as any kind of guide, not only because the meaning of these spaces has changed since he wrote but also because I'm not fully in step with his sensibility, his way of thinking about the world. I have never quite believed that all that is solid must melt into air. So when he describes the "intoxication" of the *flâneur*, for whom "with each step, the walk takes on greater momentum; ever weaker grow the temptations of shops, of bistros," until he stumbles "utterly exhausted" into a room he can barely recognize as his own — well, I can't help thinking that if he were less of an anchorite, if he would only remember to eat and drink, then the city itself would not seem to swim so dizzyingly before his eyes. But the more I walk in these arcades the more my skepticism fades, the closer to Benjamin I come, and I start to share his appreciation for the way brick and stone can splinter into evanescence. There are no landmarks inside, and I can't remember the names of the stores, they almost don't have names, or ones that you learn only when you hold a receipt in your hand. Numbed by the superfluity of merchandise, sleepy from fluoresence, stunned by the greenhouse heat of a skylight, you walk bewildered past cafes whose permanent and yet transitory clientele there seems no reason to join. Fugue; and you ignore your thirst until it's too late and the headache's throb fills the city around you.

No one can absorb *The Arcades Project* fully, it's no more possible to follow its every divagation than it is to absorb every piece of the city itself. The more I read, however, the more I find that almost every page can be usefully rubbed against my own experience. Even those moments when it looks most alien, as in Benjamin's dream of stumbling "upon an arcade myth, with a legendary source at its center — an asphalt wellspring arising at the heart of Paris," even those seem instructive, in the very contrast their pavement reveries provide to the workaday sites these places have now become. Workaday, though still fantastic. "False colors are possible in the arcades . . . Everywhere stockings play a starring role." While boredom is the outer face of luxury, "a warm gray fabric lined on the inside with the most lustrous and colorful of silks." Which brings me back to the "peculiar irresolution" of the *flâneur*, the way in which "doubt" forms his proper state. "The path of one who shrinks from arriving at his goal will easily take the form of a labyrinth," Benjamin writes, of a chaos of wandering, an endless circle of goals unreached and choices one fails to make, in which the "magnetism of the next streetcorner" seems "ever more irresistable." And so one walks on into the long light evenings of summer for hours after the shops have closed, the mind vacant of all but the next step: the *flâneur's* exhaustion, the perverse exhaustion of one who has no reason to stop and no place he must be.

✸ SIX

Hauptstadt

Take the subway—the tube, T, Metro, U-Bahn—and mole your way beneath the city, dropping down into darkness and popping up again in a street that doesn't match the one you left behind, into rain you didn't know was happening, a view that seems suddenly all park, or all slum. Come up the stairs and blink in the light, if there is any, hoping that you've picked the right stairs, that you won't be separated by two intersections from the direction in which you want to go. The city discontinuous: which way to turn? Yet, however disorienting, the tube provides the subterranean thread that stitches the place together, and its tracks are a mirror on the invisible city upstairs. The veins coursing down the long tongue of Manhattan, the slow clanking Circle around Central London: they tell you how the city sees itself, about what it thinks it needs.

Berlin's transit map at first looks dominated by a bundle of lines that run from the old Prussian East to the nineteenth century's new moneyed West, Alexanderplatz to the Zoo and beyond—the urban spine that the Wall had severed. A spine, not a center: for look more closely and what you see is sprawl, tracks running everywhere, so confused that some lines seem to cross themselves. That tangle points to Berlin's early history as an agglomeration of villages, a reminder that this old capital is the youngest great city in Europe, a place that during its Wilhelmine explosion grew very nearly as fast as Chicago. It's got a big footprint, Berlin. It's got too many parks and rivers, most of its buildings are low, and even before the bombing of the Second World War its urban fabric wasn't especially tight, not compared to Paris, say, or even to London. And its combination of size and relative youth makes for whole quarters that look as if they could be anywhere, anywhere in Germany at least, neighborhoods as interchangeable as Wal-Marts, characteristic and anonymous at once.

So one spring afternoon I came up into the air at Sophie-Charlotte-Platz, wondering who she'd been, and looked around me at an intersection I didn't know but where I seemed already to have stood a hundred times before. Wide streets and fast cars, wide sidewalks, too, and trees, a lot of them and not scraggly either, with each corner a cluster of green, lindens and chestnut and beech. The buildings were all stuccoed in sherbet pinks and yellows, there was a kiosk selling cold drinks and kebabs, and benches that served a mixed crowd of old people and young women with strollers, but few men of employable age. Ostensibly I had a mission here, an Italian restaurant to investigate, a place we might go on this mid-April break in *die Hauptstadt*. But I'd written nothing down and discovered, once I started to look, that I could recall neither its address nor its name. So my job almost immediately unmasked itself. It was an excuse for wandering, nothing more: a chance to take the U-Bahn out to some place figuratively off my map and walk until the city's pieces began to run together, until the streets became recognizable and I could fill in the empty spaces of the world above the ground.

I made a loop of a few blocks out to the west and back in, Horstweg to Sophie-Charlotten-Strasse to Knobelsdorfstrasse, bought a roll at an organic bakery, drank a bottle of water, got bored. Nothing about the area looked promising, it was too far from our hotel and too drab, a neighborhood of one-man shops, in which all custom is local. There wasn't even a Turkish fruit stand. But when I came back to the main road, a few hundred yards north of my starting place, I found that the street's character had changed. Now it was a boulevard divided by a tree-lined strip of hard-packed earth, and every fifty yards or so there was a knot of men playing *pétanque*, an immigrant game though the players here weren't. I watched as one tall and frizzily blonde man put down his cigarette to make a throw, grasping the metal ball from above as though he were planning to drop it, and then swinging his arm out stiff to release it, the motion so awkward and ungainly that it was hard to credit the accuracy with which it rolled to its target. A muttered curse from his opponent, an American-style high five to his partner: an attractive game, its object immediately clear, not only the bowling but also all the standing around and talking. Still, it wasn't a spectator sport, and so I walked on, until I saw in the distance a yellow baroque gleam that told me where I was.

Charlottenburg. It was the name of the district but also of that building taking shape through the trees, the Hohenzollern's summer palace, unexpectedly attractive and not nearly so grand as the ones that many lesser princes had built for themselves; Prussian thrift. I had been there a few months before, wandering through a series of china-encrusted state rooms and then out into its compact park — nothing I needed to see again. Not in the palace *qua* palace, at least. But there was also a picture gallery I liked, a small and coherent collection of early nineteenth-century canvases — a gallery, not a museum — and so I walked through the gates, across a parking lot once meant for soldiers on parade, and then into the building by a small side door.

Half a dozen rooms, with period furniture, pastel walls, and large windows open onto the park behind: rooms that fit the paintings. Or maybe it was the other way around. They were quiet scenes, these pictures, and they looked as though they had been here always, as perhaps indeed they had. The dates on the labels suggested that some of the Friedrichs in particular had gone directly from his easel into the royal collections. There were his familiar, and indelible, images of blasted oaks and ruins in the snow, of skies at twilight that looked to hold every possible shade of violet: landscapes that seem always to have caught their breathe in stillness. Two men stood on the shore, though Friedrich's palette was so dim I found it impossible to tell just where, exactly, the beach faded into the water. They had their backs to us, silhouettes in a haze of moonlight, and wore loose cloaks and hats of a soft velvet floppiness, the whole scene looking posed and timeless and theatrical, and all the more mysterious because of it. I was glad to see it again, and there was a sense of surprise in having come here by accident that made me want to linger. So after I was done with my favorites I wandered back past the entry kiosk, with its modest rack of postcards, and into a room I hadn't visited before, where I found myself pulled up by a very different kind of painting.

It was an 1853 view of Unter den Linden, a few miles away to the east, the grand processional way that ran from the Brandenburg Gate to — well, it wasn't clear any more what it did run to. Once it had gone past a clutch of embassies and hotels, past an equestrian statue of Frederick the Great and the University and the Staatsoper and the Arsenal, on its way to the domed Berliner Schloss. The Communists had pulled that down, even though it hadn't suffered much from Allied bombing — much less, in fact, than had the reconstructed rooms where I now stood. And they'd replaced it with the cast concrete of the Palace of the Republic, now itself condemned, its asbestos insulation providing the environmental Band-Aid for a political decision. That palace too would be torn down someday, but the exact future of the site remained still uncertain, and though the embassies and hotels and even the mounted Fritz were today all back in place, the street now just zipped past them, an overly wide main road on its way to nowhere in particular.

The picture in front of me showed a different city with near-photographic precision, its vanishing point so deep that I could almost fool myself into thinking that the painter had worked with a wide-angle lens. It was the middle of the nineteenth century beneath a cloudy but unthreatening sky. The road's surface was swept clean despite the passing horses, a street of crinolines and carriages, with Frederick off to one side, then the opera house, and the Schloss fading to gray in the distance. There were a couple of dogs running loose, lindens, of course, and a sentry at a corner, with a few officers talking on the sidewalk. I recognized the buildings, almost all of them, we'd watched spandexed rollerbladers glide past them a couple of days before, a Sunday when the street was closed to cars. But I had never seen Unter den Linden looking so untrafficked or so finished, and for a brief hallucinatory moment I wondered what had happened to all the construction, to the dust and scaffolding and cranes, to the shiny plastic pink and blue water pipes that now ran around the street at eye level and made the whole place look like an especially confusing piece of installation art. The avenue hanging on the wall before me was ordered and clear, grand and yet without quite enough people to fill it, in a way that made it seem intimate as well: less like a street than a kind of enormously extended courtyard. I suppose in a way it had been.

The painter's name was Eduard Gaertner — not an artist of whom I'd heard, though the gallery had a few of his other things, including a fine, Bellotto-like view of some houses along the Spree. Later I learned that he began his career working on porcelein for KPM, the Prussian equivalent of Meissen. But he soon developed into a skilled painter of architecture, and in that visually impoverished city — for painters Berlin had a rich future but no past — he quickly found important patrons, the Prussian monarchs among them. And what at Charlottenburg I thought so affecting was the doubtless stylized but still powerful image he provided of a city that looked entire and whole — a city that seemed the very opposite of any of the many Berlins we have come to know since. Though it wasn't just his own skill. Gaertner had been lucky in his moment as well, for he set to work right as the great architect Karl Friedrich Schinkel had finished remaking Prussia in his own neoclasical image, designing everything from its theaters and museums to furniture and the Iron Cross. Gaertner caught the city at a moment, perhaps its one moment, of equipoise: just when Schinkel was done, but before Berlin had industrialized and before the commercial explosion of its western suburbs. His pictures show us a small and stately capital, its buildings grand but not grandiose: pictures that speak of the hushed moment of the Biedermeier peace, of a world that was gone with his last brushstroke. For the past here literally was another country, and in my own walks around Berlin I found it almost impossible to believe that this city had ever once been so coherent and whole.

Oh, the place, or rather its masters, have wanted it, how they have wanted it! In the century and a half since Gaertner worked, Berlin has aspired to a permanence which in the end has always and thankfully proved illusory. Schinkel's lovely squares and colonnades gave way to the bombast of Bismarck's empire, to the ponderous cathedral built for Wilhelm II and the Victory Column in the Tiergarten. Hitler disliked the city itself — too many socialists, too many Jews — but that didn't stop him from making plans for it. He wanted to rename it "Germania" and to rebuild it around an intersecting pair of boulevards even wider than the Champs Elysses, with a square to hold a million people and a domed hall with a volume sixteen times that of St. Peter's. It was a dream, as Brian Ladd writes in *The Ghosts of Berlin*, of a "timeless, static city," and for a while the postcard-painter may even have thanked the Allied air forces for helping with the demolition his plan required. Then came the Wall, and it was as though the city's face had been gouged. That, too, was meant to last. For a century and more the rulers of Berlin tried to build themselves into eternity, envisioning a city that was meant to last forever. But they have failed, all of them, and if I had today to pick a single place to serve as an emblem for Berlin's shattered history, it wouldn't be the Brandenburg Gate or the Reichstag, it wouldn't be the Alexanderplatz or Charlottenburg or the glitter of the Kurfürstendamm, but rather the broken Hellenistic statuary of the Pergamon Altar a few miles across town.

It is the Teutonic version of the Elgin Marbles: ripped in the nineteenth century from its original site in Asia Minor, installed in a Western capital, and today the subject of controversy; though the Germans, unlike the English, do at least plan to return their spoils. And yet Berlin has been an appropriate home. Pergamon was famous for its wars of conquest, and this altar has been one of Berlin's main attractions ever since it was installed in its own purpose-built museum. In the tourist season a polyglot line wraps itself around the corner of a building never meant to handle such crowds, while a staff of East German holdovers works as slowly as possible in making change and taking coats. Why do so many people come? I suppose their guidebooks tell them to, as mine did, and yet I can't imagine that very many of them find it rewarding. For the altar's central importance lies in what seems at first an almost entirely illegible frieze, a hundred meters of chopped-up sculpture that once depicted a battle between the gods and the giants.

Headless bodies and heads without bodies, cloven torsos with their muscles rippling like comic book heroes', sliced-off faces and snapped-off fingers, legs and arms unconnected to trunks, and trunks that are themselves without limbs. A disembodied hand, like an empty glove. Shields, shattered. Bits of wings. Beasts that look half horse and half fish, but which have themselves been halved by time. Other bodies cut clean away, their edges sawn smooth, victims of the excavators' tools. Some faces have been reconstructed, while other statues have had their pieces put back where they should be, but with spaces left for the missing bits: an arm and then an emptiness where the shoulder should go, before we reach the breastplated torso. You can see the cracks, every one, the cracks and splits and fissures and fragments that time has wrought, and so it is with Berlin too, a city whose own splinters are permanently on show. Even the outer walls of the museum itself have been chipped and riddled by the bullets of 1945.

Yet it's different now. I leave the Pergamon and walk through streets loud with construction to catch the S-Bahn at Friedrichstrasse, one of the main switching points between East and West in the days of the divided city. I'm going west for lunch in Savignyplatz, and the train heads over the Spree and glides past one inscrutable building after another, the cranes waving in the air all along the path of what had been the Wall, filling in that gouge with stone and steel: we will always see the scars, but the face will again be able to work. I look out the window at the Reichstag, its restoration not quite yet complete, and then we pass sandpits and lakes of evacuated groundwater, and it strikes me that post-*Wende* Berlin knows that tomorrow won't be like today. The city now embraces its cracks and admits its own impermanence, its texture different from year to year, and sometimes from week to week, fugitive. A derelict department store becomes an edgy nightclub and then a tourist attraction, the great synagogue of the Oranienburgerstrase is restored and reopened, shops and restaurants flare into life along streets of Stalinist apartment buildings. It's no wonder, then, that Gaertner's canvases are now so compelling, for in them the city looks complete, as it has never has been since and certainly isn't today. The work had just been done, there was a moment as still as a candle, but it would not last.

It took me a couple of visits to begin to like Berlin. I first went there in the summer of 1993, staying in a hotel, now closed, that a colleague had recommended because it was cheap. It was in the Auguststrasse, in what I then called the East and now call Mitte; in what used to be and is today once more the city's historic center. The place was run by the Lutheran Church, one of the safety valves for other faiths that the Communists had allowed, and the rest of the clientele appeared to be school groups. The fittings were so threadbare that they couldn't help but be clean, and the woman behind the desk wore horn-rims on a steel chain around her neck, like an elderly teacher from the fifties. One morning I asked her for directions out to the museums in Dahlem, far away to the west. She couldn't help me, she'd never been there, and the idea that she could in fact now go seemed strange to her: the different parts of the city had remained separate, however freely one might once more move between them.

By day the neighborhood was faceless and drab, a place where it was difficult still to buy food; I remember the aggrieved and bedraggled look of the apples in the one corner market I found. At night my hotel's pinched respectability was belied by the streets around it. Oranienburgerstrasse, a minute away, had already started to turn itself into seventies Soho, a neighborhood with a dark incipient glamor that would in a few years become simply fashionable. Some of its edge came from the squatters who had moved into empty buildings. And some came from the prostitutes who stood along the sidewalk, facing out toward the trawling cars: hookers who had here found their Platonic form, wearing thigh-length boots and silk bomber jackets and not much in between. There were bars that stayed empty until midnight, and were then crowded until four: one of the liveliest was in a Kosher vegetarian restaurant attached to the synagogue, newly rededicated but not yet reopened. For this district had once been the center of Berlin's Jewish life, and that very fact seemed inseparable from its post-*Wende* revival.

But I didn't like Berlin, not then. The neighborhood fascinated and intimidated me at once, and in the rest of the city the distances seemed too great for comfort. I walked, my first day, from the hotel to the Brandenburg Gate, where I bought a Red Army badge from a street vendor, and then down along the edge of the Tiergarten, along the line of the Wall itself. Were some chunks still standing? I don't quite remember, or rather I don't quite trust the memory that tells me they were. I was heading toward the Philharmonie, hoping for a ticket, and walking because public transportation didn't yet get there from here. The trees in the park to my right looked scrawny and ill, and to the left there was nothing, just a waste that had once been filled with guard towers and barbed wire, and flood-lit at night: the shoot-to-kill zone known as the death strip. No, Berlin was too large, too blasted, and it felt rather oddly American—a city of empty spaces between pockets of interest, and where you needed a car—like Atlanta but bombed.

So my fondness for it dates from a later time, when I went there with Brigitte and our students for a week near the start of our year in Hamburg. The buses and trains had by now knit themselves into a coherent system and the once-empty ground that marked the path of the Wall had become a Pandemonium of earth-movers and cranes. But I still found the city too big and confusing, and my *flânerie* would regularly find itself at a literal dead-end, with the way forward blocked by construction. Then something stuck. Maybe it was the cows in Prenzlauer Berg. We were trudging, in a cold October drizzle, through streets that seemed longer than they should have, heading toward the Kollwitzplatz, the center of a neighborhood that under the Communists had been as bohemian as the regime would permit. Inevitably we passed a bar, in Berlin you are always passing a bar, but this one bordered an empty lot, and as we walked by I saw there was something strange about the building itself. Half a dozen cows were walking up its exposed side wall, browsing away on the perpendicular. Fiberglass of course, and of colors not found in nature; looking closely we could see the bolts that held them in place, and there were flowers and cow flops painted there as well, a cartoon of a field. "Kuhuunst," a sign said, *Kuh Kunst* or cow art, and both the pun and the building itself would have been inconceivable anywhere else: a mark of the way in which German culture can push even a joke to a dogged extreme. Still, there was something puckish about it, as if that thoroughness had learned to laugh at itself. A hundred yards on, we turned back to look again; and the distance made those impossible beasts look real.

Perhaps it was then that I fell for the city: at any rate I went back as often as I could, sometimes with Brigitte and sometimes on my own for a night or two. Only the Berlin I found wasn't the one about which my earlier reading had taught me, even if it does remain the one city in Germany for which Anglo-American literature has provided a detailed image. Or several images. There's Isherwood with that self-effacing narrator who calls himself a camera, with Sally Bowles and Mr. Norris and the decadent bars that the ones now on Oranienburgerstrasse do their best to echo. Though Isherwood himself isn't much read today, and what we know instead is the movie of *Cabaret*: the *Berlin Stories* as refracted through the paintings of Georg Grosz and Otto Dix, the city brutal of gartered thighs and porcine faces. Then there is the flayed metropolis of the *Null Stunde*, the human rats climbing up from the ruins in the Zero Hour of May 1945, a desperate place even when played for Hollywood laughs: the city of Thomas Berger's underrated first novel, *Crazy in Berlin*, and of Billy Wilder's *A Foreign Affair*. But that city slides almost imperceptibly into the one we know best, the Berlin of the Wall and its Cold War thrillers, of John Le Carré and Len Deighton, Checkpoint Charlie and Potsdam's Glienicke Bridge, where the important prisoners got swapped. And these different cities have each left an aftertaste. Maybe you'll stop for coffee at the Café Adler just a few yards away from Checkpoint Charlie, and try to remember which imaginary disillusioned spy did the same thing while waiting for someone to cross over. Or you can walk down Nollendorfstrasse to see the plaque on the house where Isherwood lived, and at the local U-Bahn station find yourself accosted by a male prostitute.

These images cling to our minds, and there are others, other tropes, and darker ones, in the rhetoric of Berlin, there is the history into which Isherwood's city falls and out of which the

Cold War emerges. There is the Gestapo bunker now known as the Topography of Terror, where you may read a xeroxed copy of the minutes from the Wannsee Conference, or the spot on the Grosse Hamburgerstrasse where the city's Jewish citizens were collected for removal to what was euphemistically called "the East." And it is that Berlin, far more than the one with the Wall, that provides the terms for the often bitter debates over the intersection of architecture and history that the city has known since the *Wende*. Knocking the Wall down may have allowed for this belated conclusion to the city's postwar reconstruction. But the battle over an appropriate form for that reconstruction remains grounded in reference to the Third Reich: a battle traced by Ladd in *The Ghosts of Berlin* and Michael Z. Wise in *Capital Dilemma*, by Jane Kramer's *New Yorker* reporting or James Young in *At Memory's Edge*.

For "what kind of architecture," as Wise asks, "is appropriate for a country whose past has rendered patriotism suspect?" Or as Kramer puts it, in Berlin even a department store atrium may find itself described as too "'authoritarian'" for a town with this particular past to tolerate. These debates are primarily concerned with the public — the official — city of squares and commemorative spaces, with the rebuilding of Potsdamer Platz and the plans for the city's Holocaust memorial. Should the Reichstag have a dome? Is Daniel Libeskind's Jewish Museum, for all the unnerving brilliance of its spaces, entirely suitable for the exhibits it's meant to house? Such questions seem to fuse the postwar and the post-Wall. It's as if the city as a whole had remained frozen in the *Null Stunde*, however extensive the rebuilding of its separate halves, and though the common wisdom holds that Berlin has too much history, I'm tempted to reply that in another sense it doesn't have nearly enough. The different pasts that matter here all came so quickly; if they were spread out over centuries they'd be easier to sort through. Yet while those questions about the city's public space, its architectural reckoning with the past, do need to be asked, they have remarkably little to say about the city's quotidian life. For Berlin has now thawed beyond its own teleology. The apocalyptic city my reading had prepared me to see wasn't the one in which even this conscientious traveler was spending the bulk of his time, and I quickly felt the need for some other guide, some other way of comprehending the enthralling streets around me.

A couple of nights after my serendipitous walk to Charlottenburg, with Brigitte gone back to her desk in Hamburg, I took myself out to a sleek Italian restaurant on the Rosenthalerstrasse in Mitte. It was a crowded air-kissing place, the kind derisively called *Schicki-micki*, and when I asked for a spot for one, the pouting hostess told me that I'd have to be gone by ten. She dropped me at a table marked "*Reserviert*," and I leaned back on a taupe leather banquette, ordered something to go with red wine, and opened my book. At first, however, I found myself distracted by the full room of expensive skinny people, out for a night of urban pleasure unmixed with angst — historical angst anyway. Germans enjoying themselves over *tagliatelle al salmone* and a glass of Pinot Grigio — a frightening idea, perhaps, but I was used to it by now. And Mitte was clearly no longer what it had been just a few years before. It wasn't the East anymore and had instead become what it had been many decades ago, a stylishly bourgeois playground, trendy but not in the least *alternativ.* Two women sat down next to me, one in a cherry-colored bustier and both of them wearing a lot of gold, made up with enthusiasm for a long night out. They looked with a studied absence of curiosity at the American alone with his book, and I turned back to my novel and read its first sentence.

"In the middle of the 1870s, just at the crossing of the Kurfürstendamm and the Kurfürstenstrasse, diagonally across from the 'Zoological' could still be found a large vegetable garden, stretching a distance away from the street." As if to say, Times Square! I took a sip of Valpolicella and tried to work out exactly what was there now, what has replaced the market garden where Theodor Fontane's 1887 *Delusions, Confusions* begins. I wasn't even certain that crossing still existed as such, and when I got back to my room and opened a map I found that the intersection is now filled by the Europa Center shopping complex. Nevertheless it is one of the busiest corners in Europe and as close to a city center as anything in all of West Berlin, a square dominated by the stumpy, flame-blacked tower of the bombed-out Gedächtniskirche, with the Zoo Station just a couple of minutes walk away. But that church wouldn't get itself built until the 1890s, and as I sat in the restaurant trying to graph that opening sentence onto the city today, I felt as though I were caught inside a palimpsest, between that city and this one, and all the different Berlins that had come between.

The one thing I felt certain of, as I moved deeper into the novel, the one thing I knew for sure, was that no vegetables grew there now. For I'd walked all across that site, in fact as nearly as I could tell that garden would have run back to what's now Ka-DeWe, Berlin's biggest department store. I tried to imagine asparagus beds and pear trees beneath its foundation, and failed. Commercially successful market-gardening, on that corner, at that late date—the detail reminds us how young a city Berlin is and how quickly it has changed. Indeed Fontane's first sentence lets us know that the city he describes has already vanished—"could still be found." A place as gone as the Wall; it seemed an ironically appropriate thing to read in a chic restaurant that couldn't have existed here just a few years before. While other moments in the book suggest the novelist's awareness that his Berlin, like ours, remains unfinished: the male lead, Botho von Reinäcker, moves into an apartment on the Landgrafenstrasse, "which in those days still had only one row of houses."

In English Fontane is best though barely known as the author of *Effi Briest*, a book whose eponymous heroine is a kind of runner-up in the tragic adultery sweepstakes, a distant third to Anna and Emma. Only this one doesn't kill herself, she dies of consumption instead, worn down by her years of living in shame, with her own small daughter trained to think of her as a sinner. And yet her husband would have been happy enough to keep her.

Effi's one affair has been over for years by the time he discovers it, but he believes he hasn't a choice in challenging her lover to a duel, despite feeling no trace of a "'thirst for vengeance.'" Duty compels him, though it isn't his duty to himself so much as that which he believes he owes to his "'whole society . . . If it were possible to live in isolation, then I could let it pass.'" So the husband shoots the lover dead and destroys a double-handful of lives for the sake of what he himself considers a social fiction.

I had picked up Effi's tale earlier that year in Hamburg, admiring Fontane's landscape painting, his account of the windy Baltic coast, admiring as well his portrait of Effi's fondly dim parents, who want the best for their girl but haven't the least idea of what that might be. All the same, I wasn't quite convinced. If this was the best German novel between Goethe and Mann . . . well, it seemed easy enough to name a dozen of his contemporaries in English who'd done better. *Delusions, Confusions — Irrungen, Wirrungen* in German — was my second attempt at reading him, and this time it worked. It is a slighter book than *Effi Briest* perhaps and set in a far more congenial and forgiving world. Nevertheless its sheer historical specificity offered something that *Effi* didn't, and its sense of an ever-altering urban fabric seemed to capture the very warp and weft of the city I was dining in now.

I read through the meal, lingering until the hostess' pout turned into a glare that told me that my table's rightful owners had appeared, then on toward midnight at my hotel, and across the city the next day, with each trip on the U-Bahn good for another chapter. That evening marked the beginning of a passion that took me through whichever of his books I could find, with *Delusions, Confusions* leading on to *The Poggenpuhls* and *Jenny Treibel,* to *L'Adultera* and *The Stechlin,* back even to *Before the Storm,* his historical novel about the Prussian fight against Napoleon. Once again I found myself regretting the weakness of my own German, for Fontane's descriptions of Brandenburg's ruined abbeys and mysterious tree-shrouded lakes made me more than ever want to read the many volumes of his *Wanderungen.* And the more I read, the more I found that *Effi Briest* seemed atypical, that the intransigence of its conclusion was something Fontane characteristically avoided.

Delusions, Confusions provides an example. Botho von Rein-äcker has been courting Lene Nimptsch, a seamstress of uncertain parentage. They're well-suited in everything except social class, and for neither of them is the attachment a light one, as shown by Lene's consternation when, after a night at a riverside inn, they meet up with a few of Botho's fellow officers, out for a day with their mistresses. Is that, she wonders, how other people see her? Then the young man's mother issues her commands: he has to marry, and for money, the family's estate will irrevocably suffer if he doesn't. He gives in — and that's when the novel's real interest begins. Botho's wife is the airhead twin of my restaurant's hostess, full of gossip about balls and cures and regiments, incapable of serious talk, and Fontane shows him getting used to it. Or almost used to it, for Botho never quite loses his sense of how much his family duty has cost him. And Lene? Where *Delusions, Confusions* differs from an English novel — from, say, *Adam Bede*, which it in some ways resembles — is that Lene doesn't get pregnant; there isn't the dreadful consequentiality of George Eliot. After a few years, she meets an older man, and though at first she answers his proposal by confessing her history, the book does end with their marriage. Neither Botho nor Lene are as happy as they might have been: as they might have been, if only their whole world were different. But they make do with what they have in what Fontane calls "our dear old Mark Brandenburg . . . a province where thrift is called for."

Things sort themselves out. That is the dominant note of his work: that, and a city in constant flux. *Effi Briest* may present Bismarck's Germany at its most rigid, but it's balanced by *L'Adul-tera*, in which a complaisant husband agrees to a divorce that will let his wife marry her lover. Still, most of Fontane's books are without such drama. Whole chapters in his late masterpiece, *The Stechlin*, turns simply on rides through the country, on tea parties and preparations for visitors. Nothing much happens, except talk: conversations in which his characters discuss the quirks of their friends and try to remember who's related to whom; conversations that make these Prussians more pleasant than I would once have thought possible. These Germans are good Germans still. Reading Fontane can suggest what Austen would have been like if she'd been a man and lived to be old. He values kindness as she does and he has her shrewdness, too, and he has as well the equanimity of Trollope, and a bit of Eliot's all-forgiving sympathy. There's even a touch of Eliot's broad comedy, a taste of Mrs. Poyser in the sharp-tongued regional satire of *Jenny Treibel*, where the title character looks with horror on the idea of a Hamburg daughter-in-law.

Fontane's Berlin is a boomtown, with new streets and new construction in every direction, a city "panting for developers . . . already land prices were on the rise." But those words aren't his — they belong instead to Günter Grass, who in his post-*Wende* novel, *Too Far Afield*, takes his predecessor's work as a guide to the city today. In Fontane's world the very streets seem to change by the minute, just as Berlin does now. The Treibel villa lies in a part of the city "where there had once been only factory buildings," while the Poggenpuhls live in a flat so new that it's "still damp in the walls" when they take it. Fontane locates the apartment so precisely that you can find it on a period map: a shabby place in a quarter notable only for its rail yards. It's hardly a suitable address for a family that's produced at least four generations of officers, but the Poggenpuhls' city is changing in more than physical terms. It's still a garrison town, where the land that's now Tegel Airport serves as a firing range. And it is more than ever a court city, with its emperor and protocol and parades, a place full of generals and ministers, and ministerial tea tables as well. But small gentry like the Poggenpuhls can see themselves losing their place at those tables. For Berlin has become more than its court, it's also an exploding commercial capital in which all values seem to fluctuate, not just stocks but social ones, too. And not all of them are on the rise.

In the 1812 of *Before the Storm* the landowner Berndt von Vitzewitz maintains that one must be free to disregard the orders of the king himself if the survival of the nation depends on it, and his words have a direct bearing on the Officers' Plot of 1944. Fontane's other characters, however, the ones in the novels he set in his own day, might be less willing to make that claim. At the center of *The Stechlin,* written when he himself was almost eighty and near death, is an old man who knows that his own beliefs and assumptions have become passé. The settled agricultural world in which Dubslav von Stechlin has spent his life now seems irrelevant to the blustery dynamo of the new German Reich. He isn't entirely sure he likes the country that his own generation brought into being and misses his old Prussia, whose hegemony over the rest of Germany has come at the price of its own particular identity. Still, that independence strikes even Dubslav as no longer quite desirable, and the only way he can maintain it is to retreat to his own estate, a retreat that is only confirmed by his son's Woldemar's decision, after the old man's death, to resign his commission and to live in the country as well. On its own terms, and in its own time, that quiescence may seem a principled dissent from Germany's late nineteenth-century course. But it's apt now to make us pause, and it almost seems, in reading *The Stechlin* today, as if Fontane had had some uncanny premonition of the inner emigration into which so many of his countrymen would travel in the years to come.

"Yes, Berlin is becoming a world city," says Uncle Eberhard in *The Poggenpuhls*, squeezing lemon over a breaded sole, and while he's a bit put out by the city's new "fuss-pot" manners, it's not enough to keep him from enjoying his dinner. Reading those words now and knowing of the storm that was to come, we may have a sense of trepidation mingled with nostalgia for a time in which the future was not yet inevitable. Yet Fontane isn't looking back on anything, it's we who look back on him, and rather than recording a long-vanished world what he does is to capture a society that is both vanishing *and* coming into being at once. I read *The Poggenpuhls* in a café a few steps away from the Auguststrasse, where years before I had first stayed in Berlin. The building where my hotel had been still wore its faded sign, but the place itself was shut, the Lutherans vanished, and the neighborhood was now almost unrecognizable, with galleries that showed contemporary photography and courtyards lined with boutiques. Some workmen were putting a new façade on the building across the road, there was the noise of a jackhammer, and a temporary covered sidewalk doglegged around an open pit, while next door was a milliner's shop with its window full of hats as bright and gauzy as confectionery. Uncle Eberhard's *Weltstadt* looked to be coming alive around me, and for one dangerous moment, as I looked at the damp new-plastered walls across the street, I tricked myself into thinking that the century in between simply hadn't happened.

Travelers are supposed to dislike change. Returning to Rome in 1872, Henry James found himself regretting the loss of what he called "old Rome," a phrase he used to denote not the Rome of Caesar or even Michelangelo, but the preunification city of his first visit just three years before. He wants the place to stay just as it was, maybe even as it was before his own arrival, and so too we continue today to seek the unspoiled, the authentic, the original. We long for empty beaches and regret the hotels that let us visit them, we complain about churches wrecked by restoration and Third World villages ruined by television; I suppose some people even think that England's gone off, now that the food is edible. By those standards, Berlin has always been a fallen world. In another sense, however, the place can never be spoiled, for change itself has always been its most characteristic and permanent feature: a city eternally marked, as the historian Peter Fritzsche writes, by its very "experience of transience." So Fontane's city offers a paradox: what you want is for things to be different, which will in turn tell you that it's all stayed the same. You come back here to check up on what's changed, and even those visitors who know—knew—the town well can find themselves turned into the most rubbernecking of tourists.

Oh, some things do remain—things I'm glad to find are still around. I think of a hushed corner off the Fasanenplatz, where I wandered one morning into an antique store, drawn by a vase in the window, only to find myself thinking hard about a set of six faultless Biedermeier chairs. For a moment I saw them in my Massachusetts dining room, and perhaps I'd see them there still, if only my credit had been up to it. Or there are the foodhalls at the KaDeWe, the *Kaufhaus des Westens* or Shop of the West, a place full of everything the East was once denied. My nose fills with the heady odor of all the world's cheeses at once, chèvre in every shape imaginable, Roquefort marbled in blues and grays, and the salt smell of an old Gouda; I count three brands of Pont L'Évêque, ten of Camembert. Eggs lie loose in baskets, there are cherries as large and dark and lustrous as any I've seen, a deli case stacked with white asparagus, and others that seem to offer Germany's entire inventory of charcuterie, all arranged by region, the hams and blutwurst and salami, the sausages of different lengths and thicknesses, some shaped like loaves of bread, others in the form of rings, a few molded like cannonballs. There are tanks of live fish and a counter for offal, chocolate chip muffins and a display of Middle Eastern pastry that could choke a sultan, and at the top of the escalator, a scale-model of the Reichstag the size of a schoolteacher's desk, constructed entirely out of marzipan.

A couple of years after our time in Germany, I went back to Berlin, taking a week in the middle of June to check up on what was new. The vendors of Soviet paraphenalia who'd once clustered around the Brandenburg Gate were pretty much gone, a long-running nostalgia act pushed out by the district's expensive new hotels. Potsdamer Platz was now finished, with theme restaurants and cinemas and a shopping arcade of downmarket chainstores, but the whole complex was disappointing, more White Plains than Manhattan and not yet fully integrated into the city around it, if indeed it ever will be. The Reichstag had reopened, with long lines waiting to ascend its crystal dome, the ground had been cleared for the Holocaust Memorial, and the Jewish Musuem was offering its first tours. And I went once more to see the pictures at Charlottenburg, only to have my friend Manfred tell me that they wouldn't be there much longer.

"They're moving," he said as we sat waiting for dinner in an anonymous Indian restaurant, "they're going to Mitte." Manfred teaches English at the Freie Universität in the far west of the city, and his wicked crinkling eyes make him look like a cross between Santa Claus and Machiavelli. Charlottenburg's paintings, he scowled through his beard, were going to be ripped, simply *ripped*, from the delicate period rooms for which they were so well suited, and flung into the money pit of the East. The old Nationalgalerie on the Museum Island was being fixed up for them, part of an attempt to consolidate what the city's budget-minded officials saw as a redundancy of culture, with museums and opera houses in each of Berlin's pre-*Wende* halves. I'd heard of Easterners who missed the Wall, but Manfred was one Westerner who seemed to as well, and my *saag paneer* came with an aria on the evils of unification, the difficulty and expense of absorbing a whole ungrateful nation in which everyone was either a Stasi informer or a neo-Nazi, and sometimes both. But he enjoyed the grumbling, and kept smiling as he conducted the song with the stem of an unlit pipe.

Still, he was right enough about the pictures: they left a few months later, at the end of 2000. And he was right, too, about what that move implied, about the tidal pull of the East, sucking the city back to where it used to be. Students from western Germany who came to Berlin now tended to choose the Humboldt University on Unter den Linden over Manfred's own F.U. Indeed he had felt that pull himself and, on first moving to Berlin, had thought of buying a flat in Prenzlauer Berg, that eastern neighborhood of wide quiet streets and unrestored prewar buildings. That was back in 1990, however, and with the Wall only just down he hadn't been able to see himself on the cutting edge of gentrification and having, as he put it, to live with "the social resentments of my neighbors."

Manfred's son Dominic had joined us for dinner, a slightly dreamy medical student in his twenties, and now he spoke up to define a reaction among his friends, not against the East but against what he called the *Schickification* of the East, of Mitte in particular. It was too slick, he said, too full of beautiful people: I thought of the restaurant where I'd fallen at last for Fontane. It had become a place for West Germans, for those relocating to Berlin from other parts of the country; while he and his friends, who had been teenagers here, now stayed in the old West and spent their evenings in Schöneberg or Kreuzberg instead, as people had done when the Wall was still in place. And Manfred took up the theme as well, adding that though they had moved to the city after the *Wende,* he had lately started to think of himself as a *West* Berliner: an unexpected identity, and one that in the early nineties he would have thought outmoded and irrelevant, retrograde. It was, he admitted between bites of *naan,* much harder now to tell people apart on the basis of their clothes or speech, and yet even so East and West had remained separate, not only nationally but within the city itself. "*Wir sind ein Volk?*" I asked, quoting the words that the crowds had chanted in the days before the Wall had opened. We are one people. "*Noch nicht,*" he said, "not yet."

Talking to them gave me an increased awareness of unification's dropped stitches, of the seams that remained open even as the city knit itself together physically. Indeed the critic Andreas Huyssen has suggested that since unification the "abyss between East and West Germans seems larger than ever," and while economic dislocation explains a part of that divide, it doesn't explain it all. Perhaps even more important is the degree to which East Germans "now experience themselves as second-class citizens, as colonized by the victorious West." We ourselves had seen an example of Western condescension in that Magdeburg parking lot, in a way that made sense of Huyssen's suggestion that "the whole *Ossi-Wessi* split [had] symptomatically" found expression in an "infantilized language," as though the very terms themselves were the name-calling of nursery school. And that ever-increasing resentment beween East and West has had "an insidious hidden dimenson," insofar as it has contributed to a growing level of "physical and verbal violence against foreigners," a violence Huyssen interprets as a displacement of the antipathy that East and West continue to feel toward each other — "one state, but two nations," and each of them looking for someone to blame.

Such issues do receive some attention in the American press, but not nearly so much as do those aspects of life in Berlin, or in the Eastern *Länder* in general, that touch more directly on the Second World War. Antiforeigner violence gets covered because it can be linked to neo-Nazis, but the "abyss" that Huyssen defines as an "inner-German problematic" remains largely ignored. And perhaps the American press isn't the only one to blink at the complexities of the German present. The Wall limited the scale of Berlin's postwar reconstruction; it seemed to freeze the past into place and, as I have already suggested, the city is only now having the full discussion of the relation between public memory and architecture that Hitler's war requires. In the divided city there could, for example, be no Berlin Holocaust memorial as such: a memorial that will inevitably become the nation's as well. Or take the rebuilding of the Reichstag, destroyed by fire in the first months of the Third Reich. In pre-*Wende* Berlin its burnt-out hulk stood as the visible mark of history's wounds, the ruined seat of a national government that must have seemed doubly canceled.

Still, there's a problem here. For it isn't quite clear, now, just which wounds its refashioning might attempt to heal. It's hard, as you stand on the Reichstag's terrace with a coffee and look out at street after street of new government office blocks, to avoid the sense that both the city and the country see themselves as getting around to a job that, except for the Wall, they would have finished long ago. No wonder the Eastern resentment! One can't simply go from the *Null Stunde* to the *Wende* and skip over everything in between, and yet the rhetoric of Berlin's renovation does indeed threaten to occlude the intervening half-century. This latest makeover remains grounded in reference to the war. Nevertheless it takes its motive force from the opening of the Wall, and the only reason the Second World War seems so immediate here still is because the Cold War remains so present as well. It is as though the earlier war had absorbed its successor. If Berlin, and by implication Eastern Germany as a whole, is set for a protracted period of what's called *Vergangenheitsbewältigung,* of overcoming or mastering the past, then the danger is that only a part of that past will get dealt with: a part that for all its horror may here, in this city, no longer be the most pressing.

Or it will be thought — has been thought — that overcoming the Wall can be done with money alone. Though perhaps that is indeed how it will happen. I don't mean that facetiously — at least, not entirely. Let me conclude my impressions of Berlin by describing two walks in the eastern part of the city, or rather the same walk twice, the same street at a distance of a few years. A lot of Berlin's streets have had many names: this one used to be known as Frankfurter Allee. It suffered heavily from wartime bombing and afterwards was rebuilt and renamed: Stalinallee, a grand processional road, enormously wide and flanked with apartment buildings so massive and long that, in Ladd's words, they "function as walls enclosing the street." Krushchev later softened the name, calling it Karl-Marx-Allee, and that's still what it's called today. The boulevard was intended as something like the Champs Elysses of the Warsaw Pact, and its apartment buildings, with their façades "profusely ornamented with classical detail" and their upper stories covered with Meissen tiles, stood, as Ladd writes, for "the promise of a new society in which ordinary workers would enjoy the comforts of the old bourgeoisie." Western modernists, in contrast, at first detested it, seeing the street as "the worst kind of overwrought kitsch . . . the epitome of Communist centralization, regimentation, and false pomp." Today, however — but let us go there.

In the fall of 1997 I took a walk along that road, catching the U-Bahn at the Alexanderplatz and getting off three stations and a couple of miles to the east, all ready to walk back in. And what I remember above all is the smell. The East smelled different, or at least its subway tunnels did. I write that sentence knowing that smell has always functioned in travel writing as a trope around which to organize a sense of otherness, a way to define the exoticism of that other East that lies beyond this one: the smell of Egypt, the smell of India. So I wish that something else had impressed itself upon me, but no: this U-Bahn line had an odor in its tunnels and corridors that I didn't recognize from anywhere else in Berlin, not even other stations in the east. It was at once pungent and stale, an acrid heavy smell of burning rubber and melting plastic, but more than that, of rubber that seemed tired, fatigued, as if it were about to disintegrate: a smell that had hung around for a while, even after the burning was over.

Brigitte had described the Karl-Marx-Allee as a triumph of urban planning, but once I came up into the air I felt belittled and exposed by an architecture so out of human scale that it seemed cruel, as oppressive in its way as the Gauforum in Weimar. Some of its buildings looked as long as supertankers beached on Berlin's sandy soil, and the road itself ran flat and dead straight for miles. The sidewalk was as wide as the street, spotted in places with undergrown trees but most of it empty, and the street was empty too, with so few cars that it seemed you could simply wander across; the whole of it, from one canyon wall to another, was almost as wide as a football field is long. And as I walked I started to feel an overwhelming impression of absence. There seemed no shops, no restaurants, nothing at street level to relieve its sheer massiness, not until Strausberger Platz, over halfway in, where a solitary greengrocer had put up a sidewalk display of apples, lettuce, and long white radishes. It was loud and colorful and run by Turks, people who understood retail and had seen an opportunity. Though they were wary, they weren't letting people choose their own fruit, as we did at our local markets in Hamburg. Here there were mustached young men to wait on you, men who shouted and joked with an aged clientele unused to such openness, and seemed with each bunch of grapes to be offering a lesson in how to live.

When I returned, in June 2000, I went out again along the Karl-Marx-Allee, and knew as soon as I entered the U-Bahn that things had begun to change. This time there was nothing to smell. The air seemed refreshed and renewed, the same air as in the furthest reaches of Charlottenburg, and once up above the ground I saw that other things had changed as well. Even the architecture seemed less oppressive, and I found in consequence that I could now begin to see it. The buildings here are so huge that the street and its attendant sidewalks—setbacks, really—need to be wide: any narrower and you wouldn't be able to appreciate the scale of the place, to see one of those buildings whole. Some of the apartment houses have their ground floors pierced by colonnades, like a Stalinist fantasy of a seaside hotel, and they are all liberally sprinkled with balconies—though not all balconies have been created equal. A lot of the tilework is patchy, with missing bits, while other buildings could use a scrub. But when I got out of the U-Bahn at the Frankfurter Tor, I found my heart lifted by two gleaming and fully restored structures, with high towers like lighthouses that seemed to announce one's entry into the city. Still, there was a reason for the sparkle: they were now owned by an insurance company that clearly saw that spiffiness as good advertising.

Such investment has taken a long time to come here, longer perhaps than elsewhere in the city's eastern quarters. "The day before German unification," Ladd writes, the government of East Berlin "declared the entire former Stalinallee a protected historical landmark." With tight limits on redevelopment, few businesses chose to open, and others stayed away for more mundane reasons: a lack of parking, a lack too of free-spending customers in a district where many people lived on old-age pensions. Some of those difficulties seemed to have vanished in the two and half years since my first visit. There was, it's true, a sign on every building that announced its protected status, and warned against graffitti: a warning that had been mostly obeyed. But the ground floor of most buildings now looked given over to commerce, to travel agents and fancy kitchen stores, a multiplex cinema and a McDonald's and a chain Mexican restaurant, shops for clothing and shoes, drugstores: all the activity that seems so normal elsewhere, and so new here. The street was still relatively empty, with fewer cars and pedestrians than in the city's other quarters. Through a colonnade came the loud shouts of a school playground, but most of the people out walking were old, and one could also trace the neighborhood's character — as well as the nature of East German health care — in the stores that sold walkers, crutches, and canes.

I passed some young men drinking beer on a stoop, the long-term unemployed for whom this development hadn't provided an answer. Moving between and around them, however, were teams of blue-overalled masons, busy with the job of renovation. It is a dangerous business, to read hearts and minds from the look of a street, but that is a chance that any travel writer must take. Benjamin notes that as a child he saw the city "only as the theater of purchases," and I'm suspicious of the way I seem here to be doing the same, suspicious of the direction in which my second walk along the Karl-Marx-Allee has taken me, with the opening of shops and markets as providing in itself a way to master the past — though given the road's name, I do enjoy the irony. And, of course, I know that with Germany a decorous pessimism remains the proper thing. It's a place you worry about and worry at, where we've been trained to look out for the alarming and to distrust any pleasure it might offer; and what's true of the country as a whole goes double in its capital. Yet how often do we get to watch a great city come into being? Berlin carries an impossible burden of meaning. Nevertheless it is the one place in this country where an overabundance of history has created a present so exhilarating, so all-enveloping, as to let you forget for a moment about its past.

Or rather its pasts. One of the new shops on the Karl-Marx-Allee was a spacious, airy bookstore, all blonde wood and bright lights, cookbooks and classics, new novels still in their shrink-wrap, and a revolving rack of maps before which I found myself transfixed. They were published by a firm of Berlin cartographers named Pharus, and one of them was in my pocket already, a current map of the city that I'd bought in a souvenir shop at Checkpoint Charlie. That one was for sale here, too, but there were also facsimiles of the city maps from 1902, 1903, 1926, '28, '36, '40, '47, '48: a new release, it seemed, of every edition that Pharus had ever published. Match 1928 against 1936, and see how the Nazis changed the names of the streets; match anything early against anything later, and watch the building or the rebuilding of neighborhoods. You can buy maps of London or Paris as they were, but I'd never seen anything like this profusion of different pasts on offer. And their very existence spoke of Berlin's fascination with its own turbulent and omnipresent evanescense, with the nineteenth-century explosion in size that had put an end to Gaertner's world and which Fontane had recorded; and with other and later explosions too. I bought the edition for 1902, where the Kurfürstenstrasse still ran into the Kurfürstendamm, and the Zoo Station hadn't yet been built. It's open on my desk now as I write, held flat with coffee cups and pens and a library copy of *The Poggenpuhls,* and with my map from Checkpoint Charlie spread out on top.

✸ SEVEN

Family Chronicles

We had our regular beats in Hamburg, a choice of long walks and short ones, a clutch of neighborhood restaurants, a set of streets and stores where we did our marketing. We had our preferred places to buy coffee and flowers, got bread at one bakery and rolls at another. There was the brasserie at the hotel a few hundred yards down the Rothenbaumchaussee, and up the road in the other direction was the Turkish market from which we bought mineral water by the case, with the shopkeeper's young cousin wheeling a loaded handtruck down the street and onto our building's elevator. When six months into our stay I saw him one evening on an U-Bahn platform, and we spoke for a minute in our differently accented German, I felt for a moment as though Hamburg really was where I lived.

And untied from a desk, and with a great city to explore, I developed my own routines beyond the ones that Brigitte and I shared. I liked sometimes to wander through the brick fantasia of the Speicherstadt, the late-nineteenth-century "warehouse city," a dozen cobbled blocks tucked along the Elbe that had all the hush of a cathedral close, its warehouses occupied even now by caviar importers and dealers in oriental rugs. I discovered the *halal* butcher shops of the Sternschanze, and a block in St. Pauli where every other door led into a Portugese restaurant, and buildings on the waterfront that did their best to look like ships, with brick poop decks and prows. There were the bookstores and the arcades — sometimes bookstores in arcades — and there was always my bicycle. The Alster was too big to walk around with any regularity, but it was easy enough for a cyclist. Every second or third day I made its loop and came to learn not only the way the water changed color with the weather, but also every inch of its human geography: the spots where you sometimes saw campers or small boys fishing; the different tendencies in the clothes and class of those walking on one bank or another; the place where tour buses could park, and those pathways too exclusive to be reached by public transportation; the stretch of road where an old boat club looked across to a newly gilded mosque.

Then, in the city's gray and snowless winter, when the daylight seemed barely to last beyond lunch, we found ourselves with a new destination on our schedule. Every couple of weeks we would walk down to the taxi stand at the hotel and take a ten minute ride out to an appointment in Eimsbüttel, not far from my friend Helga's apartment. How the taxi went would depend on the traffic and the time of day, but the destination was always the same, and one that, at forty, we approached with a mixture of longing and fear: the obstetrics ward of the Elim Hospital. The Elim had its specialities, the oddest of which was hand surgery, so that we were perpetually meeting people with casts on their arms, and it also had some connection to a religious order, though which one remained unclear. By American standards its pace was unhurried. The waiting room was never full, and the people sitting there did their best not to look at one another, as though a smile were an invasion of privacy. From one standpoint the place looked understaffed — there weren't many nurses or technicians — and yet from another it wasn't, for it was a teaching hospital and there seemed always an abundance of doctors. Nothing was rushed, there was none of the popping in and out so common in medical practices at home, and Brigitte's physician drew her blood samples himself, instead of handing the job to a nurse. And he was confident, a short wiry man in his sixties whose character was marked by a kind of sardonic reassurance: so utterly confident that when, after an amnio, he ordered us to drink a glass of champagne, we were happy to take his prescription.

After her appointment we would, in the early months at least, walk slowly toward home, testing out names and debating the fine points of strollers; later I sometimes walked back alone, while Brigitte took a cab. I don't know how it is for other people, but the prospect of having a child made my mind turn in the direction of Ecclesiastes, of the generations passing and to come. So on those solitary walks back to the Rothenbaumchaussee I found myself thinking with a special force about my own childhood and parents, and in particular about my father, already ten years dead. And those thoughts led in turn to others, to the memory of a college classroom twenty years before, of a moment peculiarly appropriate, not only to the fact of my own impending fatherhood but even to the place in which I was going to become one. The class had met in the science center, an awkward room with the professor walled off from us by the demonstration counter he had to use for a lectern, setting his notes down between its two sinks. The chairs were the kind whose writing surfaces swiveled up and down, and I always had the sense of locking myself in when I lowered the desktop and got out my notebook. Modern European Social History. We learned about wandering journeymen and the difference between a revolution and a rebellion, read about the world we have lost and the crisis of the aristocracy and how peasants were turned into Frenchmen; we studied the making of the English working class and the persistence of the old regime.

We were reading *Buddenbrooks,* the bell that tolls the end of the nineteenth century, the tree in which one can trace the descent of Thomas Mann. The novel opens with a housewarming in 1835. The Buddenbrook family, grain dealers in the Baltic port of Lübeck, have just moved into a grand seventeenth-century structure on the Mengstrasse: a house whose purchase from an older family, now "broken and impoverished," marks the growing strength of their name. At the table that day, sitting over their loaded Meissen plates, are three successive bearers of that name: the past, present, and future masters of the family firm. There is Johann — old Johann — who has made their fortune, supplying the Prussian army in the Napoleonic wars. He is a rationalist, an energetic man of the Enlightenment, who in his seventies still powders his hair and has "never in all his life . . . worn a pair of trousers," preferring instead the breeches of his youth. His son Johann, Consul for the Netherlands, is the current head of the business: pious and prolix, tough-minded but unimaginative, someone who sees no distinction between profit and Christian duty. He too has a son, the ten-year old Thomas, whom a guest describes as a "very solid chap. He'll have to go into the business, no doubt of that." Thomas will, however, be a bit too refined for the world he will inherit, a man with a taste for Heine, who marries a foreigner and orders his clothes from Hamburg. Under Thomas, the business reaches its peak. He is the first and only Buddenbrook to become a senator in Lübeck's ancient mercantile republic. And under him it also goes smash.

There will be another generation, too, in little Hanno the music lover, Thomas's son and Mann's stand-in: the one who is simply too sensitive to live. What we've got here, I remember my teacher saying, is a typical bourgeois family history, a pattern enacted time and again, in place after place, a way of life in which the firm and the family are inseparable. But that can only last so long, he added, such a life has its own natural span, eventually the firm is sold off or frittered away, eventually the heirs grow unsuited for business and do something else, become artists, enter the professions. And now I was listening hard.

From the outside the place where my father worked looked like a particularly dingy storefront, with its unwashed plate-glass funneling into the mouth of a wide door set some way back from the

Bank Street sidewalk. The windows themselves were always hung with posters advertising the circus—we got free tickets in trade for the space—and the door stood open all day long, no matter the weather, with boxes and bags and men and handtrucks going perpetually in and out and in again. Inside was a short hallway and, on the right, an office that contained a bookkeeper with an adding machine and not much else. Then the corridor opened out into a long, high-ceilinged interior, one that I remember as always dark, though there was a bit more light—bare bulbs—over the counter where my father did his work. This was simply a few planks attached to the wall, piled with telephones and legal pads and order books, where he sat on a stool next to his cousin Joe, a pencil tucked behind his ear.

Behind them, deeper in the store, were stacks of boxes and crates. Bananas, cabbage, tomatoes, carrots—basic stuff, what Joe called "the hardware." Halfway back on the left, the wall had been broken down into the smaller shop next door. This room was mostly potatoes in fifty-pound burlap bags, the contents of the monthly railroad car from Idaho, though the space also held a cooler in whose dry air we stored fruit. At the back of the main room—a hundred feet? probably less—was another, bigger icebox, this one kept moist, with celery and lettuce and everything that might wilt in the summer's heat. In a corner stood the bagging machine, a hopper fitted out with a scale, which we used to weigh out potatoes into five-pound plastic sacks. I felt very proud that each bag was printed with our family name.

Three nights a week my father rose at midnight and went to buy in the regional market at Hartford. The other days he got up at four. Most of the time he would be home by early afternoon, but after a nap he would spend another hour on the telephone, or in the summer, two. And at the shop itself the physical labor was hard. Trucks would park along the sidewalk, in a space marked "Loading Zone: Police Take Notice," but there was no loading dock, no ramp, no way to roll a stack of boxes directly on or off. Everything had to be handed up or down, lifted off the truck that brought it to us, stacked on a handtruck—the doorway wasn't wide enough for a skid—lifted and stacked again when we sold it and sent it out for delivery. A case of cantaloupes weighed ninety pounds, cabbage and carrots ostensibly fifty though usually more, but a bushel basket of peppers only thirty-five.

I think I was puzzled by what my father did. I knew that he sold fruits and vegetables, that he owned six trucks, that his customers didn't come off the street but were restaurants and schools and grocers. I knew that though he sometimes called his place a store, it wasn't one in the usual sense. But I didn't know what else to call it, or rather what to call him, not as I knew terms like "fireman" or "doctor." My mother said he was a merchant. But that at first meant nothing, not until one morning when she told me, after I said that I wanted to go see him and "all his merchants," that the other men who worked there should instead be called "the help." So my earliest awareness of class came in the form of a definition, a linguistic distinction used to mark a social one. When later I had to describe what my father did, I said that he was a fruit and vegetable wholesaler, and in the family we always called the store the "wholesale," turning the adjective into a noun. In college and after, with more reading and more pretension, I said he was a wholesale greengrocer.

After I started school, my teachers would sometimes ask which Gorras we were. The family was large—once extended, now attenuated—and in our coastal Connecticut town its two main branches had started in different businesses, one in fruit and the other in women's clothing. The Gorras in clothing were tall, with rich olive skin and fine strong noses. They had been the first to come over from Lebanon, and it showed: now they looked settled and even urbane. The Gorras in fruit were shorter and dumpier, their skin was sallow and their faces slightly squashed. My paternal grandparents had been cousins. My grandmother, from the clothing side, had as a young woman gone into business for herself, selling linens to the big shorefront houses. My grandfather Michael was a fruit Gorra, who began with his brother in a corner market. My father wasn't tall but he had the bones of his cousins in clothing, though with blue eyes and lighter skin — Crusader genes, my mother joked. Eventually the fruit business added a wholesale, and eventually the two split: the retail shop was still alive when I was a boy and people would sometimes mistake the two. After my grandfather died, my father — he was then twenty-one — took over the wholesale, running it at first for his mother and then later for himself, though he always had relatives working for him.

When I was eleven my father moved from Bank Street to a larger place on Jefferson Avenue, a building with a five-bay loading dock and a parking lot. It's only in writing this, however, that I've realized he moved not just to make the work easier but also because that first store cramped his ambition to grow. It would not have been possible, from that storefront, to do the amount of business he almost at once began to have: not possible to load the trucks fast enough, to store and to ship so many packages. He bought more trucks, pneumatic jacks, a third cooler, then a fourth. He added a good line in frozen cheesecakes, and we gave up the slow work of bagging potatoes. He bought the failing gas station next door, doubling his floor space, and refrigerated most of it, so that he could begin to order soft fruit by the trailer. Over the years, "the help" grew in number from seven or eight to fifteen.

And it was in his first year on Jefferson Avenue that I began to work myself, on summer mornings from eight to twelve: he paid me a quarter an hour. I had wanted to start the year before, but my mother had stopped that. I used to think that was because the work was too hard, and in truth I couldn't yet do much lifting. But, of course, the problem was Bank Street. It was a wholesale district of candy and groceries, two meat distributors, another fruit wholesaler, a banana importer: immigrant businesses, all of them owned by Jews except for the bananas — a Greek — and ours. Across the way was a Sicilian grocery whose owner always paid our bills from large rolls of cash; next door to us was an all-night market called Patsy's that paid in third-party checks. There were a couple of bars, though the tough bars, the ones for hookers and sailors, were a few hundred yards further down, near the restaurant where my father had his 4:30 breakfast. But there was a bookie around the corner, at one of the meat wholesalers, and once my father got arrested there, though he always said he hadn't — that time — been betting. He owed his second arrest to his competitor Ben Steinman, who complained that we — that he, but the plural still comes so easily — were violating the Connecticut Blue Laws by opening for a few hours on Sunday mornings. I was eight and puzzled: why should a Jew care if a Catholic opened on Sunday? My father made his defense on other grounds, but though the judge was sympathetic, he still paid a fine.

It is, of course, almost inconceivable that a Buddenbrook might get himself arrested. Oh, their in-law Weinschenk goes to prison in an insurance scam, and Thomas's brother Christian, the one who can't settle to business, who fathers a bastard and does impressions and winds up mad — Christian might well know the police rather better than he should. But the head of the firm, Consul Johann or Senator Thomas? That would be impossible, and not only because of the grinding probity in which they live. It would be impossible because in the world Mann describes they are themselves the police, or rather the embodiment of a business world that seems inseparable from civic order. In *Buddenbrooks* — in the Lübeck of Mann's ancestors — merchants are also and inevitably public officials to the precise degree of their business success. They think of themselves as burghers. They are in fact an urban aristocracy, who shepherd their fortunes as though trade were a landed estate, and entailed for generations to come. Business alliances are brokered over the marriage bed — the Buddenbrooks with the Krögers, the Möllendorpfs with the Hagenströms — and dowries go to increase a firm's "working capital." And it is within this closed shop, this narrow "circle of ruling families," that all public affairs are settled. These merchants serve as consuls — and the position is often hereditary — for the countries with which they trade, they sit on committees that deal with the questions of "customs, rates, construction, railways, posts, almonry." They even, in those days before Bismarck, work as diplomats, negotiating treaties and tariffs with other German states, or indeed with Denmark and Sweden. But then with what aren't they concerned? Thomas moves to replace the city's "miserable old oil lamps" with gas, and even interests himself in restoring "the old monuments out of our great period."

The Senator knows that such a period will not come again, yet though he has "the intellect . . . to smile at himself for the ambition" he nevertheless wants to "give his city greatness and power within her sphere." That ambition must be seen in terms of Lübeck's history: the pride of its merchant aristocracy grows from the fact that it has never known another one. Thomas's city remembers always that it too was once at the center of its world, independent and self-governing centuries before either Hamburg or Bremen: a free imperial city, subject to no external authority beyond the nominal and faraway rule of the Holy Roman Emperor. It moved the creation of the Hanseatic League, the trading confederation whose influence spread from Riga to London, and in that League it played the leading role: the "great period" to which Thomas refers is that of the Hansa's fifteenth-century peak. Even after the League's decline Lubeck on its own managed to fight Sweden to a draw, and in Thomas's day the traces and memories of that power lingered still. He knows that its population is now little more than half its late-medieval high, and that the city has been long outstripped by its rival Hamburg, for the simple reason that the Atlantic is bigger than the Baltic. Yet Lübeck kept its status as a free city throughout the nineteenth century, and it still today has an air of being somewhere in particular, closer in spirit to an Italian city-state like Verona or Lucca than to anything else in Northern Europe.

I would have gone there anyway, *Buddenbrooks* alone would have made me want to catch its herring-scented tang. But Lübeck is just forty minutes from Hamburg by train, and it became a regular trip, so regular that I even developed an itinerary, a set list of stops through which I would march our American visitors. From the train station we would walk through the glazed brick of the Holstentor, whose red and black round towers lean in toward each other, the ground beneath having subsided in the five hundred years since it was finished. Then it's over a bridge and into the center, a mile-long, egg-shaped island in the River Trave, a core that in the sixteenth century was already built from one end to the other. Our first stop lies down a twisted little alley, the Petrikirche, with its whitewashed nave so short and wide as to seem squat. But the attraction here is the tower and the view it offers of the surrounding city: the spires of its churches, the gardens hidden behind gabled rowhouses—a world that looks so self-contained and whole as to seem medieval still.

There are other stops to make, other churches known for their rood-screens or seamen's memorials, there is the Burgtor at the north end of the island, which looks impregnable still, and the water meadows to the south. I'll take my guests to Niederegger, the *Konditorei* that claims to have perfected marzipan, and we'll order *Kaffee und Kuchen* to eat in the kind of dining room where women still leave their hats on. And with every step we take, I'll wonder how anyone could possibly understand Mann's novel without coming here first, without seeing on the ground how exactly he has reproduced his hometown. He never gives the novel's city a name, and that is in itself one of the book's great strokes: how shrewd, to know that he could make Lübeck the world if only he didn't mention its name! But the Rathaus in the novel is where it is in fact. When his characters leave the city they do so by the Holstentor, the street names are the same—Breite Strasse, Sandstrasse, Fischergrube—and the Heiligen-Geist-Hospital is an ancient almshouse in the novel and in history both. Thomas enjoys showing guests the old guildhall of the Schiffergesellschaft, whose stepped gabled façade dates from 1535 and whose interior—"little altered," as my 1900 *Baedeker* says—has long housed a restaurant. The great church in both the novel's city and the real one is called the Marienkirche, where Buxtehude was once the organist: a structure that, in the guidebook's words, owes its size "to the ambition of the citizens to have their principal church larger than the cathedral of the bishop."

Today the Marienkirche's high walls and verdigris towers still dominate the low-built city, so out of scale with its surroundings that even now it inspires a trace of the awe with which its first worshippers must have seen it. The region is without workable stone and so, like all Lübeck's churches, it is built out of brick. This sometimes disconcerts visitors from other parts of the country. My friend Frank tells me, bemusedly, that the churches here simply look wrong to him. He comes from the Rhineland, where they build in a creamy pink sandstone, and claims that brick belongs to commerce, that he can't accept the idea of using the same stuff for a nineteenth-century warehouse and a medieval church. And it is indeed hard to resist the obvious jokes about the business of sanctity and the sanctity of business in the Hanseatic world. Despite its materials, however, the Marienkirche is a place for which the clichés of Gothic description might have been invented: the grove of pillars that separates the apse from the altar, the dark recesses of its aisles and chapels, the bewildering height of its nave, with the ribs of its vaulting picked out by a floral design, like the pattern around the rim of a plate. The ground here has subsided as well, so that the church slopes toward the west: you could roll a ball down the nave. It was bombed out in 1942, on the night before Palm Sunday, in a raid mounted by the RAF in explicit retaliation for the Luftwaffe assault on Coventry. Yet while Coventry built a new cathedral next to the burnt-out shell of its old one, Lübeck chose to reconstruct the Marienkirche as fully as possible. Some paintings were lost, some memorial stones as well, and you can buy postcards of what the church looked like before and also of the building in flames. Still, everything that could be put back together has been, with one extraordinary exception. Below the south tower lie two bells that fell sixty meters to the floor that night, bells warped and twisted by the heat, cracked and smashed by the fall, and the stone floor beneath them smashed as well. They have been left where they landed.

In 1948 Mann donated his German royalties toward the Marienkirche's reconstruction. For it isn't only Lübeck's most important church, it was also his own family's place of worship, and just across the Mengstrasse, staring full into its long ruddy flank, sits what is now called the Buddenbrookshaus: the very house in which the novel opens and in whose rooms so many of its great scenes take place. Mann changed some of the family history. His father was indeed named Thomas, but in writing he eliminated some of his relatives, his own siblings in particular, and set the novel back half a generation, so that it ends in the year of his own birth. Nevertheless he put the family house where in fact it was, at Mengstrasse 4: his grandparents' house, where his father was born and where the family firm for many years had its offices, with the loaded wagons rolling through an archway into what's now a municipal parking lot.

Nothing illustrates the civic position of Mann's family better than the physical position of this house. Its very location suggests how closely his heritage, his earliest identity, was entwined with Lübeck's corporate life. It is a grand house, with a baroque façade whose gray stucco distinguishes it from the brick Hanseatic gables of its neighbors. Since the family left it has been both a bookstore and a bank, and it offers today a museum devoted to the life and work of Thomas and Heinrich Mann. It's a good exhibit, one whose well-mounted photographs and documents trace the brothers from childhood to the ends of their careers. There's a model of the house as it was in the nineteenth century, the newspaper announcing Thomas's Nobel Prize, and a poster for *Der Blaue Engel*, the movie based on Heinrich's novel *Professor Unrat*: the poster features Marlene Dietrich, and it makes me wonder what, in their American exiles, she and Thomas thought of one another. On the day I was there the house seemed full of *Gymnasium* students making notes on Mann's family tree, copying out *Buddenbrooks'* timeline, studying its sales figures. One label quotes from a 1926 essay in which Mann states that despite a thirty-year residence in Munich he has always and in everything written as a Lübecker; in another, he defines his ambition as that of giving "epic character" to a novel of Hanseatic burgher life. And then there is the newspaper advertisement that Mann's Uncle Friedrich, the model for Christian Buddenbrook, took out in 1913: a protest against the book's portrayal of himself and his relatives, in which he describes his nephew as a bird that fouls its own nest.

My father had neither the time nor the inclination to make in his own life the Buddenbrooks' close identification of commerce and public affairs. But some businessmen did go into politics, sat on boards, ran the city council. A young lawyer would find that getting elected to something was good for his practice. On rainy childhood afternoons I would look through my father's high school yearbooks and catch the buzz and hum of what does indeed seem a Lübeck-like civic order, finding under an adolescent's picture a name I knew as that of a local doctor or school principal. I heard stories of once strong but now broken partnerships, learned how this shopkeeper had gotten his start and how that one had cheated in school. The young Buddenbrooks — Tom and his sister Tony — know "everybody in town . . . the labourers and the clerks . . . butchers, dairy women . . . grey-bearded craftsmen." But that's really to say everybody knows them, and so it seemed to me as well. People knew our name: they saw it painted on the sides of our trucks, they bought dresses from my cousin Joseph, and my father's business made him recognized at every restaurant in town. All this was, of course, on a more limited scale than the Buddenbrooks', the business far more modest. My parents' friends weren't the town's lawyers and mill owners but salesmen and high school teachers; the grandest of them was a Greek who ran a supermarket, the only person we knew who drove a Mercedes. And like most immigrant families we had no sense of the past. I never heard my father mention his grandparents' names, and certainly we had no equivalent of the "stout leather portfolio" in which the Buddenbrooks keep their family papers, the history book of their deaths and marriages.

One aspect of the Buddenbrooks' life seems so different from ours as to make me wonder about the limits of Mann's representation. Their employees are almost entirely absent. Some of them do figure by name: the confidential clerk, Herr Marcus, a warehouseman or two, the captain of one of the firm's ships. They are present enough to suggest that the firm employs a great many people, and yet the Buddenbrooks never talk about them, never have problems with them, never voice amusement or exasperation at — or even interest in — those who depend upon them. It's tempting to read that absence historically. Perhaps the family's position is so lordly that their employees no more exist to be talked about than do the servants in Jane Austen. Perhaps it's a mark of an increasing separation between work and home, and between the world of men and women. Certainly it's easier to imagine old Johann talking over "the help" with his wife Antoinette than to see his grandson Thomas discussing them with his violinist spouse Gerda. But I nevertheless wonder if actual German burghers would have been so silent, if perhaps this isn't simply an area of business life about which Mann himself remained incurious or even perhaps ignorant.

My father's employees were in contrast a major part of our lives. Many of them stayed with him for decades, and I can still name almost everyone who worked on Bank Street when I was six. Our cousin Joe was my father's deputy, the only other person to know, not only the price of everything we sold but also how much it might vary from one customer to the next. Charley Muscarella had worked for my grandfather and tricked me into eating chili peppers in exactly the way he had tricked my father thirty years before. Harry Chiappone spent his whole working life with our family and died alone of a heart attack in the Jefferson Avenue store as he prepared one night to go to the Hartford market. Chet Lemanski ferried my younger brother and me home from Sunday school when our father was at the shop. Bob Parker was the first black man I ever knew and thrilled me with scabrous stories about my relatives. Johnny Higgins bought me my first copy of *Playboy*; I was twelve, and hid it in the truck. Afterwards there were other men, too, and then still later a few boys my own age, high school dropouts, the only ones I've ever known. And my father always hired extra help for the summer, most of them the teenaged children of his friends, and then eventually the friends of his children. Those schoolboys and our relatives aside, my father didn't see his employees away from work, and though they all called him by his first name, they never used my mother's. But at home we talked about them almost every night. What this one said to that, their problems with their families, their bad backs and their ulcers. One worked hard, another was lazy, and at fifteen I thought at least two of them should be fired. But the only people my father ever did fire were the ones he caught stealing.

Once I started work it took me two years to learn what to do. The hours from eight to noon seemed bitterly long. I counted out lemons by the dozen, weighed peppers, built muscles enough to hoist a bag of potatoes, and found I didn't yet like coffee. At thirteen I began to enjoy myself. My body felt hugely strong and seemed as though it might stretch forever. I ran madly around the shop, doing every task at double-time and stupidly carrying two crates of lettuce at once, just because I could. I learned to drive the blade of a handtruck underneath two hundred and fifty pounds of boxed potatoes as easily as a spatula slides under an egg, and found I could take that loaded handtruck down a set of wet stairs, leaning back against its weight and lowering it a step at a time. I developed a particular skill for stacking watermelons, and on breaks I ate bran muffins and talked baseball and read the

New York *Daily News*. My hourly pay went up a quarter each summer and my hours grew longer as well, so that by the time I hit minimum wage I was punching the clock at six. That was the summer I learned to drive, starting out on an International pickup truck that was old enough to drink. The horn no longer worked, neither did the heat, and it had never had a radio, but none of that kept either it or me from making our deliveries to pizza houses and grocery stores.

I was sixteen then—the same age at which Thomas Buddenbrook is ready to leave school. He has been enrolled on the modern, the commercial, side of the city's old high school, "marked from the cradle as a merchant and future member of the firm," and at sixteen his future can no longer wait. His father takes him down to the office and the warehouses, introduces him formally to the family's employees, men with whom he has "long been on the best of terms," and installs him in a revolving chair of his own. He does not appear to have been given a choice, though there is, admittedly, no suggestion that he would, at that age, choose differently if he could. Already Thomas looks "forward seriously and eagerly to his career . . . enter[ing] upon his tasks with devotion, imitating the quiet tenacious industry of his father." Many years later, however, the Senator will voice a regret that his life was so soon committed. "How foolish we were," he says to his friend Stephen Kistenmaker, "that we went into the office so young, and did not finish our schooling instead." And Kistenmaker agrees with him: "You're right there. But how do you mean?"

One of the things Thomas means is that without having "taken the classical course at the gymnasium" and becoming a "professional man" he can never "succeed to the first place in his little community." He is the Burgomaster's right hand, but he will never be the Burgomaster himself: under the city's constitution that office is reserved for those with legal training. The very stupidity of Kistenmaker's response, moreover, suggests another reason for Thomas's dissatisfaction. Business in these last years no longer exhilarates him, and the firm's fortunes have begun their decline, though which is the cause and which the consequence remains a nice question. He has more than once had to sell "a large quantity [of grain] very much at a loss," and his rivals no longer take him seriously. He has too soon touched "the high-water mark of his life." Thomas has always, Mann writes, "done a great deal of historical and literary reading. . . . he was conscious of being superior to his circle in mind and understanding." Late in the novel, he will be ravaged by a few pages of Schopenhauer. In Lübeck, however, it is no help for a merchant to be brighter than his fellows. That kind of "inward culture" is a disadvantage, it serves only to make him restless, rubbed raw by his tight little world; the Senator tries without success to dissipate his nervous energy with Russian cigarettes, with the "thousand trifles . . . of his house and his wardrobe." But he dressses too well, and his "faultless exterior" makes him a joke with other men. Over time he comes to realize that he has neither his father's confidence nor his resilience, and on the day of the firm's hundredth anniversary wonders if he will have "a single minute to relax the muscles of his face."

Watching Thomas one knows—*he* knows!—that the Buddenbrooks have hung on too long. Nevertheless he enters his son Hanno "on the mercantile side of the school—for it went without saying that he would . . . take over the family business . . . The firm needed a successor." By now the family exists for the sake of that firm, and not the other way around. Yet Mann's best example of that sense of a corporate identity involves not Thomas but his sister Tony. Early in the novel, she receives a proposal from a Herr Grünlich of Hamburg, and though she detests his fawning manners and scented yellow whiskers, her father nevertheless ask her to think about it. From the firm's point of view, the alliance looks like a good one, and so he sends her off to Travemünde, Lübeck's little Baltic resort, for a few weeks of quiet meditation, reminding her that "we are not born for . . . our own small personal happiness. We are not free, separate, and independent entities, but like links in a chain . . ." Once away from home, however, Tony quickly falls in love with a medical student of modest family but such brilliant prospects as to suggest his career will end either at the height of his profession, or on the barricades of 1848. But such a romance lies on an "unregulated path." As soon as it's discovered Tony finds herself fetched home, and eventually her resistance fails. One morning she sees the "leather portfolio" that contains the family's history lying upon the breakfast table. She turns its pages, reads of the family's origin in sixteenth-century Rostock, finds the date of her parents' wedding and the record of her "own tiny past," the notation of her birth and "childish illnesses" in her father's "small, flowing business hand." "Like a link in a chain," she thinks, and then trusting that thought, yet hopeless just the same, she writes in the date of her betrothal to "Bendix Grünlich, Merchant, of Hamburg."

What Tony does here is to act against her own desires on behalf of what she believes will be best for her family. My own father fit more comfortably into his world than do any of Johann Buddenbrook's children — or so it always seemed, for writing these words has made me realize how little I know about the inner contours of his early life. I know that as a teenager he wanted to become a sportswriter, that before joining the National Guard at the time of Korea he spent two years as an English major at the local branch of our state university. I know that the Guard let him out when his father died, so that he could keep the family's failing business alive. He liked the Giants and the Knicks, enjoyed John Le Carré, and thought Fred Astaire a great artist, though he also once spoke sharply to me about playing jazz on Christmas morning. Early on he acquired a rigorous sense of duty, but he was also usually tired, worn thin by the people with whom he worked. He had a hot temper that he nearly always managed to keep in check, though I suspect it would not have burned so high if he had let it flame more often. I do believe it shortened his life, though so, too, did the brutal hours that the business made him keep. But if in my teens I began to understand what Hanno sees about his own father — "how cruelly hard it was upon him" — I never heard him complain about the shape of his life.

Most of the people we knew assumed I would someday enter my father's business. It was a good business, it made money, it went on making more money every year until he died. My aunt up from Brooklyn would announce at Sunday lunch that she thought sons should work with their fathers. His employees would speak of my taking over and giving him a rest, and he himself said that so long as he was supporting me, he expected me to support him by showing up for work on Saturdays and during school vacations. Clearly he wanted me to join him. At the same time, he was an American of immigrant stock who wanted his son to have an expensive education, and I do not know when he began to see that those desires might conflict. Thomas distrusts the one thing his Hanno loves, the "passion for music" that threatens to draw the boy away from the "sphere of his future activities." He takes the boy "down to the harbour . . . [and] into dark little warehouse offices," into a world of ships and granaries that smells of "fish, seawater, tar." But he cannot keep himself from seeing "that the son was hostile, not only to the surroundings and the life in which his lot was cast, but even to his father as well." It was not — not quite — so bad with us, but at no time after the age of thirteen did I look forward to entering the fruit business. I was only afraid that I might, or might have to. I would never have chosen it, I would only have failed in the struggle toward something else, and I thought about law school as a way to square the family circle.

Then one July morning after my first year of college my father came out of the office, a brown-haired balding man in his forties, and gestured for me to follow him. We walked along the loading dock and down to the other end of the store, past the trucks and the men working, down to the far end where there was nothing but watermelons and skid after skid of potatoes. Then he stopped and looked at me, and said a few simple sentences. He hoped I would want to work with him but knew I might not; whatever I did, I had his blessing. The following summer I found a Capitol Hill internship; the summer after that I taught at a boarding school in New Hampshire. All I could think of then was myself, but now it's my father who seems more interesting. It was a kind of surrender, and so sudden — what made him do it? And yet his motives were the same as Tony Buddenbrook's: he acted against his own desires to do what he believed was best for his family. Except that with a century and an ocean lying between them, the definition of what that "best" might be had changed.

Though in generational terms Thomas Buddenbrook stands in place of Mann's father, and mine, the novelist also described the character as "my father, my brother, my double." For Mann is the artist who recognized in himself a bourgeois, and he often relied on a grotesque doubling of his characters: the Aarenhold twins in "The Blood of the Walsungs," the shipboard meeting of Aschenbach with a painted old man at the start of "Death in Venice." In *Buddenbrooks* the dissolute Christian is everything his brother Thomas fears he might become, were he indeed to "relax the muscles of his face." Yet perhaps that face is also the one that Mann came himself to wear over time: the form, the mold, of bourgeois propriety into which he poured the willfull rage and longing of his art. I can find myself in the boy Hanno and see in his relations with his father certain moments in my own, but it is indeed with Thomas Buddenbrook that I feel a deeper kinship. Thomas is what I might have become, had I entered our family's business. Thomas is who I might have been, had my own father been in the end more like him.

That first encounter with *Buddenbrooks* remains one of the central reading experiences of my life. There is more, much more, I might say about it, beginning with the way Mann makes the winding up of the family firm presage the end of the family itself. There is more, much more, I might say about my own family, for the road from that July morning was neither simple nor straight. Still, by the time I met up with that novel a possible future had become clear, and I knew that I would not be entering my father's business. I think now that what made my initial reading of *Buddenbrooks* so memorable wasn't just the fact that I saw so much of my own family in it. Rather it was my teacher's sense of the sheer normality of this family history, a normality that seemed to license the choice I'd made. It told me that my decision wasn't strange or perverse—no, my desire not to be the next link in a descending chain of fruit dealers was entirely to be expected. Typical, even down to the guilt I felt. And that very typicality was like a salve.

Buddenbrooks was the first German novel I ever read, and I tried to write about it soon after we arrived in Hamburg, to ping-pong between the book's family and mine. Many pages came, but they never found a conclusion, and I can only suppose that I was, without knowing it, waiting for the sense of finality that would come with the birth of our child in a Hansestadt of our own: a child not even yet conceived when I first tried to bounce between the book and the life. "In my end is my beginning," as the poet wrote—or is it the other way around? To journey out is to journey within; the trip abroad will also take one home. These are the truisms—the truths, rather—of travel literature, the first things one learns after realizing that any description of a foreign land is never simply that alone. Even Germany can provide the occasion, or the excuse, to talk about something else. Or to borrow from T. S. Eliot once more: "the end of all our exploring/ Will be to arrive where we started/ And know the place for the first time."

But the clichés of travel writing weren't the only ones in play at the end of our time in Hamburg. You will have a beautiful daughter, Brigitte's doctor had said, and we do: a little girl whose beginning stands as both the symbolic and the actual end of this story, for we returned to the States just a few weeks after her birth. I suppose we felt like all new parents, one of Tolstoy's interchangeably happy families, and our Miriam's birth was like other births. Though would there really have been nine people in an American delivery room? Brigitte, me, the doctor, anesthesiologist, midwife, two nurses, and an obstetrics resident whose strong forearms, along with those of an orderly, took the place of stirrups when the time came: nine people to help a tenth one come out. I'm grateful for every member of that crowd, and yet it did make me feel as if I were back at the beginning of the year, and noting the ways in which German norms differed from my own: the change placed on the counter instead of in my hand, the absence of double beds. Indeed the whole business of having a child made the people around us seem somehow more German than usual, more stereotypically themselves, as though we'd been smacked in the face by those very things that make the country's own citizens all want to go as often as possible to Italy.

"You Americans," a banker tells us at a dinner party, "so superficially friendly." To which Brigitte replies, with a Teutonic asperity of her own, that it's better than a superficial unfriendliness. "But if we are nice with everyone," he answers, "how can we save ourselves for our real friends?" People here often make a rigid distinction between the private life and the public face, a zero-sum in which the warmth of the one finds its necessary balance in the sternness of the other. Civil society isn't often civil, and when not positively rude maintains what seems at best a cool formality. Take, for example, the childbirth class we attended in the months before our daughter's birth. We've gone around the room and introduced ourselves, and now with our shoes off we stretch and bend and lie on the floor, breathing deeply, trying to float on a sea of calm, all of it pretty much as *What to Expect* . . . has taught us to expect. What I don't expect here is friendship of the kind that I'm told will sometimes emerge from similar classes back home. But camaraderie, a group heading off for an after-class coffee? That might be possible, even if we do all *Siezen* each other. Or rather it seemed possible until the end of the first meeting, when with nods more curt than cordial each couple went off on its separate way.

Your pregnancy is your own business—at least until either it or the resulting child becomes the business of the authorities. My German was good enough to let me follow the midwife who taught the class, though now I remember just one detail: the word *Kaiserschnitt*, the emperor's cut, what in colloquial English we call a C-section. But my language wasn't up to figuring out just what I was doing wrong in taking my two-day old daughter for a walk down the hospital corridor. The ward has maybe a dozen rooms, all of them occupied, and all of them with their doors shut—there's been no visiting between rooms, no admiring of each other's babies, and no conversation the day before when the newborns were all taken, *en masse*, for a check-up. It reminds me of the hallways at the Hamburg University, where every office door remains firmly closed—*Innerlichkeit* of a different kind. I walk the corridor once, twice, hoping to let Brigitte sleep a bit, with the child seeming much heavier at seven pounds than she will in a few months at fifteen. And then, on my third pass, there's a a barking sound and I turn to see a pair of hips-on-hands nurses glaring at me. Do I hear the word *verboten*? Not quite, but that's what they mean, back in your room, no babies in the hallway. "*Ich verstehe Sie nicht,*" I say, I don't understand, except that I do, I understand enough to know I must retreat. But they wake up Brigitte anyway and tell her, too, though at this point even her own German fails. It's something about germs, but is it that the hallway isn't as sterile as our room, or that the child isn't as sterile as the hall?

Weddings and funerals, births and birthdays—maybe all moments of passage or ceremony bring out something distinctively local. When we returned from the hospital, two bouquets of tight-furled sweetheart roses were waiting on our sideboard: a large one for Brigitte, bound by a pink ribbon to a small one for Miriam. No American florist I've asked has encountered a similar arrangement: that was the attractive side of German formality.

The less attractive side showed itself when ceremony met bureaucracy. Miriam needed a birth certificate, and so I took the little form with the doctor's signature that the Elim Hospital had given me and went off to the municipal offices. I'd been there once before, to register our address—you can't move in Germany without letting the government know—and while waiting had noticed that the functionaries in charge entered the office by one door and the rest of us by another. Our papers hadn't then been in order: we claimed to be married but did not present a certificate to prove it. Could we have one faxed from America?

Nor were our papers in order this time. Brigitte had hyphenated her name on our marriage license, but she never used the hyphenated version, she always used her birthname, and on the hospital forms we had forgotten all about that nominal complexity. The woman at the counter nodded pleasantly, seemed to think there was no trouble, took our passports and the sheet from the Elim, typed out the paperwork, and took it all away to be stamped and signed. And from an inner office came a voice like a potato peeler that told me we had trouble. What trouble, I didn't yet know. It was simply the timbre of his voice, he could have asked me the time and I would have known he would let no irregularity pass. After some protest I was shown into his office—though that was itself an irregularity—and found a man with aviator glasses and a pudding bowl haircut on the other side of the desk, his face caught between a squint and a scowl. He looked like someone who would stand waiting at a trafficless red light, would wait if he were alone, and would wait even more determinedly if there were people jaywalking around him—a face not aggressive so much as aggrieved, frowningly on guard against a world in which *alles* is not in *Ordnung*. But the problem wasn't what I expected. He tapped Brigitte's red-jacketed Swiss passport with distaste. Her name in this document—one issued before we had even met—it wasn't at all the same as that on the marriage certificate. How could he feel confident she was the same person? Perhaps if we first regularized her passport, he could then register the birth, though that might be difficult, too; he was not sure Swiss law would recognize the hyphen. . . .

We had been away a year, we wanted to show our daughter off where it would matter, we were eager to be home. Yet even if we hadn't been, our small dealings with the German state would have made us want to go anyway. They made my neck prickle, I felt in them both the vestiges of an age-old petty legalism and the shadow of a more recent past. Neither of those things had played much of a role in our daily life here; now they did, or seemed to. Yet though I was tempted to explain the man with the aviator glasses in terms of some essential flaw in the national character, I also knew I was overreacting, even as I exploded over the telephone to an official at the American consulate. We got the birth certificate in the end, though it took a few days, while our bureaucrat invented a form to cover himself, an affidavit in which we declared that we wished our names to be governed by American law, not Swiss. He seemed to think it a very odd choice indeed.

Before we left I had one final visit to pay. I went back to Lübeck, not to the Buddenbrookshaus this time, but to the vast and drafty hall of the Marienkirche to stand and gaze once more at those ruined bells, the bells that had fallen silent. There have been several churches in this book already; this will be the last. I entered by the south portal, where the previous October I had found a large sheet of paper nailed to the door, a new set of Ninety-Five Theses, though these dealt somewhat more than Luther's had with questions of social justice. They deplored the shortage of jobs and the tendency to see all thing in terms of their economic value; admonished us, in our comfortable lives, against turning our backs on the world outside; demanded equal treatment for foreigners. By now that sheet had long been taken down, but the kiosk inside still had xeroxed copies, and I picked one up as I entered the mustily cool air of the church itself, looking it over as I stood and wondered which way to go. I didn't want to get to the bells too quickly, and yet leaving them aside, the Marienkirche isn't usually a place where my eye lingers on particular details. Rather it's the whole that stirs me, the bare brick columns on which you can still find a trace of their earlier whitewash, the sense of space and of recesses within that space: a place that seems the more sumptuous for being, now, so spare.

This time I made myself look at things. There were monuments to the families of the city's merchants: memorial tablets and tombs and the chapels they had left in their names. I found a cross listing the names of those parishioners who had died in the First World War, but I saw no equivalent for the Second, though I'd learned by now not to expect one. A sandstone Madonna, wall-paintings, a baptismal font like a wine barrel sawn in half — I took in each detail, the chrome pipes of the organs, the filigree wood of the gilt altarpiece in the ambulatory. In the north aisle was an astronomical clock, one of those automata around which human figurines march at particular times of day. It was a simplified version, my guidebooks said, of a grander one that had burned in 1942, and on the wall next to it was an image of that burning: a pair of stained glass windows that showed devils and ghouls dancing around a set of burghers and prelates. One of the latter had on a modern fire helmet along with his Franciscan habit. It was a dance of death, meant both to replace and to commemorate the loss of a fifteenth-century painting of the same subject. I bought a black-and-white postcard of the old one, and saw Lübeck itself and indeed the spires of this very church painted in the background. And there they were again in this twentieth-century stained glass, six panels showing the city in flames.

"A serious house on serious earth" — so Philip Larkin had apostrophized the subject of his "Church Going," and so the Marienkirche has always seemed. I turned away from the windows and walked down the nave toward the rear of the building. It was uncrowded and quiet, and because the rubber soles of my shoes had no echo it felt, as I moved from point to point, as though I couldn't even hear myself walk. Then I stood once more before a wrought iron screen and looked through its bars at the bells and the crushed floor beneath them. Two bells, with their clappers rusted, though more from centuries of use than anything else. One bell had lost its top, pulverized in the fall, so that a metal knob the size and shape of a human head poked out. The other seemed more intact, if only because one whole face had survived while the rest of it was in fragments: on its blackened surface I could see a few lines of an inscription in what looked, from here, like a mix of Latin and German. The bells lay over crushed memorial tablets that had once been set like paving stones in the church floor, a floor that now looked dusty, even rusty in one spot, while new brick had been laid around the edges of the chamber. No, not a chamber. A chapel rather, except that there was no altar, and indeed what altar could compete with that twisted mass of bronze? On the back wall hung a set of beribboned memorial wreathes, though the only one I could read from that distance was in honor of the Lübeck dead. Then I caught a gleam of silver in the corner of my eye and turned to see two stainless steel spikes, put one against the other in the shape of a cross. The nail cross of Coventry, it's called, made out of metal from the ruins of that city's cathedral: a gesture of reconciliation from the city that Hitler destroyed to the one on which the British took their vengeance.

Shards and fragments, a place so mute and still as to tease me out of thought; one that makes me feel I am back with Friedrich's wanderer, looking out over those fluff-covered hills and wondering if the fog is gathering or clearing, wondering too at what is hidden within. "What's this?" I heard the German tourist next to me ask his wife. "Bombs," she answered, as if that were answer enough, and maybe to him it was, for they almost immediately moved away. Everyone who visits the church stops here, for a moment of what is usually silence, and almost nobody has much to say about it. I heard a young father tell its history to his son — just the bare anecdote: the bells left where they had fallen, but with no attempt to define what they meant. A tour guide came up, leading a group of elderly English, and began her spiel with Coventry. Indeed she spent most of her time explaining the cross of nails, and merely glanced at the bells, and though given her audience that might have been understandable, it still missed the interest, and the difficulty, of this place. So then I started to ask people what had happened here, how they understood this site, moving away after every encounter and then circling back to a new crowd of visitors, and asking my question again. Sometimes I spoke in English and sometimes in German, but my opening query was always as naïve and open and unprobing as possible. Yet their being German gave no special insight to the people I asked. All most of them could tell me was bombs, their words as uninflected as a guidebook description, though one older man misheard my accent and apologized, in quizzical and ironic English, for having to tell me that those bombs had belonged to the RAF.

The site is clearly one of mourning, of memory. But what, exactly, does it remember? Does it commemorate what Lübeck itself suffered, or does it mark the suffering of war in general? Does it tell the city that "this was done to us by them," or does it perhaps declare that "this is what we brought upon ourselves?" There's no placard or label to tell us how to see this place: maybe it simply says that these particular and much-loved bells used to ring, and now can't. At the same time, the prominence given to that cross of nails suggests that anger plays little role in the public memory of the city's destruction. In Coventry it still does. There the ruined walls of the old cathedral stand as the eternal token of a crime. Here one is presented instead with a more abstract sense of the visitations of war, of a cruelty that seems to proceed from nowhere and no one, like an earthquake, a hurricane. Which begs a question in itself, or several of them. My friend Helga grew up in Lübeck, and says that as a girl she was brought here with a group from her school, as though the place were important for children to see. Important — which isn't to say that they were encouraged to think about what it meant. "It was all so curiously unexamined," she told me one afternoon as we pushed our strollers along the Rothenbaum-chaussee. "So ahistorical. Nobody spoke about why it had happened. There was no sense that the city deserved it, but also no sense that there was anyone at all to blame."

I myself want—sometimes I want—to see the bells as a silent scream, a German recognition of German culpability, of the curse that the Nazis laid upon their own house. And some people here have always shared that view, even during the war itself; even then some Germans, in Sebald's words, saw "the great firestorms as a just punishment . . . an act of retribution on the part of a higher power." Yet that view is in its own way extreme; at other moments, I recall the sense of stunned surprise, the sharp intake of breath with which I first saw these bells. They made the destruction of war seem real in a way that texts and photographs never quite had—so pitiably, tearfully real, that my heart was full for anyone, or anyplace, that had suffered so. The bells remember, but what they remember remains unsaid. Or rather, these found objects say many things, in different measure to different people, and their enigmatic power depends on saying no one of them exclusively. They stir and disturb me even more than Weimar does, they turn the Marienkirche into one of the most quietly troubling places I know. For I distrust the way in which I am brought to sorrow by their mute sublimity, and then in turn I distrust that distrust and want simply to mourn with this city, with Germany, not because of it.

But nothing about this place will ever be so uncomplicated. Our year was over, and with it my last visit to Lübeck. I had gone there first for *Buddenbrooks*, yet it was the bells that kept pulling me back: the bells that have now, for me, been laid on top of the city's earlier meaning. Nor is it their silence alone that draws me. For that silence reminds us too of the long centuries when they rang the hours of the world before their fall, and in doing so makes me wonder how we might locate ourselves now in relation to that earlier time. How can we see it, comprehend it, even at times admire it, without feeling ourselves crushed by that unheard roar?

I stood in the church and remembered some words of Lübeck's own great son:

> Events do not happen all at once, they happen point for point, they develop according to pattern, and it would be false to call a narrative entirely sad because the end is so. A tale with a lamentable close has yet its stages and times of honour, and it is right to regard these not from the point of view of the end, but rather in their own light, for while they are the present they have equal strength with the presentness of the conclusion.

Mann wrote that as Hitler came to power, words that anticipate the issues about which any student of German culture is still today required to think. History would perhaps be simple if we could always and only read it backwards, a teleology in which the *Sonderkommando* were inevitably prefigured by the *Sonderweg*. Mann denies us that grim satisfaction, but he offers something in return. To him the past is more than a foreshadowing of the future, it has a life of its own, a value that remains independent of its contribution to a "lamentable close." Its narrative develops "point for point" and moment by moment, with its "stages and times of honour" and pleasure and even instruction — maybe more instruction, for our present, than that time of horror for which we inevitably see it as a preparation.

For those who lived in it, however, that earlier world wasn't a prelude to anything. It was simply life itself: an end, not a means. And it too has its right to exist, to impose itself on our attention, uncanceled by what was to come. Yet though we ourselves may now have lived beyond the "lamentable close" of which Mann spoke, though we may acknowledge such earlier "times of honour" as those contained in Lübeck's own history, so too must we admit the claim of those moments and years of nightmare. They too impose themselves, they too are now a part of our past, forever present even as we live on into another world. Other bells may ring, but these will stay silent.

✸ Sources and Suggestions
for Further Reading

A bibliography of the travel books, uncited elsewhere, that have shaped my sense of the form can be found at the end. I have not included citations for such readily available poems as Auden's "The Shield of Achilles."

PREFACE
The Wanderer Above the Sea of Fog

Almost all books on Caspar David Friedrich simply adopt his name as their title. Werner Hoffman's (London: Thames and Hudson, 2000) is probably the best and certainly the most sumptuous; I am particularly indebted to its account of the cover of *Der Spiegel* for 8 May 1995. See also Joseph Leo Koerner, *Caspar David Friedrich and the Subject of Landscape* (New Haven: Yale University Press, 1990). Friedrich's work is virtually unviewable outside of Germany: there are some canvases at the Hermitage, but only a single painting at both London's National Gallery and the New York's Metropolitan, the latter acquired as recently as 2000.

Over the years, I have learned a great deal from Jane Kramer's reporting for the *New Yorker*. Some of her best work is gathered in *The Politics of Memory: Looking for Germany in the New Germany*, a set of pieces, focusing on Berlin, that runs from oppositional Kreuzberg in the 1980s, through unification, and on to the first plans for a Holocaust memorial in what had, by then, become the nation's capital once more (New York: Random House, 1996). Her subtitle also serves to define the travel books that German writers have produced about their own country in recent years, a form of *Heimat* literature inflected by an acute awareness of historical change: books that attempt to locate the essence of home in a country where the end of the Wall has altered everything. See, for example, Ralph Giordano's rather wistful *Deutschlandreise* (Köln: Kiepenheuer & Witsch, 1998) and Irina Liebmannn, *Letzten Sommer in Deutschland: Eine Romantische Reise* (Köln: Kiepenheuer & Witsch, 1997.)

Colin Thubron's account of the travel writer will be found in "Both Seer and Seen: The Travel Writer as Leftover Amateur" in the *TLS* for 30 July 1999. James Young's words about German "countermonuments" are taken from p. 27 of *The Texture of Memory: Holocaust Memorials and Meaning* (New Haven: Yale University Press, 1993).

CHAPTER ONE
Cultural Capital

The literature on Goethe's Weimar is so voluminous that even in English it makes the complications of Bloomsbury look small. But a good place to start is with the first two volumes of Nicholas Boyle's *Goethe: The Poet and the Age:* Vol. 1, *The Poetry of Desire, 1749–1790* (1991); Vol. 2, *Revolution and Renunciation, 1790–1803* (2000; both Oxford University Press). Boyle's biography has not yet reached the period covered in Johann Peter Eckermann's *Conversations of Goethe* (1837–48), a record of the poet's table talk in the last years of his life; the standard English translation (1850) is by John Oxenford. Those who want the most exhaustive of portraits may consult the eight volumes of Robert Steiger's *Goethes Leben von Tag zu Tag* (Zurich: Artemis Verlag, 1982–1996.)

Thackeray made his visit to Weimar in the fall and winter of 1830–31. His letters from it are in the first volume of Gordon Ray's Harvard edition of 1945–46; but see also his 1855 memoir of the place in Ray's third volume, pp. 442–45. Eliot's "Three Months in Weimar" first appeared in *Fraser's Magazine* in 1855; it will be found in any dusty library edition of her collected works. Her description of Liszt comes from p. 155 of Gordon Haight's 1968 biography. James's 1903 "The Birthplace," is most readily available in the Library of America edition of his *Complete Tales, 1898–1910*. For the *Elective Affinities* (1809) I have used R. J. Hollingdale's 1971 Penguin translation; for the *Italian Journey* (1816–17, but based on Goethe's trip of thirty years before) the Penguin edition of W. H. Auden and Elizabeth Mayer's 1962 translation. Devotees of Goethe's travel writing might also enjoy his meditation on mountain landscapes in the 1780 *Letters from Switzerland*. Dr. Johnson made his claim about the Scotch on 6 July 1763.

My comparison between Stendhal and Goethe is indebted to Dennis Porter's *Haunted Journeys: Desire and Transgression in European Travel Writing* (Princeton: Princeton University Press, 1991); see, in particular, pp. 132, 136, 140. Porter's book stands as the most wide-ranging and theoretically suggestive account of travel writing yet produced, especially in its account of such limit cases as political witness and ethnography. In some passages I have also borrowed Porter's smoothly readable translation of Stendhal in preference to that of Richard N. Coe's 1959 version (London: J. Calder). At the time of his death in 1980, Roland Barthes was at work on an exquisite piece about Stendhal's travel writing; I have quoted the older writer's claim that Italy is but an excuse for "sensations" from "One Always Fails in Speaking of What One Loves" in *The Rustle of Language* (trans. Richard Howard; New York: Hill and Wang, 1986) Graham Greene's 1936 *Journey Without Maps* is readily available from Penguin.

Thomas Mann wrote a number of essays on Goethe; his account of Goethe's "middle-class . . . carefulness" can be found in the 1932 "Goethe as Representative of the Bourgeois Age," collected in *Essays of Three Decades* (trans. H. T. Lowe-Porter; New York: Knopf, 1948). In Weimar itself I had the benefit of a good local guidebook, Siegfried Seifert's *Weimar: A Guide to a European City of Culture* (Editions Leipzig, 1994) and also Sabine and Harry Stein's 1993 *Buchenwald: A Tour of the Memorial Site*. My quotation from Saul Friedländer comes from *Memory, History, and the Extermination of the Jews of Europe* (Bloomington: Indiana University Press, 1993), p. 2, a collection of essays on the historiography of the Holocaust; see also Inga Clendinnen, *Reading the Holocaust* (Cambridge: Cambridge University Press, 1999). James Young's discussion of Buchenwald can be found on pp. 72–80 of *The Texture of Memory*; Timothy Garton Ash's account of the Goethe Oak is on p. 51 of *The File* (New York: Random House, 1997). Eric Hobsbawn's analysis of the tension between history and memory is drawn from his *Age of Empire, 1875–1914* (London: Pantheon, 1987), p. 3.

There are many accounts of imprisonment in Buchenwald: Bruno Bettelheim's 1960 *The Informed Heart* (Glencoe, IL: The Free Press, 1960) remains valuable, despite the many controversies about his career; but see also Jorge Semprún's lightly fictionalized *The Long Voyage,* trans. Richard Seaver. (1963; repr. New York: Grove Press, 1964). Ian Buruma's description of visiting Auschwitz is on p. 70 of *The Wages of Guilt: Memories of War in Germany and Japan* (New York: Farrar, Straus and Giroux, 1994); see pp. 209–19 for an account of Buchenwald. Lawrence Langer's words can be found in the introduction to *Admitting the Holocaust* (Oxford: Oxford University Press, 1995), p. 6.

CHAPTER TWO
The Peculiarities of German Travel

Christopher Isherwood's 1939 *Goodbye to Berlin* forms one-half of his *Berlin Stories*; the other is *The Last of Mr. Norris* (1935). There is an omnibus paperback from New Directions. See also his *Christopher and His Kind* (1976), which puts the homosexuality back in. James Fenton's "A German Requiem" is in his *Children in Exile* (New York: Vintage, 1984). Isaiah Berlin's belief that "cultures are comparable but not commensurable" is a cornerstone of his work, and throughout this chapter I am indebted to his 1976 essay on "Herder and the Enlightenment." It is most readily found in *The Proper Study of Mankind* (London: Pimlico, 1998); the particular line quoted here is on p. 398.

Fynes Moryson's description of bed linen comes from his *Itinerary* of 1617; I've lifted it from the invaluable *Traveller's Dictionary of Quotations*, ed. Peter Yapp (London: Routledge & Kegan Paul, 1983). Twain's account of the same thing is on p. 65 of the 1997 Penguin edition of *A Tramp Abroad*. John Murray describes the invention of the modern guidebook in "The Origin and History of Murray's Handbooks for Travellers," *Murray's Magazine* 6 (Nov. 1889). But the pages of his guidebooks themselves are double-columned, and I prefer the more easily legible German competition. These English-language editions of Baedeker have proved an essential reference: *Northern Germany* (1900), *Southern Germany* and *Berlin and its Environs* (both 1910), and *Rhine* (1911).

In addition to those volumes already cited, the following books have shaped my initial understanding of the historical issues with which contemporary Germany is faced: Gordon Craig, *The Germans* (New York: Putnam's, 1982), John Ardagh, *Germany and the Germans* (Penguin, rev. ed. 1991), Marc Fisher, *After the Wall* (New York: Simon & Schuster, 1995), Tina Rosenberg, *The Haunted Land* (New York: Random House, 1995), David Blackbourn and Geoff Eley, *The Peculiarities of German History* (Oxford: Oxford University Pres, 1984), and Charles Maier, *The Unmasterable Past* (Cambridge: Harvard University Press, 1988).

Jerome K. Jerome's 1900 *Three Men on the Bummel* is available, bound with his funnier *Three Men in a Boat*, from Oxford World's Classics. Henry James's German essays are in *Collected Travel Writings: The Continent* from the Library of America. Boswell was in Germany through the summer and fall of 1764; see *Boswell on the Grand Tour*, ed. Frederick A. Pottle (New Haven: Yale University Press, 1953). Jules Laforgue's *Berlin: The City and the Court* was published posthumously in French in 1922; its English translation by William Jay Smith appeared only in 1996 (New York: Turtle Point Press). Patrick Leigh Fermor's *A Time of Gifts* (New York: Harper & Row, 1977) is one of the century's great travel narratives, a central book in the revival of the form that took place in the 1970s. See also its sequel, *Between the Woods and the Water* (New York: Viking, 1986), in which the young Leigh Fermor walks through Hungary and beyond, though his pages have yet to bring him to Constantinople.

Michael André Bernstein's *Foregone Conclusions* (Berkeley: University of California Press, 1994) stands as a model of critical urgency. It has been crucial in shaping my view not only of the Holocaust but also of the contingent German past that preceded it; the quotation here come from p. 41. Mann's words about the "musicality of the German soul" are drawn from a lecture called "Germany and the Germans" delivered at, and published by, the Library of Congress in 1945; my quotations from *Buddenbrooks* come, as they do in chapter 7, from H. T. Lowe-Porter's 1924 translation. Michael Stürmer's *The German Empire,1870–1918* (New York: Modern Library, 2000) provides a succinct and elegant guide to the making—or not—of a modern nation-state; see in particular pp. 45–48 on the persistence of regional differences.

Historical works on Hamburg itself remain scarce in English. The great exception is Richard J. Evans's magisterial *Death in Hamburg: Society and Politics in the Cholera Years* (Oxford: Clarendon Press, 1987). Evans uses the cholera epidemic of 1892 to illuminate the city's move from a system of "amateur government by local notables"—what he calls a "night-watchman state"—to a professionally run administration capable of providing modern social services. It was a transformation in which, to enduring Hanseatic chagrin, the city found itself forced to follow a model established by Berlin: the victory, in Evans's words, "of Prussianism over liberalism." Especially valuable is Evans's opening overview, "The World the Merchants Made"; my quotations on the fate of the city's cathedral and the advice of contemporary guidebooks are taken from pp. 36 and 37, respectively. I have also learned from Edwin J. Clapp, *The Port of Hamburg* (New Haven: Yale University Press, 1911).

For James's sense of the usefulness of streets and inns, see p. 515 of *Collected Travel Writing: The Continent*. No work of criticism has taught me more about travel's complicated morality than James Buzard's *The Beaten Track* (Oxford: Oxford University Press, 1993); the analysis of guidebooks quoted here will be found on p. 174. Barthes's essay on the Blue Guides is in *Mythologies* (trans. Annette Lavers 1972; repr. New York: Hill & Wang, 1981), and my quotation from Ruskin can most readily be found on p. 147 of J. G Links's 1960 abridgement of *The Stones of Venice,* currently in print from Da Capo. For that fictional wise man Otto Cone, see Salman Rushdie, *The Satanic Verses* (New York: Viking, 1989), p. 295. The brief passages from Isiah Berlin that follow are taken from *The Crooked Timber of Humanity* (New York: Knopf, 1991) pp. 5 and 80, while the chapter's last quotation comes from the essay on Herder already cited, p. 413.

CHAPTER THREE
Visible Cities

V. S. Naipaul's single-sentence description of his wife is on p. 23 of *An Area of Darkness* (1964; repr. New York: Vintage, 1981); Anthony Powell's rather more extended account on p. 97 of *Casanova's Chinese Restaurant* (Boston: Little, Brown, 1960), the fifth volume of his *A Dance to the Music of Time.* For Bishop Bernward's Hildesheim, see the two volumes of *Bernward von Hildesheim und das Zeitalter der Ottonen,* ed. Michael Brandt and Arne Eggebrecht (Hildesheim: Bernward Verlag, 1993). Gibbon's comment on the origins of the *Decline and Fall* is in the 1796 edition of his *Autobiography,* as edited from a manuscript the historian left unpublished at his death; later editors have found textual warrant for omitting an account of the friar's feet.

Roman Jakobson's "Two Aspects of Language and Two Types of Aphasic Disturbance" is in *Language in Literature* (Cambridge: Harvard University Press, 1987); see in particular pp. 109–114. For Curtius's account of metaphor, see *European Literature and the Latin Middle Ages* (trans. Willard Trask; New York: Pantheon, 1953), p. 128. Conrad's account of going up the Congo is one of the great set-pieces in all his work, and by now a set text in any postcolonial analysis of European literature; it can be found in chapter 2 of *Heart of Darkness.* Eric Cheyfitz provides a thorough if overstated account of the political weight of figurative language in *The Poetics of Imperialism* (New York: Oxford University Press, 1991); see chapter 2, "The Foreign Policy of Metaphor," esp. pp. 35–36.

James's 1879 catalogue of American absence is on pp. 351–52 of *Essays on Literature: American Writers, English Writers* in the Library of America edition. Calvino's 1972 *Invisible Cities* is available from Harcourt Brace in William Weaver's elegant 1974 translation; John Updike's *New Yorker* review of the most inexhaustible short book of the twentieth century can be found in *Hugging the Shore* (New York: Knopf, 1983), pp. 457–62. Eleanor Clark's *Rome and a Villa* (1952) is at once the most mannered and the most profound of postwar American travel books. It is currently available from the Steerforth Press, and the passage I've quoted is on p. 156.

Boyle's account of the Holy Roman Empire is on pp. 9–10 of his first volume. Goethe and Schiller's comment about the difficulty of finding Germany comes from their journal *Xenia;* see Boyle's second volume, p. 403. Mann's words about "provincial . . . cosmopolitanism" are drawn from his 1945 Library of Congress lecture. James Sheehan's *German History, 1770–1866* (Oxford: Oxford University Press, 1989) is an extraordinarily readable synthesis of the period, and one in which social and cultural history weigh as powerfully as politics. See especially p. 15 on the structure of the old empire. Wilhelm Heinrich Riehl's *The Natural History of the German People* (1851–55) received an English translation from David J. Diephouse in 1990 (Lewiston, NY: The Edward Mellen Press.) See in particular chapter 6, "Centralized Land," pp. 103–117, while the epigraph for this book as a whole will be found on p. 45. There is a useful discussion of Riehl's work in Simon Schama, *Landscape and Memory* (New York: Knopf, 1995), pp. 113–16; and Eliot's essay on what she called

"The Natural History of German Life" appeared in the *Westminster Review* of July 1856. Donald R. Howard's *Writers and Pilgrims: Medieval Pilgrimage Narratives and Their Posterity* (Berkeley: University of California Press, 1980) provides a graceful and learned account of that early form of travel narrative; his description of St. Bernard is on p. 24.

CHAPTER FOUR
The Dentist's House

Daniel Jonah Goldhagen's *Hitler's Willing Executioners: Ordinary Germans and the Holocaust* (New York: Knopf, 1996) is by now the subject of a large secondary literature as well as many useful journalistic responses. Clive James's *New Yorker* review (22 April 1996) is especially valuable, as is Josef Joffe's account of the book's reception in Germany (*New York Review of Books,* 28 November 1996); also worth reading is Goldhagen's sometimes intemperate response to his critics, "Motives, Causes, and Alibis" in the *New Republic* (23 December 1996). See too the scholarly papers gathered in *The Goldhagen Effect,* ed. Geoff Eley (Ann Arbor: University of Michigan Press, 2000) and Norman G. Finkelstein and Ruth Bettina Birn's *A Nation on Trial: The Goldhagen Thesis and Historical Truth* (New York: Metropolitan Books, 1998). Goldhagen's own description of German cognitive difficulties will be found on p. 34 of *Hitler's Willing Executioners*. His account of the death marches is in chapter 14, "Marching to What End," and his judgment that the German behavior was "autistic" comes from p. 403. Saul Friedländer's *Nazi Germany and the Jews: Vol. 1: The Years of Persecution, 1933–1939* (New York: Harper Collins, 1997) describes, among other things, the juridical techniques through which the Nazis declared Jews to be nonpersons; his dispassionate prose is in marked contrast to Goldhagen's reliance on heart-rending rhetorical questions.

Walter Benjamin's description of the inextricability of civilization and barbarism forms the seventh of his "Theses on the Philosophy of History"; see *Illuminations* (trans. Harry Zohn; New York: Schocken, 1969), p. 256. Bill Bryson's 1992 *Neither Here nor There* is available from Avon Books, and my quotation from Nigel Leask's *Curiosity and the Aesthetics of Travel Writing, 1770–1840* (Oxford: Oxford University Press, 2002) is taken from p. 10. On the inability of Germany to sustain the comic, see Kramer, p. xxiv. Jonathan Raban's memorable description of the unruly genre to which this book belongs is taken from "The Journey and the Book" in *For Love and Money* (London: Collins Harvill, 1987), p. 253. Colin Thubron's words come from the *TLS* essay cited previously, and Paul Fussell's attempt at a definition will be found in the conclusion to his *Abroad* (New York and Oxford: Oxford University Press, 1980); see pp. 202–3.

For *A Little Tour in France,* I have used the Library of America edition of

James's travel writing, p. 3. Stephen Greenblatt's discussion of Montaigne is drawn from pp. 146–47 of *Marvelous Possessions* (Chicago: University of Chicago Press, 1991), and Tzvetan Todorov's words on Tocqueville come from pp. 67–68 of *The Morals of History*, trans. Alyson Waters (1991; repr. Minneapolis: University of Minnesota Press, 1995). Jane Kramer's account of shopping forms the opening sentence of her "Living with Berlin" in *The New Yorker* (5 July 1999), an essay that strikes me as the best succinct presentation of the issues that rebuilt and perhaps overly conscientious city has faced in trying to find an historically responsive architecture. Marc Fisher's description of Bärbel Bohley will be found on p. 12 of *After the Wall*. Katie Hafner's *The House at the Bridge* was published by Scribner in 1995; Frederick Kempe's *Father/Land* came out from Putnam in 1999.

For Goldhagen's account of Police Battalion 101, see his chapters 7 and 8. Christopher Browning's account of group conformity will be found on p. 185 of *Ordinary Men: Reserve Police Battalion 101 and the Final Solution in Poland* (New York: Harper Collins 1992), while his concluding judgment is made, appropriately enough, in the book's last sentence. The photograph of Vera Wolhauf is on p. 143 of *Hitler's Willing Executioners*. Richard Hamilton's analysis of Hamburg voting patterns is in chapter 5 of *Who Voted for Hitler* (Princeton: Princeton University Press, 1982). James's account of the solace Isabel Osmond finds in the ruins of Rome comes from chapter 49 of *The Portrait of a Lady*. Cynthia Ozick's description of her "non-visitor's distance" will be found in her review of W. G. Sebald's *The Emigrants*, in the *New Republic* (16 December 1996); and Young's description of the Hamburg memorials is taken from pp. 37–40 of *The Texture of Memory*.

Sebald's horrifically detailed account of the firebombing of Hamburg is on pp. 26–28 of *On the Natural History of Destruction* (trans. Anthea Bell; New York: Random House, 2003), the English title given to a set of 1997 lectures on "*Luftkrieg*" — air war — "*und Literatur.*" Bell's translation appeared too late for me to do more than take a glancing account of it; still it has been enough to reshape my view of Alfred Hrdlicka's Hamburg memorial. Sebald's argument is complex, but it suggests, among much else, that the country may have rebuilt itself too quickly: the clearing away of its physical rubble allowed for a premature turning away from the mental rubble that the bombing must have left behind, and at who knows what psychic cost. These lectures were enormously controversial in Germany itself, and their reception in America has been mixed, since any attempt to probe the meaning and experience of Germany's own suffering during the Second World War is still viewed with suspicion.

Nevertheless the question of Germany responsibility is in itself the note on which Sebald ends, and Ruth Franklin's preemptive attack (*New Republic*, 23 September 2002) strikes me as mistaken; much better is James Sheehan's piece in the *Los Angeles Times Book Review* (23 March 2003). Still, these lectures have, for better or worse, broken a taboo in the German discussion of the war, and both print and broadcast media have been examining the strategy, damage, and morality of the Allied bombing campaign; one example is Jörg Friedrich's *Der Brand: Deutschland im Bombenkrieg, 1940–1945* (Berlin: Propylean, 2002). See also Günter Grass's *Crabwalk,* trans. Krishna Winston (2002; New York: Harcourt, 2003), esp. p. 103, on the way in which, for his own generation, "the need to accept responsibility and show remorse took precedence" over any attempt to find words for Germany's own hardships.

CHAPTER FIVE
Fragments and Digressions

Most readers in English first met Walter Benjamin's "Paris, Capital of the Nineteenth Century" in *Reflections: Essays, Aphorisms, Autobiographical Writings* (trans. Edmund Jephcott; New York: Harcourt, Brace Jovanovich, 1978), which printed the 1935 version of the essay; there is a somewhat different version from 1939 as well. That selection of Benjamin's work has been superseded by the edition published by Harvard University Press. The 1999 volume devoted to and called *The Arcades Project* prints both versions of the prospectus along with a range of sketches and other supplementary material; the whole has been translated by Howard Eiland and Kevin McLaughlin from Rolf Tiedemann's Suhrkamp edition of 1982. Readers of nineteenth-century French fiction will find the "Guide to Names and Terms" especially useful, and the "Translators' Foreword" provides an exceptionally lucid account of the work's textual status. Susan Buck-Morss's judgment that the *Passagen-Werk* does not in fact exist is made in *The Dialectics of Seeing: Walter Benjamin and the Arcades Project* (Cambridge: MIT Press, 1989); see especially pp. 6 and 47.

If Poe's German had been better, he would have written *"Es lässt sich nicht lesen."* I have not been able to trace the particular unreadable German book of which he claims to speak; but their name is legion. Benjamin's account of the *flâneur's* intoxication will be found on p. 417 of the Harvard edition. Eleanor Clark's account of the Roman streets comes from p. 54 of *Rome and a Villa*; Jonathan Raban, with a nod to Frances Yates, draws his analogy between the department story and the memory theater in *Hunting Mr. Heartbreak* (1991; repr. New York: Vintage, 1998), p. 53.

W. G. Sebald works through the inventory of Sir Thomas Browne on pp. 271–74 of *The Rings of Saturn,* first published in German in 1995, and in an English translation by Michael Hulse in 1998 (New York: New Directions); p. 294 provides an account of sericulture under the Third Reich. Laurence Sterne's ready acceptance of digression is quoted from p. 51 of the Penguin *Sentimental*

Journey. On "loiterature," see Ross Chambers's book of that title (Lincoln: University of Nebraska Press, 1999), esp. p. 10. Larzer Ziff's *Return Passages: Great American Travel Writing, 1780–1910* (New Haven: Yale University Press, 2000) is that rarest of things, a book of sophisticated literary criticism that one can read for pleasure, even on a plane. His argument about Twain and digression will be found on pp. 172–74, while Twain's own comments on the charms of walking comes from chapter 23 of *A Tramp Abroad.*

Bruce Chatwin's *The Songlines* (New York: Viking, 1987) has received a fine appraisal in *Tourists with Typewriters,* by Patrick Holland and Graham Huggan (Ann Arbor: University of Michigan Press, 1998). For an account of why few Australians have had anything good to say about Chatwin, see the useful untangling of fact and fiction in Nicholas Shakespeare's biography (London: Harvill, 1999). The *Atheneum Fragments'* account of the difference between ancients and moderns is number 24 in the translation by Ernst Behler and Roman Strug (University Park: Pennsylvania State University Press, 1968); the definition of Romantic poetry is number 116. *The Harz Journey* is available in a translation by Ritchie Robertson in a volume of Heine's selected prose from Penguin; the description of the Ilse is on pp. 81–83. Benjamin's account of the labyrinthine wanderings of the irresolute is taken from p. 338 of the *Arcades Project.* Those readers drawn to him may also enjoy the London walks of his contemporary equivalent, Iain Sinclair: see, among others, *Lights Out for the Territory* (London: Granta, 1997).

CHAPTER SIX
Hauptstadt

Very little is available in English about Eduard Gaertner; the interested reader will have to work with Hans Borgelt and Dominik Bartmann's catalogue for a 2001 exhibit of his work at the Ephraim-Palais in Berlin: *Eduard Gaertner, 1801–1877* (Berlin: Nicolai). The largest collection of his works is in that city's Märkisches Museum. Schinkel is the subject of any number of monographs, but Barry Bergdorf's, *Karl Friedrich Schinkel: An Architecture for Prussia* (New York: Rizzoli, 1994) is especially rewarding; the sense of a distinctively national vision conveyed in Bergdorf's title is confirmed by that of Heinz Ohff's 1997 *Karl Friedrich Schinkel, oder Die Schönheit in Preussen* (Piper). Brian Ladd's *The Ghosts of Berlin: Confronting German History in the Urban Landscape* (Chicago: University of Chicago Press, 1997) has proved indispensable for my reading of the city's layered past; see too Rudy Koshar, *From Monuments to Traces: Artifacts of Germany Memory, 1870–1990* (Berkeley: University of California Press, 2000).

Histories of Berlin suffer from a distressing tendency, for which their authors cannot entirely be blamed, to turn themselves into histories of the twentieth century as a whole. The fullest available in English is Alexandra Richie's *Faust's Metropolis* (New York: Carroll & Graf, 1998), which offers a more comprehensive version of the city's pre-Weimar history than does Giles Macdonogh's *Berlin* (London: Sinclair-Stevenson, 1997). In addition to the volume by Jules Laforgue cited earlier, readers may also enjoy the fluent and encyclopedic two volumes of Henry Vizetelly's *Berlin under the New Empire: Its Institutions, Inhabitants, Industry, Monuments, Museums, Social Life, Manners, and Amusements.* (1879: repr. New York: Greenwood Press, 1968). See especially his chapters on popular theaters and beer gardens. Koshar's *German Travel Cultures* (Oxford: Berg, 2000) uses period guidebooks to offer an interesting account of Berlin as a locus for 1920s sex tourism; those interested in that period may also profit from Norman Page's *Auden and Isherwood: The Berlin Years* (New York: St. Martin's, 1998).

An English-language catalogue to the exhibits at the Topography of Terror is available at the site; its translator, Werner T. Angress, notes that he had to resist the temptation to smooth out the "convoluted, pedantic and otherwise graceless language" behind which the Nazi leadership "camouflaged their real meaning." Michael Z. Wise's *Capital Dilemma: Germany's Search for a New Architecture of Democracy* (New York: Princeton Architectural Press, 1998) is a necessary complement to Ladd's *Ghosts of Berlin* in its focus on the city's most recent reconstruction. James Young's *At Memory's Edge* (New Haven: Yale University Press, 2000) takes up developments since the publication of *The Texture of Memory*, including Daniel Libeskind's Jewish Museum and Young's own work in selecting the design for Berlin's Holocaust memorial. Two recent volumes of photographs have enriched my sense of the city. Alan Cohen takes shots of the city streets in *On European Ground* (Chicago: University of Chicago Press, 2001) — photos of the actual streets, that is of the pavement, which his work shows as an overlay of different materials from different periods. Irina Liebmann's *Stille Mitte von Berlin* (Nicolai, 2002) collects shots of that district taken in the early 1980s. Little besides the street names will be recognizable by the quarter's current habitués.

Nothing I read while at work on this book has given me more pleasure than my belated discovery of Theodor Fontane. In English his work is shamefully hard to find: several of his major novels have not as yet been translated, let alone his travel or autobiographical writings. *Effi Briest* remains easily available from Penguin; Douglas Parmee's 1967 translation has recently been replaced by Hugh Rorrison and Helen Chambers's 1995 version. Oxford World's Classics has let a 1985 translation by R. J. Hollingdale of *Before the Storm* go out of print, and Penguin has been similarly careless with its 1996 volume containing *The Woman Taken in Adultery* and *The Poggenpuhls*. The latter, at least, is still available in Continuum's admirable German Library series, bound with *Delusions and Confusions* in a 1989 edition. There is a related Continuum volume from 1982 that contains *Jenny Treibel* along with some shorter pieces, but for both that and William L. Zwiebel's 1995 translation of *The Stechlin* (Camden House), one will need a university library. There is a useful 1999 portrait biography by Gordon Craig. Günter Grass pays an extended tribute to Fontane in *Too Far Afield*, trans. Krishna Winston (New York: Harcourt, 2000); the German title of this 1995 novel, *Ein weites Feld*, is itself a quotation of the last words of *Effi Briest*.

Peter Fritzsche's *Berlin 1900* (Cambridge: Harvard University Press, 1996) is a lucid and sophisticated account of the city's Wilhelmine explosion in size; his reading of the popular press is especially suggestive, and my quotation comes from p. 31. Andreas Huyssen's shrewd "Nation, Race, and Immigration: German Identities after Unification" is in *The Power of Intellectuals in Contemporary Germany*, ed. Michael Geyer (Chicago: University of Chicago Press, 2001); see esp. pp. 327–28. Brian Ladd's account of the Stalinallee is on pp. 178–88 of *The Ghosts of Berlin*; and Benjamin's account of the city as a "theater of purchases" comes from "A Berlin Chronicle" in vol. 2 of the Harvard edition of his *Selected Writings*.

In 2001 the paintings from Charlottenburg were moved back to the Museum Island. They look every bit as good as they used to.

CHAPTER SEVEN
Family Chronicles

The literature on Thomas Mann is now approaching Goethean proportions, which would have pleased him. Biographies in particular have proliferated, though even in German he does not yet appear to have found an equivalent of Ellmann on Joyce or Lee on Woolf. I have used Anthony Heilbut's *Thomas Mann: Eros and Literature* (New York: Knopf, 1997), which follows Mann's life and career closely through his receipt of the Nobel Prize in 1929, and in an abbreviated form thereafter. H. T. Lowe-Porter's translations of Mann please few Germanists, and her work on *Buddenbrooks* in particular has been replaced by John E. Woods's 1993 version; nevertheless I have kept on with Lowe-Porter because hers was the voice in which I first encountered Mann's world.

On Lübeck's greatest church, see Max Hasse, *Die Marienkirche zu Lübeck* (Munich and Berlin: Deutscher Kunstverlag, 1983), a book notable in particular for its selection of prewar photographs. See p. 217 for an image of a funerary monument that now exists in fragments only, while p. 234 shows a view from *behind* the smashed bells, looking down the bombed-out aisle toward the apse. W. G. Sebald's words about air raids are taken from *On the Natural History of*

Destruction, p. 14. I first encountered Mann's meditation on the nature of history's narrative in Heilbut, p. 545. The passage comes, in Lowe-Porter's translation, from *Joseph and His Brothers,* initially published in 1933 as the *Die Geschicten Jaakobs* (New York: Knopf, 1938), p. 220. The consonance between Mann's pre-war views and the reading of Holocaust narratives in Michael André Bernstein's *Foregone Conclusions* seems uncanny.

TRAVEL NARRATIVES
A Selective Bibliography

Bedford, Sybille. *A Visit to Don Ottavio* (1953. New York: Counterpoint, 2003)

Byron, Robert. *The Road to Oxiana* (1937. New York: Oxford University Press, 1982)

Holmes, Richard. *Footsteps: Adventures of a Romantic Biographer* (New York: Viking, 1985)

Krakauer, Jon. *Into Thin Air* (New York: Villard, 1997)

Lawrence, D. H. *Sea and Sardinia* (1921. Penguin, 1999)

Lévi-Strauss, Claude. *Tristes Tropiques* (1955). Trans. John and Doreen Weightman (London: Jonathan Cape, 1973)

McCarthy, Mary. *Venice Observed* (New York: Reynal, 1956)

Magris, Claudio. *Danube.* Trans. Patrick Creagh (New York: Farrar, Straus and Giroux, 1989)

Matthiessen, Peter. *The Snow Leopard* (New York: Viking, 1978)

Mayes, Frances. *Under the Tuscan Sun* (New York: Broadway Books, 1997)

Mayle, Peter. *A Year in Provence* (New York: Knopf, 1990)

Newby, Eric. *Round Ireland in Low Gear* (New York: Viking, 1988)

O'Hanlon, Redmond. *In Trouble Again* (Boston: Atlantic Monthly Press, 1989)

Raban, Jonathan. *Old Glory* (New York: Simon and Schuster, 1981)

———. *Bad Land* (New York: Pantheon, 1996)

Theroux, Paul. *The Great Railway Bazaar* (London: Hamish Hamilton, 1975)

Thubron, Colin. *The Lost Heart of Asia* (London: Heinemann, 1994)

West, Rebecca. *Black Lamb and Grey Falcon* (1941. Penguin, 1982)

❀ Acknowledgments

Earlier versions of sections from this book appeared in the *Threepenny Review* (Fall 1998 and Fall 2001), the *Southwest Review* (vol. 86, no. 4), the *American Scholar* (Summer 2002), and the *Harvard Review* (no. 23, Fall 2002). My thanks to the editors of these journals for their gracious permission to draw on their pages.

I could neither have begun nor finished this project without the help of my friends in the Department of German Studies at Smith College. Margaret Zelljadt taught me what German I know, Jocelyne Kolb was my first guide to Hamburg, Gertraud Gutzmann shared generously of her experiences and contacts, while Hans Rudolf Vaget read the manuscript in its entirety and set me right on any number of important issues. As always, Smith College has provided generous institutional support. My thanks to its Committee on Faculty Compensation and Development, and in particular to the long series of deans who signed when they were asked to: John Connolly, Susie Bourque, Don Baumer, and Charles Staelin.

Margot Livesey was the first reader of the first pages I wrote, and told me I had to go on with them. Later, Anthony Giardina, Sigrid Nunez, James Wood, and especially Pamela Petro provided similar encouragement. In Germany itself I could not have done without the kindness of Helga Schwalm, Manfred Pfister, Graham Huggan, Frank Schulze-Engler, Liselotte Glage, Christiane Thurner, Jutta Gutzeit, Karin Graf, and above all the friendship and hospitality of Indira Ghose and Walter Wullerweber. At Princeton University Press, Mary Murrell has been the epitome of editorial encouragement and patience and tact; and my thanks as well to the Press's anonymous readers.

Without Brigitte Buettner I would not have been in Germany at all. To her, and to Miriam, I owe thanks beyond words.

✿ Index